The Bible in the Renaissance

The Bible in the Renaissance

Essays on Biblical Commentary and Translation
in the Fifteenth and Sixteenth Centuries

Edited by

RICHARD GRIFFITHS

Ashgate

Aldershot • Burlington USA • Singapore • Sydney

Published by
Ashgate Publishing Limited
Gower House
Croft Road
Aldershot
Hants GU11 3HR
England

Ashgate Publishing Company
131 Main Street
Burlington VT 05401–5600 USA

Ashgate website: http://www.ashgate.com

British Library Cataloguing in Publication Data

The Bible in the Renaissance: Essays on Biblical Commentary and
    Translation in the Fifteenth and Sixteenth Centuries.
    (St Andrews Studies in Reformation History)
    1. Bible—Criticism, interpretation, etc.—History. 2. Bible—
    criticism, interpretation, etc.—History—Sixteenth century.
    I. Griffiths, Richard, 1935–   .
    220.6'7

Library of Congress Cataloging-in-Publication Data

The Bible in the Renaissance: essays on biblical commentary and
    translation in the fifteenth and sixteenth centuries.
        p. cm. (St Andrews Studies in Reformation History)
    Includes bibliographical references and index.
    ISBN 0–7546–0394–6 (alk. paper)
    1. Bible—Criticism, interpretation, etc.—History—Congresses.
    2. Bible—Translating—History—Congresses. 3. Renaissance—
    Congresses. I. Griffiths, Richard. II. Series.
    BS500.B547   2001
    220'.09'31—dc21   2001022812

ISBN 0 7546 0394 6

This book is printed on acid free paper

Typeset in Sabon by Bournemouth Colour Press, Parkstone and printed in Great
Britain by MPG Books Ltd, Bodmin, Cornwall.

Contents

St Andrews Studies in Reformation History

*The Shaping of a Community: The Rise and Reformation of the
English Parish c. 1400–1560*
Beat Kümin

*Seminary or University? The Genevan Academy and
Reformed Higher Education, 1560–1620*
Karin Maag

Marian Protestantism: Six Studies
Andrew Pettegree

Protestant History and Identity in Sixteenth-Century Europe
(2 volumes) edited by Bruce Gordon

*Antifraternalism and Anticlericalism in the German Reformation:
Johann Eberlin von Günzburg and the Campaign against the Friars*
Geoffrey Dipple

*Reformations Old and New: Essays on the Socio-Economic
Impact of Religious Change c. 1470–1630*
edited by Beat Kümin

Piety and the People: Religious Printing in French, 1511–1551
Francis M. Higman

The Reformation in Eastern and Central Europe
edited by Karin Maag

John Foxe and the English Reformation
edited by David Loades

The Reformation and the Book
Jean-François Gilmont, edited and translated by Karin Maag

Penitence in the Age of Reformations
edited by Katharine Jackson Lualdi and Anne T. Thayer

The Faith and Fortunes of France's Huguenots, 1600–85
Philip Benedict

Christianity and Community in the West:
Essays for John Bossy
edited by Simon Ditchfield

Reformation, Politics and Polemics:
The Growth of Protestantism in East Anglian Market Towns,
1500–1610
John Craig

The Sixteenth-Century French Religious Book
edited by Andrew Pettegree, Paul Nelles and Philip Conner

Music as Propaganda in the German Reformation
Rebecca Wagner Oettinger

John Foxe and his World
edited by Christopher Highley and John N. King

Confessional Identity in East-Central Europe
edited by Maria Crăciun, Ovidiu Ghitta and Graeme Murdock

List of Figures

List of Figures

Preface

This volume is the product of a conference held in London, under the aegis of the Institute of Romance Studies, on 7 May 1998. This was the eighth and last of the annual Renaissance conferences that had been organized for the Institute, in the years 1991–98, by Professor Helder Macedo and myself. To the papers given on that day have been added one by Luc Borot, who had contributed very effectively to the conference from the floor, and one by Michael O'Connor, which was given to the Institute's conference on Savonarola which took place the next day, 8 May.

One thing was agreed by all present: that this interdisciplinary conference had been remarkably coherent, with the same themes recurring from paper to paper, subtly different in each context, but giving rise to most fruitful discussion after each paper and at the 'Round Table' at the end. Sadly, these discussions were not recorded; but the contributors have incorporated into their chapters some of the issues that emerged, and these and other issues will be alluded to in the Introduction.

My thanks are due above all to the Institute of Romance Studies, and to Helder Macedo, the perfect 'partner in crime' who made our collaboration on these annual conferences not just a professional, but also a personal pleasure. I also wish to thank the contributors for their articles, and for their forbearance in the face of my innumerable queries, suggestions and pesterings; Ceri Davies for inserting the Greek quotations into the typescript; Christine Trevett for transliterating the Hebrew quotations; Alison Aiken for translating the Portuguese quotations; and Bruce Gordon of St Andrews, for his encouragement in this venture.

Richard Griffiths
Penarth, 2001

Notes on Contributors

Luc Borot is Professor of Early Modern British Civilisation, Centre d'Etudes et de Recherches sur la Renaissance Anglaise, Université Paul-Valéry – Montpellier III. His research fields are political and religious ideas and mentalities; the interface between ideology and representation in the sixteenth and seventeenth centuries; and rhetoric. He has edited and produced articles on Hobbes, More, Harrington, Milton, etc.

Ceri Davies is Reader in Classics, University of Wales, Swansea. He was a member of the New Testament and Apocrypha Panel, *Y Beibl Cymraeg Newydd* (*The New Welsh Bible*) and is the author of *Rhagymadroddion a Chyflwyniadau Lladin, 1551–1632* (*Latin Prefaces and Dedications, 1551–1632*), University of Wales Press, 1980; *Latin Writers of the Renaissance*, University of Wales Press, 1981; and *Welsh Literature and the Classical Tradition*, University of Wales Press, 1995.

John L. Flood is Professor of German, University of London, and Deputy Director of the Institute of Germanic Studies. He has published extensively on the history of the book, and on literature in the Early Modern period. Recent books include *The German Book 1450–1750* (edited with W.A. Kelly), 1995; and *Johannes Sinapius (1505–1560), Hellenist and Physician in Germany and Italy* (with D.J. Shaw), 1997.

Richard Griffiths is a Fellow of King's College London and Emeritus Professor of King's College London and of the University of Wales. He was the organizer, with Professor Helder Macedo, of eight annual Renaissance conferences, 1991–98, for the Institute of Romance Studies. He has published books and articles on French Renaissance rhetoric, tragedy and poetry.

Michael J. Heath is Professor of French Literature, King's College London and is the author of books on Renaissance history and on Rabelais. He is a contributor to Toronto University Press's *Collected Works of Erasmus*, for which he has translated ten works, including five Psalm commentaries.

Michael O'Connor studied theology at the Pontifical Gregorian

University, Rome, and historical theology at Oxford. His research interests centre on religious thought in the Italian Renaissance and Reformation. He has taught theology at Ushaw College, Durham, 1996–98. His D.Phil. thesis was concerned with 'Exegesis, doctrine and reform in the biblical commentaries of Cardinal Cajetan, 1469–1534'.

Paulo Cardoso Pereira is Lecturer in Portuguese Literature, University of Aveiro. His research areas include the medieval *exemplum*; the medieval rhetorical tradition and hermeneutics; and Galician–Portuguese lyric poetry.

Vincent Strudwick is a Fellow of Kellogg College, Oxford, Canon of Christ Church Cathedral, and Tutor in Theology in the Oxford University Department for Continuing Education. He was formerly Sub-warden and Tutor in Reformation History at Kelham Theological College. The focus of his teaching and research has been sixteenth-century English historical theology.

Henry Wansbrough, OSB, has been a member of Oxford University Faculty of Theology and Master of St Benet's Hall, Oxford, since 1990. He is Editor of the *New Jerusalem Bible*. He has also edited *Jesus and the Oral Gospel Tradition*, 1991; and *Benedictines in Oxford*, 1997. His books include: *Event and Interpretation*, 1967; *Theology in St Paul*, 1968; *Risen from the Dead*, 1978; *The Sunday Word*, 1979; and *The Lion and the Bull*, 1996, as well as commentaries on Genesis and Luke.

List of Abbreviations

CWE	*The Collected Works of Erasmus* (Toronto, 1974–)
GW	*Gesamtkatalog der Wiegendrucke* (Leipzig, 1925–40; Stuttgart, 1968 and 1978–)
KJV	King James Version (Authorized Version) of the Bible
MOPH 9	Monumenta Ordinis Praedicatorum Historiae, vol. 9
STC	A.W. Pollard and G.R. Redgrave, *A Short-Title Catalogue of Books Printed in England, Scotland and Ireland ... 1475–1640*, 3 vols (London, 1976, 1986, 1991)
VD16	*Verzeichnis der im deutschen Sprachbereich erschienenen Drucke des 16. Jahrhunderts*, ed. Irmgard Bezzel, 24 vols (Stuttgart, 1983–97)

List of Abbreviations

CHAPTER ONE

Introduction

Richard Griffiths

No single book could ever pretend to cover all the aspects – cultural, intellectual, spiritual, exegetical, linguistic, social and even polemical – of the history of the Bible in the fifteenth and sixteenth centuries. This volume, the product of a conference on the subject, makes no pretence of being all-embracing, consisting as it does of a series of 'soundings', from different countries and from differing points of view, which produce a series of insights into some of the major issues involved. These issues include the interface between classical learning and the translation and interpretation of the text; the blurred nature of the transition between medieval and modern when it came to methods of exegesis; the complication, at times, of distinguishing between Catholics and Reformers in their attitudes towards the Bible; the ways in which the reading, translation and interpretation of the Bible could serve the specific and often practical aims of those involved; the social, political and religious impact of the translations of the Bible in the sixteenth century; and the issue (crossing the Reformation lines) of the extent to which the Bible should be available to the people, and the extent to which they needed to be led in their interpretation of it. This introduction is an attempt to recapture the debates that took place at the conference, after the individual contributions – debates which revealed the recurrence of these major issues from paper to paper.

The interface between humanist learning and biblical scholarship is nowhere better epitomized than in the writings of Lorenzo Valla (1407–57), who is so often mentioned in the chapters of this book. Valla it was who first challenged the Latin Vulgate New Testament attributed to St Jerome. He was the first person to apply humanist skills (philological and exegetical) to the Bible, treating it as he would any other ancient text. In his *Collatio novi testamenti* (1444) he returned to the original text, making a critical comparison between the Vulgate and the Greek New Testament. The other side of the coin was that he was also, as a humanist, concerned with the beauties of the ancient tongues, and appalled by what he saw as the barbarities of the Latin Vulgate translation. These two sides to Valla can be seen, to greater or larger extent, in all those concerned with translation in the succeeding century.

As Michael Heath points out, Erasmus owed much to Valla, whose *Collatio novi testamenti* he published in 1505 as *Adnotationes in Novum Testamentum*. In 1516 Erasmus published the first-ever printed Greek text of the New Testament, together with a new Latin translation and his notes, the *Annotationes*. This was to be of great effect upon all later translations of the Bible into the vernacular. Luther, for example, used Erasmus's New Testament in the preparation of his German translation. In Italy, Santi Pagnini owed much to Erasmus for his translation of the Old and New Testaments. Tyndale relied heavily on Luther. The first Welsh translator, William Salesbury, used for his New Testament Erasmus, Luther and Tyndale (together with later editions of the Greek text of the New Testament).

So the desire to return to the true sources was very real (even if Erasmus' translation was found to be based on later Greek manuscripts inferior to those Jerome had used). By the sixteenth century it was generally agreed that the Vulgate was often inaccurate, marred as it was by errors, omissions and interpolations, and that scholars should return to the original Greek and Hebrew. But while the return to the Greek of the New Testament was solidly based in the translators' knowledge of the language, the return to Hebrew was initially less so. Much was made of the new 'trilingual' culture (Latin, Greek, Hebrew), with trilingual colleges being founded, and the greatest praise of a scholar being that of *vir trium linguarum gnarus*; but the reality at times failed to match the ideal. Henry Wansbrough notes that though Erasmus praised Corpus Christi College Oxford for its *bibliotheca trilinguis*, in 1537 the only Hebrew book in its catalogue was Reuchlin's Hebrew grammar, *De rudimentis hebraicis*. Erasmus himself was seriously deficient as far as the knowledge of Hebrew was concerned. In 1504 he had written to Colet that 'his effort to take up Hebrew [had] faltered through lack of time and the strangeness of the language', and he was later to say that his knowledge of Hebrew was 'only a brief taste ... with the tip of my tongue as the saying goes'.[1] For his Expositions of the Psalms, as Michael Heath has pointed out, Erasmus declared himself obliged to rely on 'those who know the Hebrew tongue'. Luther, too, though much more at home with Hebrew, still needed the assistance of scholarly friends such as Matthæus Aurogallus for his translation of the Old Testament.

Most of the major translators of the Bible, from Tyndale onwards,

[1] Dominic Baker-Smith, Introduction to *Expositions of the Psalms*, ed. Michael J. Heath, Collected Works of Erasmus, 63 (Toronto, 1997), p. xlvii.

were, however, familiar with all three languages, and by the mid-sixteenth century a knowledge of Hebrew went hand in hand with that of Greek and Latin. William Salesbury, for example, was typical of the 'multi-linguists' of his time.

For most of those involved, the translation of the Bible, and the establishment of a reliable text, were not just a question of humanistic scholarship, however. They were an essential tool to foster a better knowledge and understanding of the faith among Christians. This aspect of the new learning was not restricted to the Reformers or to those, like Erasmus, who took reformist attitudes within the Catholic Church; as Michael O'Connor points out, Cardinal Cajetan, whose biblical commentaries have been wrongly seen as ripostes to Luther, had in fact an agenda not remarkably different from the Reformers: 'calling for reform: for a renewal of fidelity to the words and commands of Christ, as contained in the Gospels and the teachings of the apostles; for reform of liturgical and devotional life, of theology and of patterns of leadership'. As Master General of the Dominicans, Cajetan 'declared Scripture to be the centre of the intellectual life, reform and mission of his order'. Cajetan shows just how much we can be misled if we try to categorize sixteenth-century attitudes too rigidly.

One of the major concerns of the Reformers, however, was to make the Scriptures for the first time available to all, by translating them into the vernacular. Erasmus famously expressed the wish that everyone, men and women, should be able to read the Gospel and the Epistles, the farmworker singing parts of them at the plough, the weaver at his shuttle. This was echoed by Tyndale's confident assertion that he would cause the boy driving the plough to know more about Scripture than a learned divine. Similarly, Luther lamented that God's word had too long 'lain under the bench ... almost destroyed by dust and moths'. Like Erasmus and Tyndale, he wanted the Bible to be written in the vernacular as spoken by the people, 'the mother in the house, the children in the street, the common man in the market place'.[2]

Savonarola, of course, as Michael O'Connor tells us, 'unlike Erasmus ... did not seek to put the Bible into the hands of every Christian', and was not so much concerned 'with the Scriptures as read [as] with the Scriptures as preached'. Savonarola, however, is in some senses, from the biblical point of view, a harking-back to a previous era rather than part

---

[2] The references for the quotations from Erasmus, Tyndale and Luther are to be found in the chapters by Vincent Strudwick, Henry Wansbrough and John Flood. It has been my policy, throughout this Introduction, not gratuitously to repeat such information.

of the humanist wave. His forte was exhortation rather than teaching, magisterial rather than trusting in the good sense of the individual Christian.

It is misleading, however, to see Savonarola's case purely as a question of chronology. Some later Renaissance biblical scholars differed equally from Erasmus' attitudes. For some, another part of Valla's legacy, the cultivation of the Bible as literary language (already evident in Erasmus' rhetorical analysis of the Psalms), took precedence. In some cases, the Renaissance concern for scholarship clashed with the need to communicate with the people, with the latter losing out. John Flood tells us that 'there were some among late fifteenth-century humanists who believed that the only way to improve the quality of German writing was to model it closely on the style of Latin, the idea being that if one followed the example of Cicero, the result would perforce be elegant Ciceronian Latin'. In Wales in the 1560s, William Salesbury went even further. It was not just Latin style that he copied; he also produced a self-consciously 'Latinate' Welsh language which often bore little relationship to everyday Welsh and that would in many respects be ill understood by the people. 'The consequence', Ceri Davies tells us, 'was that an outstanding work, remarkable accurate in its rendering of the Greek text and brilliant in the way it embraced the whole range of Welsh vocabulary and creatively extended it, was vitiated by excessive learning.' The Renaissance obsession with scholarship, often for its own sake, dominated Salesbury's work.

The best of the Renaissance translations were, of course, those which combined a directness of communication, in the popular language of their own day, with a profound literary sense. Luther's, Tyndale's and Bishop Morgan's Bibles are literary marvels in their own right, and have had a lasting effect not only on the religious life of subsequent generations, but also on the literary and cultural lives of the countries concerned – Germany, England, Wales. In the case of Bishop Morgan's Bible, the effect has been even greater, as it was one of the greatest factors in the survival of the Welsh language.

The main thrust of the new efforts to translate the Bible lay in a concern for the emancipation of the people, who would now be able to read it for themselves, and not rely on the teachings of others. It was for this reason that the new trends appeared dangerous in some circles. Though there was, in Catholic humanist circles such as the Dominicans under Cajetan, a humanist desire to study the Bible, and to make it accessible to the people, there was also, within the Catholic Church, a fear of what such emancipation might bring. In England, in particular, the legacy of Lollardy made translation of the Bible appear a recipe for heresy – and the association of it with Luther, and the new Protestant heresy, made it even more suspect. Even humanists like Bishop Tunstall were strongly opposed to vernacular translation, and Sir Thomas More attacked Tyndale's version as 'Luther's Testament'. Tyndale was to pay for his efforts with his life; and it is interesting to note, with John Flood, that Johannes Cochlaeus, the man who betrayed Tyndale's printing of the New Testament to the city authorities in Cologne in 1525, had this to say about the new universal reading of Luther's Bible in Germany: 'Even tailors and cobblers, even women and other simple folk who had only learnt to read a little German in their lives, were reading it with great enthusiasm as though it were the fount of all truth, while others carried it around, pressed to their bosom, and learned it by heart.' This scornful tone is a far cry from the enthusiasm of Erasmus and Tyndale for working people's familiarity with the Bible.

Just as it would be misleading to equate all Catholic attitudes to this, so it would be wrong to equate all Protestant rule with unfettered access to the Scriptures.

It is true that Cranmer's great collect for the second Sunday in Advent presents us with the ideal of Christian use of the Bible: 'Blessed Lord, who hast caused all holy Scriptures to bee written for our learnyng: graunte us that we maye in suche wise heare them, read, marke, learne, and inwardly digest them; that by pacience, and coumfort of thy holy woorde, we may embrace, and euer holde fast the blessed hope of euerlasting life, which thou hast geuen us in our sauiour Jesus Christe.'[3] This was the rhetoric of the English Reformation; but, as Vincent Strudwick notes, after the break with Rome 'the slow progress of the availability of the Bible in English is surprising'. The attitude of the Church hierarchy was equivocal. On the one hand, the Bible was seen as the basis for a stable society; on the other, it was seen as potentially dangerous, and as needing to be mediated through the Church. A 1543 Act restricted Bible reading, 'on the grounds that it created disorder among the uneducated'. Only large Bibles were printed, and they were chained in church, to be read and expounded by the educated clergy. *The Book of Common Prayer* ensured that the biblical readings, and the collects that accompanied them, presented the Bible 'not as a tool for individualism, but as part of an interpretation of life which had the royal authority at its root and the unity, peace and concord of the nation as its aim'. In the same way, as Luc Borot has shown, the *Homilies* were

---

[3] *The Booke of the Common Prayer and Administracion of the Sacramentes, and other Rites and Ceremonies of the Churche after the Use of the Churche of England. Londini, in Officina Edouardi Whitchurche. Cum privilegio ad imprimendum solum. Anno Do. 1549, Mense Martii.*

printed, and were made a compulsory part of church services, for two
major reasons: to instruct the people in the Protestant faith, but also to
maintain social order and instil in the people an abhorrence of social
disobedience. The unfettered reading of the Bible was seen as being
potentially disruptive to the social order; and the split within the Church
of England over vernacular translations was, as Vincent Strudwick puts
it, 'not between conservatives who feared Lutheranism and radicals who
wanted a true church', but between those who feared the *social* effects
of such access to knowledge on the part of the people, and those who
believed that it was 'the best way to achieve a godly commonwealth'.

Nowhere is the profound ambivalence of the Elizabethan Church
towards the provision of the Bible to the people more evident than in the
case of the Welsh translations. At first sight, the State's encouragement
of such translations seems surprising; the tendency, within the new
united realm, was towards a desire for uniformity in language, both for
questions of social order and because it seemed to many, even the Welsh,
to be 'the way forward'. Yet religious concerns pulled in the other
direction. The Acts of Union of 1536 and 1543 show the stresses at
work. On the one hand, they outlawed Welsh as a language of
administration in Wales; on the other, they applied the English
Reformation to Wales, including the use of the Book of Common Prayer
and the English Bible in every church. As Ceri Davies points out, 'For
the bulk of the native population, nearly all monoglot speakers of
Welsh, this meant being compelled to worship in a language that was no
less alien to them than the Latin of the Vulgate and the old Catholic
liturgy.' The religious solution was to provide the Prayer Book and the
Bible in Welsh – the latter to be read in church and to provide, in true
Elizabethan fashion, the basis for the lessons of the clergy. An Act of
Parliament in 1563 required the Welsh bishops to arrange for
translations of both. Salesbury's Prayer Book, Psalter and New
Testament appeared in 1567, and William Morgan's complete
translation of the Bible in 1588 – its title-page, otherwise entirely in
Welsh, proclaiming in English that it had been printed by the 'Printer to
the Queenes most excellent Maiestie'.[4]

The contributions to this volume highlight many of the 'blurred edges'
of Reformation history. We have seen how sections of the Catholic
Church shared what are generally believed to be 'Reformation' attitudes
to the Scriptures; we have learnt how social concerns could make

---

[4] *Y Beibl Cyssegr-lan. Sef yr Hen Destament, a'r Newydd ... Imprinted at London by
the Deputies of Christopher Barker, Printer to the Queenes most excellent Maiestie. 1588.*

'Protestant' authorities as wary of universal access to the Bible as many Catholics were. A further area where boundaries are uncertain is that of chronology.

Paulo Pereira's chapter, for example, shows us just how slow the new ideas were in reaching other areas of Europe, such as Portugal, which the influence of Erasmus did, eventually, reach in the 1530s, brought from the rest of Europe mainly by the Portuguese expatriate André de Resende and by the Flemish humanist Clenardo. Gil Vicente's plays, written mainly in the 1510s and 1520s, share many of the qualities of the medieval theatre, not just in their use of allegory, but also (in the *Breve Sumário da História de Deus* in particular) in their similarity, as far as dramatic construction is concerned, to the tradition of the mystery plays. Any criticisms of the church and of religious communities that appear in this traditional structure are as likely to have been based on the anticlerical traditions of medieval literature as on a participation in 'modern' ideas. And though, in Vicente's form of spirituality, and in his specific attacks on the Roman trade in pardons, and so on, modern scholars have tried to see an 'Erasmian' influence, Pereira shows, in Bataillon's words, that 'this spiritualism and this evangelism were in no way unique to Erasmus [and] Vicente had no need of Luther or of Erasmus to mock [Rome's excesses]'; Vicente, he suggests, was more typical of 'pre-Reformation' spirituality. It is also interesting to note that Vicente's paraphrase of the psalm *Miserere mei Deus* was, according to Pereira, based on Savonarola's meditation on the same penitential psalm, for, as we shall see, Savonarola's exegetical techniques were essentially medieval.

Another area of 'blurred edges' is shown to us by Luc Borot, in relation to the transition from Catholicism to Anglicanism in the sixteenth century. 'Protestantism', he tells us, 'was not adopted with spontaneous enthusiasm by the English masses', and 'the English people that Elizabeth began ruling at her accession in 1558 were still a Catholic people'. It was only gradually, in Elizabeth's reign, that the new faith took hold, largely as a result of Protestant teaching, of which the *Homilies* were a major part. But, as Borot points out, the *Homilies* contained much that pertained to the old religion, with justification being made for continuing customs seen as 'papistry' by the Puritans. Also, 'the religious imagination of these sermons is still very closely related to the mind of medieval Christianity'. Nevertheless, the moderate teaching of Protestant principles, in a mode that did not offend the susceptibilities of the generations that harked back to what had gone before, was one of the strengths of the *Homilies*.

Biblical exegesis is another area that does not provide simple answers. Most Renaissance exegetes used the Bible, of course, for their own ends. Savonarola used the Bible to preach morality to the Florentines, naturally; but he also utilized the techniques of allegory not only, in the traditional way, to cite the Old Testament as a prefiguration of the New, but also to cite it as a prefiguration of what was happening to Florence in the present. Thereby his moral teachings became filled with a contemporary urgency. Erasmus, the aim of whose commentaries on the first four Psalms, Michael Heath tells us, was to expound his 'philosophia Christi', used his later psalm exegeses to more immediate ends: theological controversy, discussion of 'the most urgent geopolitical issue of the day' (war with the Turks), pleas for moderation and conciliation, proposals for theological compromise, and finally a yearning for 'universal recognition of a spiritual membership capable of transcending doctrinal divisions'. Luther's copious notes to his New Testament did, of course, express his own theological views; but the typographical techniques, and the Cranach illustrations, went further than this, producing a far more polemical message, in which the Roman Church was identified with the 'whore of Babylon'. Finally, the authors of the Elizabethan *Homilies* used biblical exegesis selectively in order to instil obedience and respect for rulers.

These differences in the utilization of the Bible hide, however, certain underlying similarities in techniques and approach. The rigid use of the medieval techniques of biblical exegesis – historical, allegorical, tropological, anagogic – was heavily criticized by Erasmus: but the underlying trend, from Savonarola to Erasmus, and to the writers of the *Homilies*, was still based largely on an allegorical link between Old and New Testaments, with the major role of the Old being to foretell and foreshadow the New. In the process, of course, the Old Testament text could be used to create a whole series of meanings suitable to the individual author's thesis – these extending, in Savonarola's admittedly idiosyncratic case, to the foretelling of specific events outside the Bible, even into the present day. The techniques of exegesis were not, in this sense, subject to the same revolution as the theology of the age; nor did the provision of vernacular Bibles lead to much change in all this, as the need for magisterial interpretations of the biblical text appeared to contemporaries to be more, rather than less, necessary.

These, then, are some of the linking themes which emerged from our discussions in 1998. It is the chapters by each contributor which have inspired these comments; and it is a reading of them that is now necessary, for a full picture to emerge.

CHAPTER TWO

The Ark and the Temple in Savonarola's Teaching (Winter 1494)

Michael O'Connor

On 28 December 1494, Fra Girolamo Savonarola concluded his sermon in the Cathedral church of Florence with the complaint that he was totally exhausted, worn out with preaching and praying for Florence; he told his listeners that he was having a short holiday and that the canons of the Cathedral had agreed for someone else to preach in his place for the coming days, and so God's work would continue (XXIII, 424–5).[1] This was the last of a series of twenty-three sermons preached over the course of the previous eight weeks, a period of remarkable and quite unforeseen change for Savonarola and for Florence.[2]

The Medici banking family had been the de facto rulers of Florence for sixty years. Before the end of the year, political control passed to a professedly popular government whose champion was, to his surprise and everyone else's, the prior of San Marco, Savonarola, a Dominican friar from Ferrara. He would remain its guiding spirit until political and religious enemies engineered his execution in May 1498. These sermons in late 1494 constitute, therefore, a turning-point in Savonarola's activity, and are well known as evidence of his changing prophetic stance and political involvement. They will here be examined for indications of the way Savonarola uses Scripture to give shape and authority to his message.

The collection of sermons for this period is known misleadingly as

---

1 *Prediche sopra Aggeo con il trattato circa il reggimento e governo della città di Firenze*, ed. Luigi Firpo (Edizione Nazionale delle Opere di Girolamo Savonarola; Rome, 1965). References in the text are to the sermon number and page number.

2 For accounts of these events and Savonarola's part in them, used throughout this study, see Joseph Schnitzer, *Savonarola: Ein Kulturbild aus der Zeit der Renaissance* (Munich, 1924), chs 9–11, pp. 163–216; Roberto Ridolfi, *Vita di Girolamo Savonarola*, 4th edn (Florence, 1974), chs 9–11, pp. 115–57 (for an English translation of the first edition, lacking the notes, *The Life of Girolamo Savonarola* [London, 1959]); Donald Weinstein, *Savonarola and Florence: Prophecy and Patriotism in the Renaissance* (Princeton, NJ, 1970), chs 3–4, pp. 112–58.

Sermons on Haggai (*Prediche sopra Aggeo*). With occasional exceptions, the sermons fall into three groups. The first group is actually concerned with Noah's Ark, continuing Savonarola's sequence of sermons on the book of Genesis from the previous Lent (Sermons I to VI). A middle section employs a variety of texts mainly from the Psalms (Sermons VII to XIII). Only then is Haggai's prophecy considered, for most of the final third of the collection (Sermons XIV to XXIII).

Two principal images dominate these sermons: the Ark and the Temple. In the first group of sermons, Savonarola appeals to the Florentines to enter the Ark, to avoid the coming chastisement. Sermon V, concerning the food Noah brought into the Ark, will be taken as illustrative of the life Savonarola envisaged for the elect within the Ark. In the final group of sermons, the rebuilding of the Temple is applied by Savonarola to the civic and spiritual renewal required of Florence after the fall from power of the Medici party. Savonarola's reading of the prophet Haggai illustrates the extent to which the whole city of Florence is now his direct concern: the city of God, the elect city, beginning with its government, must be rebuilt in peace, faith and love.

Before embarking on the examination of these sermons, an introduction to Savonarola's basic approach to Scripture is in order, drawing on remarks not only within this collection of sermons but scattered throughout other works.

Savonarola and Scripture

Savonarola always claimed to be a biblical preacher and saw himself as a restorer of Scripture to its rightful place in the life of the Church. He rails against preachers who allow the Scriptures to gather dust whilst they expound on philosophy, Dante, or superstitious fancies. Scripture is a refreshing well (IV, 69); it is the nourishing part of Christianity, 'la parte nutritiva della Cristianità', which is to be read and explained to the faithful (VIII, 125). Scripture is a consolation in this life for those who love God: in the Scriptures are hidden all divine treasures and all that can satisfy the human heart (I, 8). In the *Triumphus crucis*, a kind of catechism and apologia in one, he praises the saintly preachers of old and sees in them an example for preachers in his own time: when they confined themselves to the simple preaching of the holy Scriptures, they were able to fill their hearers with divine love, enabling them to rejoice in affliction and even martyrdom.[3]

---

[3] *Triumphus crucis*, testo latino e volgare, ed. Mario Ferrara (Edizione Nazionale delle Opere di Girolamo Savonarola; Rome, 1961), pp. 71 (Latin), 357 (Italian).

For Savonarola, Scripture is not only nourishing and consoling – it is also robust. Indeed, scriptural preaching is more powerful than Cicero's rhetoric. Scriptural preaching has a greater power to instruct, to delight and to motivate than human rhetoric not because it is more artful, but because Scripture has its origin and cause, its effects and strength (its *virtù*), not in human artifice but in God (XXI, 381–2). Savonarola is not interested in any purported use of rhetorical devices and techniques in scriptural texts, in contrast most conspicuously to Melanchthon twenty years later; the Bible is uniquely fitted to teach and persuade simply because it is the word of God. His evaluation of human philosophy and ancient wisdom, at best a qualified welcome, can at times rise to a shrill denunciation: Christ will come to burn the devil's books (V, 81–2). Preachers who discourse only on philosophical subjects, or pay great attention to oratorical effect, produce scarcely any fruit among their Christian hearers. He himself knows this from personal experience: when he was wont to discourse on subtle points of philosophy or theology, to impress the learned, he found that the people who heard him were inattentive. But as soon as he devoted himself to the exposition of the Bible, all eyes were fixed upon him, and his audience seemed to have been carved out of stone, so intent were they on his words. More surely than a two-edged sword, Scripture contains that marvellous doctrine which pierces hearts with love, adorns the world with virtue, and overthrows idolatry, superstition and error.[4]

Such comments reveal Savonarola's preoccupation with his own calling and mission. Unlike Erasmus, for example, Savonarola does not seek to put the Bible into the hands of every Christian; he is not concerned so much with the Scriptures as read, but with the Scriptures as preached. In the parable of the Good Samaritan, the innkeeper is the preacher, entrusted with the two coins of the Old Testament and the New Testament (IV, 63–4). In another image, preachers are trumpets made of gold (charity) and silver (eloquence and learning in sacred Scripture) given to the people by God to teach them the Christian life (VIII, 139–40).

Allegory and the Old Testament

Savonarola concedes that, for all the comfort and nourishment it contains, Scripture remains for many an unyielding source. He has a particular sympathy for those who are puzzled by the continuing

---

[4] Ibid., pp. 71–2 (Latin), 357–8 (Italian).

Christian use of the Old Testament, an attitude he recalls from his days as a student when he was asked, even by good people, why he was studying the Old Testament: surely it has all been fulfilled long ago, and is finished with?[5] His resolution of this problem recapitulates medieval and patristic accounts of allegorical interpretation, relying especially on the position elaborated by Aquinas.[6] Of considerable importance in this tradition is Paul's reading of Abraham's family history: according to the book of Genesis, Abraham had two sons, one born of a free woman, his wife Sarah, the other born of a slave, Hagar (Gen. 16 and 21). In his letter to the Galatians, Paul refers these details allegorically to the Christian Church, since the Church is drawn both from the Jews, the children of the free woman, and the Gentiles, the children of the slave (Gal. 4: 24).[7] This usage gave rise to Augustine's well-known dictum: the New Testament is hidden in the Old Testament, the Old Testament is revealed in the New Testament.[8] There is a logic of promise and fulfilment in the two Testaments, or prophecy and event, or shadow and reality. This harmony, Savonarola concludes, gives the Bible the dignity of an allegorical meaning. In addition to the explicit prophecies of Isaiah, Daniel, Amos and the other prophets, he argues that names, places, events and actions have a prophetic purpose beyond their immediate meaning. God has ordered these things in such a way that they foreshadow things that are to come, not just concerning the Jewish people and Christ and the Church, but even Assyrians, Medes, Chaldaeans, Persians, Greeks, Romans. In the historical narratives of Scripture, especially in the Old Testament, God has mysteriously composed living parables out of events, people and actions; allegorical interpretation is the means to unlock these mysteries. In other words, Jesus composed parables with words; God composes parables out of true happenings, so that what is true in itself also indicates something else which is to come. Savonarola confidently asserts that not one iota of what has been prophesied in this way has failed to come about.[9]

---

[5] *Prediche italiane ai Fiorentini*, 3/II, ed. R. Palmarocchi (Florence, 1935), p. 215.

[6] See especially Maximino Arias Reyero, *Thomas von Aquin als Exeget: Die Prinzipien seiner Schriftdeutung und seine Lehre von den Schriftsinnen* (Einsiedeln, 1971); Ceslaus Spicq, 'Saint Thomas d'Aquin exégète', *Dictionnaire de la théologie catholique*, xv/1 (Paris, 1946), cols 694–738. Also Henri de Lubac, *Exégèse médiévale: les quatre sens de l'Écriture*, 4 vols (Paris, 1959–64); Beryl Smalley, *The Study of the Bible in the Middle Ages*, 3rd edn (Oxford, 1983); Spicq, *Esquisses d'une histoire de l'exégèse latine au moyen âge*, Bibliothèque Thomiste, 26 (Paris, 1944).

[7] Thomas Aquinas, *Commentary on Saint Paul's Letter to the Galatians*, trans. F.R. Larcher OP (Albany, NY, 1966), pp. 137–8.

[8] *Quaestiones in Heptateuchum*, 2, 73, *Patrologiae cursus completus. Series Latina*, 34 (Paris, 1865), col. 623.

[9] *Triumphus crucis*, pp. 67–70 (Latin), 353–6 (Italian).

Savonarola commends the divine pedagogy as a fitting condescension to human circumstances: on the (Aristotelian) principle that knowledge comes through the senses, the use of figures in Scripture is more delightful ('più delettabile'), more easily memorized (XII, 192–3). Nevertheless, Savonarola is aware that allegory is a potentially undisciplined instrument; there are constraints that must be imposed in order to prevent allegorical interpretation from becoming a licence to daydream. First of all, the truth of the literal sense must be secure ('istoria vera'), unlike the fables of the poets, which possess neither truth nor allegory. Furthermore, the allegory must not be contrary to the faith, nor to morals, nor to reason; the allegory must be plausible ('verisimile'); and the original letter of the text must not be twisted or violated by the allegory (XII, 196). Thus Scripture interprets itself; it is so arranged that what is obscure in one place is explained in another. The straightforward teaching of Scripture in one place will be the foundation, the legitimization, of the allegorical interpretation of another text. In other words, the allegorical sense relies on the literal sense. For example, the Christian sacrament of baptism makes an explicit connection between salvation and water; this connection legitimizes an allegorical interpretation of the Exodus and the crossing of the Red Sea as a prophetic sign of baptism.

Allegory and prophecy

According to standard usage, the allegorical reading of the Old Testament gives depth, shape and focus to Christian doctrine about God, Christ, the Church and the sacraments. But Savonarola does not stop there; the word of Scripture does not simply look backwards, it looks forwards too, it becomes contemporary. In addition to general moral and doctrinal teaching, the allegorical interpretation of Scripture discloses God's particular word for the present, which, for Savonarola, means for Italy, for Florence, and for Savonarola himself. This idea is familiar from the pictorial arts: Benozzo Gozzoli portrayed the procession of the Magi passing through the Tuscan landscape (1459); Ghirlandaio located the birth of the Virgin Mary in a sumptuous Florentine palazzo (1486–90).

Savonarola is less optimistic: the Flood that destroyed all but Noah and his family is set to inundate Florence. God is to reform his Church and soon, and this reform will begin from Florence. Savonarola has been sent to foretell and initiate this reform (XXI, 378; XXII, 404). He is a man chosen by God, visited by dreams and revelations, a humble and inadequate but anointed vessel of divine secrets. The Florentines are confirmed, strengthened, built up by the truthfulness of his preaching; they can be firm in their hope, their patience, their detachment from the world (XIV, 232–3), since what he says will surely happen. He insists, 'See, everything I foretold has come true' (II, 32; IV, 63–4; V, 81–2; VII, 110). For Savonarola, the biblical word made contemporary through prophetically inspired allegorical interpretation is not simply a message from a distant God; it is a word which discloses the actions and purpose of God in the present: the God who provides, redeems and punishes.

Nevertheless, Savonarola was not at ease with his calling to prophecy; he fought against it, questioned it, resisted. At times he appears defensive and vulnerable; he feels like a small boy adrift in a tiny boat on a violent sea, having to confront the waves. He is also an outsider, a foreigner about whose accent the Florentines complained when he first preached to them; but this only confirms his calling: he recalls the words of Jesus, who said that a prophet who is not accepted in his own country must preach elsewhere (Luke 4: 24; John 4: 44); he compares himself with the Good Samaritan, another foreigner, who stopped to help the man who had fallen among thieves – another figure of Florence (XIX, 327). He is in Florence because God wants him to be there, not for his own good (he might even be forced to suffer the martyr's fate) but for the salvation of Florence (XIX, 329; XX, 360).

Savonarola has no difficulty finding confirmation in the Bible that his time has come. The four horses of the Apocalypse (Rev. 6: 1–8), each representing an age in the history of the Church, enable him to indicate clearly that the time for reform is long overdue: the white horse represents the purity of the time of the apostles, the red horse represents the blood of the martyrs, the black horse represents the falsehood of the heretics, and the pale horse, neither black nor white, stands for the lukewarm, the *tepidi*, those whose religion is all externals and formality, and whose hearts are not on fire with Christian love, joy and zeal; this time of lip-service, of false brethren, of coldness of spirit, has long been suffered by the Church but it is soon to come to an end in great tribulation (XIV, 234–5).[10] His own mission to speak out in such troubled times is clearly prefigured again and again – in the guise of Noah, Elijah, Moses, Haggai, even Christ.

Every threat of destruction, every promise of deliverance, every call to repentance addressed by God to Israel in the Old Testament is relayed

---

[10] Other elements of apocalyptic used in these sermons, though not in a systematic way, include: a view of history as a seven-age scheme (XIV, 235–8), persecution of Christians by the Antichrist in Jerusalem (XXII, 406), a special role assigned to 'viri spirituali' (III, 47; XVIII, 319).

by Savonarola as God's message for Florence. In times of divine chastisement, prophetic messages should be expected, since God wants people to repent and be saved. Otherwise it would be said that God seeks to destroy the Church, or that he is without mercy, or that the calamity happened by chance ('a casu').[11]

At this point, Savonarola becomes unhooked from his sober Dominican exegetical tradition. As we have seen, Savonarola argues that Scripture interprets Scripture, that what is obscure in one place is explained by what is clear in another place. The irony is that precisely in order to justify his credibility as a preacher of Scripture, he must introduce a new element from outside the text. The literal or historical sense, which normally provides the foundation to all legitimate allegory, is displaced by direct prophetic inspiration. It is only on account of the particular message he has received for Florence that he is able to interpret the book of Genesis and the prophet Haggai in explicitly Florentine ways. He cannot prove or demonstrate the truth of these interpretations; they are certainly plausible (God will indeed reform his Church), but the truth of his prophecies will only be demonstrated by their fulfilment.[12] Scripture is therefore incomplete: God continues to be active in history and continues to inspire prophets so that divine providence, foretold in Scripture, may be recognized in the present.[13] There is a circular relationship between the biblical word preached and ongoing events: the preaching of the word discloses the providential hand of God at work in history; these new actions of God, in turn, shed new light on Scripture, inciting the divinely illuminated prophet to reread certain passages in a new way, to find new meanings in them; and these new meanings, in their turn, provide the prophet with the means to interpret more authentically God's actions in the present (XX, 348). Indeed, without the continuing action of God, the preaching of the Gospel would not be fruitful at all.[14] In the development of Savonarola's reading of the Bible, the actions of divine providence in 1494 were of cardinal importance.

---

11 *Prediche italiane ai Fiorentini*, 3/II, pp. 218–19.

12 This is the prophet Jeremiah's criterion for discerning between the true and the false prophet; see Jeremiah 28.

13 *Prediche italiane ai Fiorentini*, 3/II, p. 217.

14 *Prediche italiane ai Fiorentini*, 3/I, ed. R. Palmarocchi and F. Cognasso (Perugia and Venice, 1930–35), p. 286.

The Ark

In August 1494, Charles VIII of France descended into Italy, laying claim to Naples and the South. Enthusiastic religious reformers at the French court encouraged Charles to see himself as a second Charlemagne, with a sacred mission to conquer Italy for France, reform Rome, convert the infidel and reduce the world to a single flock under one shepherd. A corresponding mood of foreboding was widespread in Italy, expressed in terms of impending political and apocalyptic catastrophe. There was no shortage of preachers of apocalypse and Savonarola was by no means the most vociferous.[15] Civic tension increased between the supporters of the Medici, the unofficial rulers of Florence, and the supporters of the French. For Savonarola, the signs were clear: Charles was the new Cyrus, God's chosen instrument to bring chastisement on his wayward people. The Medici nerve failed. On 26 October, Piero de' Medici, now in alliance with Naples, fled the city after having surrendered key Florentine ports and fortresses to the French. Great bloodshed was feared as civil war seemed inevitable between the pro-Medici and the pro-French camps in the city.

Returning to his cycle of sermons on Genesis from the previous Lent, Savonarola urges his listeners to flee into the Ark, to escape the coming chastisement. The ritornello for these sermons is the plea, 'Do penance, there is no other remedy'. On 16 November, he reaches God's instructions to Noah concerning food for the Ark, 'See that you take and store by you every kind of food that can be eaten; this will be food for you and for them' (Gen. 6: 21). Savonarola sets his listeners at the table and describes the food that is before them; what many kinds of food, of bread are these that Noah brings into the Ark. He proceeds by means of a fourfold allegory of bread, drawing on the variety of meanings given to the word 'bread' in Scripture.

The first bread he considers is that mentioned in the Lord's prayer, 'Give us this day our daily bread' (Matt. 6: 11). For Savonarola, daily bread is simple living, simplicity, *semplicità*. It is a lifestyle marked by prayer, chastity, almsgiving. 'War, famine and plague will strip you of all your vanities and pomps by force; why not give them away out of love?' (II, 42). Noah's vegetarianism is allegorized as the absence of unruly carnal desires. In the Ark, women dressed modestly and so should the women of Florence; and since the women and men are mentioned in

---

[15] Marjorie Reeves, *The Influence of Prophecy in the Later Middle Ages: A Study in Joachimism* (Oxford, 1969), pp. 429–52; Ottavia Niccoli, *Prophecy and People in Renaissance Italy*, trans. Lydia G. Cochrane (Princeton, NJ, 1990), pp. 19–23, 89–120; Weinstein, *Savonarola and Florence*, pp. 125–9.

groups, he concludes that they remained apart from one another in the Ark (V, 82–4).

The second bread is the Word of God, as in the text, 'Man shall not live by bread alone, but by every word that proceeds from the mouth of God' (Matt. 4: 4; Deut. 8: 3). This bread is essential for the well-being of the Church (V, 84). But without a breath, Savonarola shifts attention from the Bible to the crucifix: the true book is the book of the crucifix. This is the book for rich and poor alike. Here is true eloquence, a rhetoric that cannot fail to persuade. It is a book of actions, not just words; a book that can teach more than the ethics of Aristotle or Seneca. Meditation on the crucifix is a sure remedy for the *tepidi* (V, 85). In an earlier sermon he had urged his listeners to take the book of the crucifix in their hands, to read it frequently in order that their zeal and devotion be awakened; if read every day, it will be worth more than all the studies in the world. He makes it clear that this command applies to all: men, women, fathers and mothers, sons and daughters, priests and friars, clergy and religious, monks and nuns, great and small, citizens, great teachers, people of any kind or status (III, 52–3). Speaking as Noah, Savonarola urges his listeners to give their attention to Scripture and the crucifix: 'This is the bread I will give you day and night for your salvation' (V, 85). And again, 'My speciality is the crucifix alone' ('La spezialità mia è solo il crucifisso') (XII, 206). Where Erasmus sought to put the Bible into every Christian's hand, Savonarola expects to find a crucifix.[16]

The third bread is the eucharist, as in the words of Jesus, 'The bread that I shall give is my flesh for the life of the world' (John 6: 52). Again, he encourages his hearers not to be lukewarm, but to enkindle the fire of devotion by frequent reception of holy communion. Just as bodily food is taken for physical nourishment, so the sacrament of the altar restores spiritual fervour. Do not be a Christian by constraint, he tells them, going to communion only once a year because that is the minimum required by canon law; be a Christian by love, frequenting the sacrament especially on all the big feasts (V, 85–6).

The fourth bread is penance, as in the Psalm, 'My tears have been my bread, by night and by day' (Ps. 42: 3, Ps. 41 in the Vulgate). Do

---

16 See also *Triumphus crucis*, pp. 8 (Latin), 296 (Italian), where the triumphant Christ is described carrying the Cross in one hand and the Old and New Testaments in the other. On the crucifix in Dominican devotion, with particular reference to San Marco, see William Hood, 'Fra Angelico at San Marco: Art and the Liturgy of Cloistered Life', in John Henderson and Timothy Verdon (eds), *Christianity and the Renaissance: Image and Religious Imagination in the Quattrocento* (Syracuse, NY, 1990), pp. 108–31; *idem, Fra Angelico at San Marco* (New Haven, CT, and London, 1993), pp. 149–58, 203–6.

penance, to turn away God's anger. The chastisement has begun; though there has been some respite, Florence is not yet in the clear. Do penance, there is no other remedy (V, 87–8).

This is Savonarola's message to a beleaguered city, fearing the worst. There is to be a chastisement and soon; Italy and Florence will be struck. Savonarola uses the simple statement of the scriptural text, enriched through allegorical connections to other biblical texts, to describe a clear programme for discipleship in time of imminent chastisement. Those who enter the Ark are to travel light: take evangelical simplicity, the word of God (contemplated in the crucifix), the eucharist and penance.

On 23 November Savonarola began his sermon (sermon VI) evoking the scene of Noah and all his family and all the animals having entered the Ark, as commanded by God: 'and the Lord shut him in' (Gen. 7: 16). Noah had done all he had been commanded to do to protect against the rains that would fall for forty days and forty nights. Savonarola had done all he could do to prepare for the great chastisement, and now the Ark was closed. Savonarola had prepared notes for more sermons on Genesis; there can have been little doubt about their theme.

Prophecy in transition

In the days when he was preparing the Florentines for the coming Flood, Savonarola was also involved in negotiations with the conquering French king. On 17 November King Charles had marched proudly into Florence, the conquering lord. On 21 November a Florentine embassy, including Savonarola in its number, had persuaded Charles to accept a ransom and to leave the city in the reliable hands of a new council. Savonarola exhorted him to head south and on to the Holy Land, in pursuit of his divinely ordained mission to liberate the holy places and convert the Turks to Christ. The treaty was finalized on 25 November and Charles left Florence three days later. After barely a drop of rain, the storm clouds had lifted.

The salvation of the city was widely attributed to Savonarola: he had foreseen the scourge and he had turned it away. Even Ficino, who had welcomed Charles as the new Charlemagne, praised Savonarola (though his admiration soon cooled: after Savonarola's death, Ficino denounced him to the Roman curia as the Antichrist).[17] In the political vacuum left

---

17 On the alleged influence of this determination, see S. Meltzoff, *Botticelli, Signorelli and Savonarola: Theologia Poetica and Painting from Boccaccio to Poliziano* (Florence, 1987); R. De Maio, 'Savonarola, Alessandro VI e il mito dell'Antichristo', in *Riforme e miti nella chiesa del Cinquecento* (Naples, 1992), pp. 35–65.

by the flight of the Medici and the withdrawal of the French king, Savonarola's evident prophetic powers bolstered his popular power base and lent authority to his voice. He was turned to for inspiration not only in religious matters, but also in matters of civil welfare. In this new climate, although he continued to call people to the Ark (despite having already closed the door), new themes began to emerge.

Savonarola tries to make theological sense of the recent events. Had he, Noah, been mistaken? In an earlier sermon he had confessed that his understanding had been defeated by God's mercy: God is more merciful than he had ever thought possible, his mercy is greater than his justice (I, 3–4). Furthermore, he reasons, Noah's threat was not absolute, but conditional upon genuine repentance, therefore he urges the people to continue with their works of penance (V, 87–8). He explains that God allows a tyrant to rule for a time, as a just punishment on a sinful people; but God, whose ways are unfathomable, removes the tyrant as a sign of his mercy (XIII, 225).

Throughout these days, texts selected mainly from the Psalms furnish Savonarola with the means to arouse his listeners to have mercy and lend to the poor, to find them work, to pray for peace and to give thanks to the Lord who has spared them from the Flood. These psalms, he says somewhat incongruously, are intoned by Noah to those within the Ark, instructing them on the means by which they will renew their city (XII, 192). The style of these sermons contrasts with the detailed and more highly wrought allegorical sermons on the Ark. Biblical exhortation is applied simply and directly to the Florentine people. Taken by surprise at the rapid turn of events, Savonarola seems momentarily lost for words; Noah and the Ark had certainly served their purpose, but they no longer corresponded to the circumstances of the Florentine people. The city no longer feared the Flood, yet it was more in need of reform than ever. What new image, what new word of God was the prophet to give to his people? Before the month is out, Savonarola will have cast himself as the prophet Haggai, exhorting God's people (the Florentines) to rebuild the Temple which lies in ruins (their city). The first hint of this image appears in Sermon IX based on Psalm 112 (Ps. 111 in the Vulgate), whose title in the Vulgate reads, 'Alleluia pro reversione Aggei et Zachariae'. Here he commends the joy and alacrity with which the true citizens of Jerusalem rebuilt the Temple, seeing in them an example to the Florentines seeking to rebuild their government (IX, 144–6). Before putting this image centre stage, however, he tests out others, one of which deserves mention.

The story of the Shunamite woman's dead son, brought back to life by the prophet Elisha, is retold in Sermon XII. There are four principal characters in the story: the Shunamitess, her dead son, Elisha's servant Gehazi (who, using Elisha's staff, tries but fails to revive the boy), and the prophet Elisha himself (2 Kgs 4; 4 Kgs 4 in the Vulgate). Savonarola underlines the importance of his use of this text by introducing it with the lengthy discussion of allegory already mentioned (XII, 196), and by offering a sequence of allegorical interpretations of it. In the first interpretation, he suggests that the Shunamitess praying for her son represents the Church praying for the gentile peoples lost in sin and idolatry. Gehazi represents the Hebrew people sustained only with the staff of the Old Testament, and therefore unable to save the pagans. Elisha represents Christ, the universal redeemer who raised the pagans to life through the preaching of the apostles (XII, 196–7). In a second interpretation, the woman and her son both represent the Church: the woman is the virtuous Church praying for those Christians, her children, who are dead to good works. Gehazi is the wise of the world who wrongly believe that they can govern well with the staff of their own power and wisdom; and they are deceived. Once again, Elisha represents Christ who will renew his Church (XII, 197). In the third interpretation the focus is sharper still as Savonarola comes to his point: what has been said of the whole (the Church) can also be said of one part of that whole (the Florentine Church).

Savonarola begins with an etymological explanation: the designation 'Shunamite' means 'wretched and wicked' ('misera e cattiva'). He then applies these two terms to the mother and son respectively: the woman represents the zealous part of the Florentine Church, longing for the honour of God; she is said to be wretched because she is dead to the world, weeping in compassion for sinners, constantly in prayer. The dead son represents the wicked, the perverse, those dead in their sins. The good Christians in Florence pray for the wicked as for their children because they love them and desire their salvation. Gehazi now represents the wise of the Florentine world, those who hold the staff of office and who hope, by their own prudence and power, to renew Florence. They are deceived. Indeed, the boy died complaining that his head was in pain ('caput doleo', 2 Kgs 4:19), allowing Savonarola to attribute the ills of the city to its head, to wicked leadership, both temporal and spiritual (XII, 197–8).

The allegory continues by drawing out parallels between Elisha and Christ and contrasting them with the wise of the world (XII, 198–204). In this way, Savonarola uses the biblical narrative to give impetus to a spiritually inspired civic reform: the city does indeed need prayer (XII,

200).[18] At the same time, he has found a narrative that brings together the good and the wicked in a way that the story of the Ark could not do. In the earlier sermons the good were exhorted to flee into the Ark from the chastisement that would come on the wicked; now, in the person of the Shunamitess, the good are exhorted to mortify themselves and to pray for the wicked as for their own children. Savonarola's tune has changed, allowing an unfamiliar optimism to show through, at least for a time: the reform of Florence will not come about by the destruction of the wicked in the purging Flood, but by their conversion, their spiritual rebirth through the prayers of the virtuous citizens.[19]

As the storm clouds dissipate, Savonarola begins to envisage a very different future for Florence: the city has been chosen by God to be an instrument of reform, she is the new Jerusalem, the city of God. Once Florence is reformed, and this will not be achieved without first changing the way she is governed, she will lead the reform of the rest of Italy and of the whole Church. Florence is the navel of Italy ('l'umbilico della Italia') and from here reform will spread everywhere (X, 166–7). God's work, however, requires co-operation from Florence, beginning with urgent legal and constitutional reforms outlined in some detail. Savonarola pleads with the citizens of Florence to seek the common good of their city before all personal profit; and he makes them this striking promise: those who do will be rewarded more than if they had sought only their own benefit, in temporal as well as spiritual goods. They will enjoy an ever greater reputation and ever greater riches. The slogan 'Do penance, there is no other remedy' is now eclipsed by another: 'If the city of Florence becomes the city of God, then she will be richer, more powerful, more glorious than ever' (X, 157, 166, 187–8; XII, 206; XIII, 213, 221; XV, 254, 261; XVII, 300). He recognizes that his listeners might have to adjust to his new voice: he will not always be the prophet of doom ('Non sarà sempre profeta che pronunzii el male', XIII, 213).

The sermons examined in this section were preached during the first two weeks of December 1494. In these sermons, Savonarola has replaced an unequivocal narrative of segregation and flight (into the Ark) with a more diffuse message of thanksgiving, mercy, peace, intercession and reconciliation (the prayer of the Shunamitess). At the

---

18 He dismisses the saying that the State is not run on paternosters (XIII, 215). Though usually attributed to Cosimo de' Medici, Savonarola attributes it more obliquely to the wise of the world (XII, 200), to 'those who have their proverb' (XIV, 230), to the mad, the bad and tyrants (VIII, 134; XXIII, 417).

19 In a later, revised opinion, he laments that the nature of the lukewarm is beyond conversion (XVII, 290).

same time, in addition to the language of penance and heavenly reward, he has promised worldly prosperity and prestige. His understanding of God's plan for Florence could not have undergone a more dramatic shift, yet he continues to search Scripture for images that may clothe and shape this understanding. No longer preaching flight from earth into heaven, he glimpses a real opportunity to build heaven on earth. For this purpose he turns to the short book of the prophet Haggai.

The Temple

Haggai addresses a people recently returned to Jerusalem from exile in Babylon. They are despondent after a harvest ruined by drought, mildew and hail (Hag. 2: 17). The prophet's message is that, rather than decorating their own houses, they must first attend to the rebuilding of the Temple. If they do this, they will be blessed, the harvest will be bountiful and the nation will prosper. Evidently the people were reluctant; on two separate occasions, Haggai urges Zerubbabel, governor of Judah, and Joshua, the high priest, to rally the people to the task (Hag. 1: 1–11; 2: 1–5); and he encourages them by prophesying that silver and gold will come to them from all nations, that the new Temple will be more splendid than the former Temple, and that God will fill it with his glory (Hag. 2: 6–9). Haggai is a book in which civil, economic and religious outcomes are closely connected. With its proclamation of the benefits, even temporal ones, that accrue from religious reform, its bearing on Savonarola's new message is obvious. It is hardly surprising, then, to hear Savonarola say that God put the book of the prophet Haggai into his hands (XXI, 363).

Seeking to give fresh impetus to the ongoing discussions of constitutional renewal, Savonarola applies Haggai's exhortation to the immediate situation in December 1494. As the temple was destroyed and rebuilt under Zerubbabel, so the Church of the apostles which lies in ruins is to be rebuilt, starting with the reconstruction of Florence (XIV, 238). The city's previous form took sixty years to become established; it will be rebuilt in an instant (XVIII, 313). Savonarola insists on the newness of the enterprise: new forms of life require new forms of government (XV, 250). His reading of the text (full of allegory, numerology and etymology) confirms both the general direction and the urgency of his proposed reforms, and may be summarized as follows:

> 1.1 *In the second year* [that is, no longer the first, no longer the purity of the earliest age of the Church] of *King Darius, in the sixth month* [six is the number of the days of creation, of work before rest, therefore a time of exhaustion from labours, of work and

sweat, and not the sweetness of the early Church], *in the first day of the month* [in the first light of renovation], *the word of the Lord, spoken through the prophet Haggai* [a name meaning 'festivo', that is, God reveals his purposes to those who are full of peace, joy and contemplation], *came to the governor of Judah, Zerubbabel* [a name meaning 'magister congregationis', that is, leader of the people] *son of Shealtiel* [a name meaning 'those who ask the Lord', that is, good citizens pray before important decisions], *and to the high priest Joshua* [Jesus, that is, Saviour, one who is placed above the people and who does good deeds in order to save the people], *son of Jehozadak* (XIV, 240–42).

1.8 *Go up into the hill country, fetch timber and build a house acceptable to me, where I can reveal my glory, says the Lord.* [Timber represents wise counsel, everyone's best ideas, and the prayers of women, which must be brought into the chamber as the rulers deliberate how best to rebuild the city (XVII, 291–4)]

Haggai speaks first to the secular leaders and then to the high priest. Savonarola observes that the secular authorities are entrusted with the reform of the religious leaders, noting that, in his own day, the latter allow themselves to be led by the former in such a way that the religious have become secular (XIV, 242). Savonarola's implication – that a reformed and reforming civic leadership is necessary to lead the religious back to their true religious vocation – is not without irony.

Like Haggai, Savonarola encounters the complaint of the waverers who say that the time for change has not yet come. And like Haggai, he insists that the cause of peace, reform of the Church, and future prosperity, will not be served by delay. It is the wisdom of tyrants to know how to sow discord (XIV, 245) and those who oppose the reform of the city and its institutions do not have the good of the city at heart. There must be an end to all the old dissensions, to all party labels and slogans – a theme encapsulated in the call for a new public office, that of keeper of the peace (XIV, 247). Haggai's indictment of the waverers underpins Savonarola's appeal for united and immediate action:

1.2 *These are the words of the Lord of hosts: This nation says that the time has not yet come for the house of the Lord to be rebuilt.* [O people of Florence why do you say: It is not time? It is time, since all is out of place, the city is without peace, harmony, friendship (XIV, 242–4).]

Furthermore, Haggai encourages the people by reminding them of the fabled beauty of the former Temple, comparing this with the ruins before them. Borrowing this same rhetoric, Savonarola calls to mind the days of freedom before the Medici ascendancy in 1434, inviting his listeners to contemplate the ruinous state in which the city has been left:

2.3 *Is there anyone still among you who saw this house in its former*

> *glory? How does it appear to you now?* [Call to mind the year '34, a year of great ruin and division in your city ... born from no other cause than that you never made a true peace amongst you (XV, 257, 259–60). Remember when and how your liberty was taken from you, and see how it has now been restored to you (XXI, 372–3).][20]

With the text of the prophet Haggai, Savonarola has given shape to his new vision of Florence as the chosen city of God, the new Jerusalem. He has been able to characterize his reform plans as constructive of something good and enduring, because ordained by God. In addition, and here Haggai is particularly effective, he has found a text with which to silence his enemies, the waverers and murmurers who would obstruct or delay his reforms, with the words of God himself.

Concluding remarks

In the final sermons on Haggai, some of the sense of progression and sequence typical of the earlier sermons returns. There are, however, significant differences. The tone, for one thing, is not so surefooted: not only had he had less time to prepare these sermons, but their subject matter constituted a sortie into new territory. The characteristic defensiveness and self-legitimation, never completely absent, are especially common in these sermons. Furthermore, his previous message, preached with absolute conviction, had been vindicated in a manner that had wrong-footed the prophet himself. Two observations in particular suggest that Savonarola was considerably less comfortable with his new message than he had been with his old one. The first concerns the temporal benefits of reform whilst the second concerns Savonarola's continuing use of monastic paradigms.

Firstly, there is one element in the Haggai prophecy that Savonarola deals with less than consistently. Haggai had promised that if the people attended to their common purpose, the rebuilding of the Temple, rather than their individual comforts and security, the harvest would be plentiful and the nation would prosper. Even before beginning his sermons on Haggai, Savonarola had likewise promised that if the citizens of Florence put the common good before their own advantage, Florence would be richer, more powerful, more glorious than ever.

---

[20] Savonarola refrains from mentioning the Medici by name in these sermons, but his occasional use of the medical metaphor contains a pun that is surely not unintentional: Christ is the true doctor, the *medico*, come to bring healing to Florence (II, 41; X, 165–6; XIV, 244; XVIII, 306). For alternative characterizations of Cosimo, see Alison Brown, 'The Humanist Portrait of Cosimo de' Medici', in A. Brown, *The Medici in Florence: The Exercise and Language of Power* (Florence and Perth, 1992), pp. 3–52.

Furthermore, he acknowledged that personal wealth is a characteristic of a good citizen (X, 157) and promised riches from God in return for the outlawing of usury (X, 162–3). Riches are a predictable effect of virtuous living in the grace of God (XIII, 218). The reform of government will bring peace, which in turn brings prosperity at home and fear and respect abroad (XV, 254). The example of Roman republicanism bears out his case: as long as the Romans attended to the common good, God rewarded them in this world, extending their empire and their riches; only when they allowed a tyrant to rule did they lose God's favour (XVI, 276).

These promises are new; in earlier sermons he had contrasted the temporal blessings of the Old Testament (together with its greater ceremony and commandments) with the spiritual blessings of the New Testament (with its simpler life, and single twofold commandment). He had urged his listeners to be converted from an Old Testament religion in search of temporal blessings and to embrace the poverty of the New Testament (VIII, 131). With enthusiasm, he had cited from Jerome, Augustine, Ambrose and Basil to the effect that superfluous wealth is as good as theft, clearly preferring this view to the more moderate position of Aquinas, that God allows some to possess more than they need, that they might give to the poor. For Savonarola, Christ himself was poor and loved the poor: true Christians should be no different (IX, 151–3).

Such thoughts do not sit easily with the new promises of riches, power and glory for Florence, even if these are qualified as promises directed not to individuals but to the city as a whole. Growing impatient with the pace of reform, he accuses the Florentines of being less than enthusiastic about the condition of their Christian lives than they are about wealth and honours (XIV, 243). And seemingly ignoring his previous assurances, he complains that if he had promised money to them, rather than eternal life, they would have come running to hear him preach (XVII, 286; XVII, 299; XIX, 336). Although he never presents temporal prosperity as an end to be pursued for its own sake, Savonarola seems not to have been totally at ease with his new understanding, that temporal prosperity is an additional benefit guaranteed to those who pursue a virtuous life and put the common good before self-interest. He oscillates disconcertingly between two poles: promising the Florentines wealth as a motive for reform, and chastising them for being greedy. Evidently, the role of Haggai fitted him less comfortably than that of Noah.[21]

---

21 Amongst others, the prophet Moses, the legislator and harsh disciplinarian, at once populist and autocratic, was to provide more enduring inspiration for Savonarola; see Alison Brown, 'Savonarola, Machiavelli and Moses: A Changing Model', in A. Brown *The Medici in Florence*, pp. 263–79.

A second observation follows on from the first. Savonarola complains that philosophers, theologians and poets are against him. The complaint which he singles out for explicit mention touches on the motivation and consequences of his proposed reforms: must we all become friars (XXIII, 420–21)? Is this concern justified? Savonarola presents a variety of examples of the kind of society Florence should be. Although he allows that lessons of reform can be learnt from the pagans as well as from scripture (XVI, 263), Roman republicanism is the only non-scriptural society commended by Savonarola in these sermons, because of the peace it enjoyed and because of the monarchy it avoided (XVI, 263; XVI, 275; XVII, 289; XXII, 395). His preferred examples, however, are all Christian, amongst which the apostolic Church, a privileged time of faith, is pre-eminent (VIII, 128; VIII, 131; X, 162; XVIII, 304; XXI, 382); meanwhile the angelic hierarchy, a pattern of order and blessedness, provides a detailed model for the hierarchical structure of a reformed and peaceful city (XXIII, 413–17).

More to the point, scattered throughout these sermons there are hints that the forms of religious life are standards by which Savonarola measures other forms of society. The remarks are too occasional to constitute a deliberate strategy, but the fact that these comparisons rise spontaneously to his lips is revealing: life in the Ark is like a religious order, a 'religione' (V, 81); the seven pairs of clean animals signify the seven gifts of the spirit, the contemplative life; the pairs of unclean animals signify two commandments, of the active life; the Temple will be governed by the interior law of charity and the exterior law of monastic enclosure, 'clausura' (XVII, 291; XVII, 293; XIX, 328); the good citizen living in a peaceful republic is likened to a friar in a well-regulated priory (XIX, 337); civic leaders are told to fast and pray before big decisions, including the offering of prayers and the celebration of Mass in the Sala itself (XIII, 227–8). Far from explaining that he does not want to make the Florentines all friars and religious, Savonarola simply calls down divine punishment on those who would oppose God's purposes (XXIII, 420–21). There appears to be little middle ground between fleeing the evils of the city into a convent and importing the city into the convent.

Savonarola's own life exemplifies the tension between these options. His first draw to religious life was to flee the world; he prayed to be removed from the world's wickedness, carnal violence, adulteries, robberies, pride, idolatry and cruel blasphemies, and he advised others to flee, to weep and to be silent. As prior of San Marco, one of his earliest moves had been to try to relocate the priory outside the city, for the pursuit of a purer, more observant life of peace and contemplation, but that effort was frustrated and he was driven back into the city.[22] He had sought peace and contemplation and believed he would find it in the cloister, but now he was being dragged by God onto the high seas of a prophet's miserable career. Having failed to move the priory out of the city, his alternative was to absorb the city into the priory, to turn the whole city of Florence into the New Jerusalem, the city of God.

Savonarola's personal history, however, does not exhaust the possibilities of his message. Although the community at San Marco certainly flourished – growing from some twenty-five friars in 1475 to 120 friars during Savonarola's time as prior in the 1490s – the movement he initiated did not only create friars and nuns. His disciples, the 'Piagnoni' or 'weepers', included politicians, lawyers, merchants, scholars, poets, philosophers, artisans, husbands and wives, mothers and fathers. Savonarola himself was more at home in the Ark than in the Temple; his own life attests to his preference for the ideals of the monastic or conventual life. But it is the Piagnoni movement as a whole that gives a broader picture of how Savonarola's fervent theocratic republicanism might be capable of furnishing an authentic theology of and for the laity.[23]

Evaluations of Savonarola range across a wide spectrum, from inspired prophet, at one end, to cynical opportunist, at the other.[24] Even those who find his an authentic religious voice might judge his interpretation of Haggai to be too worldly, not allegorical enough; or his use of Noah's Ark to be too fugitive, not incarnational enough. Nevertheless, his words maintain their freshness and vividness (even for those who disagree with both his diagnosis and his remedy) because they record an intense struggle with the perennial questions of Christianity.

---

[22] For these details, see Weinstein, *Savonarola and Florence*, pp. 81–2, 104.

[23] See Lorenzo Polizzotto, *The Elect Nation: The Savonarolan Movement in Florence 1494–1545* (Oxford, 1994).

[24] See Donald Weinstein, 'Hagiography, Demonology, Biography: Savonarola Studies Today', *Journal of Modern History*, 63 (1991), pp. 483–503.

CHAPTER THREE

Erasmus and the Psalms*

Michael J. Heath

Erasmus' biblical scholarship owed much to the example of Lorenzo Valla. The most obvious debt was incurred in the preparation of the New Testament published in 1516. This *Novum instrumentum*, Erasmus' most original and influential contribution to biblical scholarship, consisted of the first-ever printed Greek text, accompanied by a controversial new Latin translation and by Erasmus' notes, the *Annotationes*, in which he justified departures from the canonical text based on St Jerome's version. Erasmus' labours had been greatly eased by the pioneering work of Valla's *Collatio novi testamenti*, which Erasmus published in 1505 as *Adnotationes in Novum Testamentum*. In his New Testament, a landmark in the evolution of biblical scholarship, and of particular interest to English scholars as a major textual source of the King James Bible, we see Erasmus at the height of his powers as textual scholar and theologian. While these qualities also play a role in his treatment of the Book of Psalms, they often take second place to another aspect of Erasmus' spiritual programme in whose development Lorenzo Valla again played a role. Erasmus profited from his own edition of Valla's *Elegantiae* to place humanist eloquence at the service of piety and reform.

It was natural that Erasmus should choose, for his only venture into Old Testament exegesis, the Book of Psalms. To scriptural scholars of the Renaissance, especially those of a philological bent, the Psalter appeared only slightly less fitting than the Gospels and the Pauline Epistles as a subject for commentary, representing as it did the purest expression of the Holy Spirit to be found in the Hebrew tradition. Further legitimation was provided by the prestige of those early Fathers of the Church who had devoted much energy to psalm commentary; a special incentive for Erasmus was perhaps the recollection that Origen, who had so inspired him as a neophyte theologian, had given particular attention to the Book of Psalms in his *Hexapla*.

---

* This paper is a much-expanded version of one given at Toronto in 1988 and published as 'Allegory, Rhetoric and Spirituality: Erasmus's Early Psalm Commentaries', in A. Dalzell, C. Fantazzi et al. (eds), *Acta Conventus Neo-Latini Torontonensis* (Binghamton, NY, 1991), pp. 363–70.

Erasmus' psalm commentaries are less celebrated than those of his patristic predecessors, and were certainly less influential than the comparable writings of some contemporaries, most notably Luther. Although a number of Erasmus' efforts went into several printings, and were translated into half a dozen languages soon after publication, they have been largely neglected since, whereas his work on the New Testament has continued to resonate through the centuries in the life and worship of many denominations. It must be said that Erasmus' psalm commentaries were not intended primarily as works of textual investigation, unlike for example Lefèvre d'Etaples's *Quincuplex psalterium* of 1509, and thus their impact on the world of scholarship was muted. Moreover, the central thread of Erasmus' exegesis, the underlying appeal for moderation and reconciliation, perhaps told against these works in the climate of intolerance that was developing so rapidly. This chapter sketches some of the characteristics of this forgotten endeavour to which Erasmus returned intermittently throughout his career. I shall concentrate, for reasons which will become clear, on his exegesis of Psalms 1–4. My translation of these commentaries, the first ever to be made, has just been published; it is to be hoped that the translation into English of all eleven of these works will help to establish their place in the Erasmian canon.[1]

Unlike many of his patristic predecessors, Erasmus never found time to write a complete commentary on the Psalms. His first essay, the *Exposition of Psalm 1* (*Enarratio primi psalmi*, 1515), is a somewhat isolated effort both in time and in tenor; its programme, essentially an ethical and political one, was not resumed when Erasmus returned to the genre seven years later. It has the air of an experiment, as though he were investigating the potential of scriptural exegesis as a weapon against the same targets – tyrants, warmongers, foolish princes, corrupt bishops – that he was attacking elsewhere, for example in the *Adagia* and in the *Institutio principis Christiani*, with the aid of Plato's and Aristotle's ethical treatises. In the dedicatory epistle, characteristically, Erasmus presents it as a somewhat lightweight work, a mere prelude to his projected commentary on St Paul and his edition of St Jerome, and it seems that the most compelling reason he can find for undertaking it is the coincidence between first word of the psalm and the name of its recipient, Beatus Rhenanus.

However, there is some evidence that in the early 1520s Erasmus did

---

[1] They are being published as *Expositions of the Psalms*, ed. Dominic Baker-Smith, in the *Collected Works of Erasmus* [henceforth: *CWE*] (Toronto, 1974–   ), vols 63–5. Volume 63, containing my translations of the first four commentaries, appeared in April 1998, days before the conference.

contemplate an exposition of the entire psalter, in emulation of his patristic predecessors. According to the dedication of the *Sermon on Psalm 4* (*In psalmum quartum concio*, 1525), John Longland, bishop of Lincoln, had urged him 'several years ago' to produce a commentary on the Book of Psalms and had 'returned again and again to the same theme'. At the end of his *Commentary on Psalm 2* (*Commentarius in psalmum 2*, 1522), Erasmus speaks of 'going on to the next psalm' (144),[2] and a mysterious note from Froben, the printer, hints that other psalm commentaries, begun 'a few years before', had been lost or stolen. From the dedicatory epistle to the *Paraphrase on Psalm 3* (*Paraphrasis in tertium psalmum*, 1524) it appears that Erasmus had been challenged once more, this time by the theologian Melchior of Vianden, 'to do over again for the mystical psalms what I had done for the New Testament'. It is interesting that for this work Erasmus chose the form of the paraphrase, in which he had just completed his influential exposition of all the books of the New Testament except Revelation. Was he assessing the practicability of repeating the exercise with the Psalter? It might have proved possible to continue in this vein; the *Paraphrase on Psalm 3* is much the shortest and simplest of Erasmus' psalm commentaries. But in the dedicatory epistle to Melchior he stresses the obstacles to simple paraphrase with a text so unstable and opaque as that of a psalm, which lends itself so much more readily to a freer kind of exegesis. Thus the enterprise in this form was short-lived; when he turned to Psalm 4 Erasmus chose the form of a lengthy *concio*, a sermon or public speech, though its publication in a collection with the previous three psalm commentaries does suggest some gesture towards the establishment of a corpus. But the seven subsequent psalm commentaries, most entitled *enarratio* in the style of the Fathers, were published separately, and they too are long, complex works, owing little to the style of the paraphrase as practised by Erasmus.

Despite the occasional lapse into a conversational style, the *Sermon on Psalm 4* seems far too long to have been actually delivered in church. Its form does, however, suggest the use to which Erasmus hoped his meditations upon the psalms would be put. In a sarcastic aside to the *Exposition of Psalm 1*, he hints at the necessity for a revaluation of texts which, being *matiere de breviaire*, as Rabelais's Frere Jan liked to repeat, had become stale through familiarity:

> Perhaps this passage has some relevance for certain priests who busily recite sacred psalms they do not understand, either through lack of attention or lack of education ... Anyone who does not merely read out the sacred words, but also expounds them to the

---

[2] References in brackets in the text are to *CWE* 63.

faithful – or even to the faithless – in the form of teaching, exhortation, or consolation, 'gives his own fruit'. (46)

The paraphrases on the New Testament were designed, among other things, to provide material for a new kind of preaching; such was considered to be their value as a basis for pastoral exposition that in 1547 a translation of them had by law to be in the possession of every English clergyman who lacked a doctor's degree.[3] The *Sermon on Psalm 4* provided a fully developed (not to say over-developed) example of the homiletic potential of one of the less accessible Old Testament books; Erasmus' treatment gives full attention not only to the spiritual lesson but also to the moral implications of the psalm. The first four psalm commentaries, culminating in this impressive example of the preacher's art, are the least known and least studied even of these works, but they too can illuminate the variety of Erasmus' exegetical and homiletic methods, and they have much to contribute to our understanding of his Christology. If in the *Paraphrases on the New Testament* Erasmus' exegesis had been relatively cautious and discreet, the psalms offered him freer rein, since their importance had always been liturgical rather than doctrinal, a traditional expression of corporate worship rather than the source of dogmatic certainties.

Indeed, there was much that was still mysterious about the Psalter. The text itself, both in Greek and Latin, was known in several different versions; Jerome, in particular, had left no less than three. Erasmus, unequipped to reconstruct the original text, as he had striven to do for the New Testament, was obliged to rely on 'those who know the Hebrew tongue' (unspecified), though he did make fleeting attempts to compare the widely accepted Greek version of the Septuagint with Jerome's version based on the 'true Hebrew text' (*juxta veritatem Hebraicam*). Erasmus did not hesitate to expand his exegesis at some points by making use of the variants he chanced upon; several verses of Psalm 2 provided fruitful ambiguities of this kind.

At the beginning of each commentary, Erasmus outlines other technical problems on which, as he says, there was little agreement among the earlier Christian commentators. He weighs the conflicting opinions, in particular of Saints Augustine, Jerome and Hilary, on such topics as the order and numbering of the psalms, the identity of their author, their titles and superscriptions, the distribution of the verses among various speakers, the meaning of *Selah*, and so on. But the reader senses that his heart is not in it. His resolution of a conundrum

---

[3] Cornelis Augustijn, *Erasmus: His Life, Works and Influence*, trans. J.C. Grayson (Toronto, 1991), p. 101.

concerning the numbering of the second psalm, which involves Esdras and St Paul as well as Hilary and Jerome, makes explicit where his interests truly lay: 'It is not worth agonizing over a matter which is indeed of little importance as far as our worship and our attitude towards God are concerned' (*Commentary on Psalm 2*, 72). Whatever the shortcomings of the text – and in some cases precisely because of those shortcomings – the pious exegete will not lack for inspiration. The reader is even given the impression that, for Erasmus, to dwell on textual minutiae will be to risk interrupting and disrupting the flow of elucidation.

Erasmus' exegetical method is informal and flexible, as the variety of his titles suggests. Not for him the unflagging pursuit of the famous 'four senses of Scripture', the literal or historical, the allegorical, the tropological or moral, and the anagogic or eschatological.[4] Such schemes were originally elaborated to impose some order upon the potential extravagance of figurative interpretation, but had supposedly degenerated into an arid formalism. Erasmus' heroine in the *Praise of Folly* asserts mischievously that the despised schoolmen are so besotted with this rigid and constricting system that they will apply it even to 'some foolish popular anecdote from the *Mirror of History* ... or *The Deeds of the Romans*'.[5] In his *Exposition of Psalm 1* (29), Erasmus again denounces those theologians 'with unwashed hands and feet' (meaning rash, presumptuous and irreverent) who, whenever they get their dirty paws on Holy Scripture, will force it, however reluctant and unwilling it may be, into the prescribed mould.

We do find the occasional example of the traditional analysis in his expositions. In the *Commentary on Psalm 2* (78), the story of David and Goliath illuminates the function of the historical or literal sense, which 'does not in any way obstruct the allegorical; on the contrary, it ensures that the rays of mystical knowledge, as if caught in a mirror, shine all the more brightly and clearly before our mind's eye'. Thus we may recognize in David's battle the allegorical prototype of Christ resisting the temptations of Satan, and, tropologically, the struggle of each Christian against the passions of the world. Anagogically, Armageddon is foreshadowed. Erasmus shows, in introducing his reading here, that he is not averse to using the traditional terminology:

---

[4] On the tradition, see Henri de Lubac, *Exégèse médiévale: les quatre sens de l'Ecriture*, 3 vols (Paris, 1959–64) and, for a slightly different account from mine of Erasmus' adaptation of it, Georges Chantraine, 'Erasme, lecteur des psaumes' in Jean-Claude Margolin (ed.), *Colloquia Erasmiana Turonensia*, 2 vols (Paris, 1972), ii, pp. 691–712.

[5] *Praise of Folly* in CWE 27, p. 134.

> In many psalms the theme is twofold: the historical, which underlies
> it like the foundations of a building, and the allegorical, or
> anagogical, which, beneath the cloak of historical events, conceals,
> or rather reveals, the gospel story, instruction in true piety, or an
> image of eternal bliss.

But although all four traditional categories seem to be represented here,
the effect is to establish Erasmus' habitual method of exegesis, using a
flexible twofold division into literal and concealed meaning (analogous
to the celebrated Platonic image of the Silenus given Christian overtones
in Erasmus' *Adagia*), and thus removing the obligation to 'wring the
neck of Scripture' to find all four senses in any given passage. He could
claim patristic authority for this reduction; in his manual on preaching,
Ecclesiastes, Erasmus asserts that, although the 'four senses' have been
foisted by modern commentators upon Jerome, Gregory, Ambrose and
Augustine, the early Fathers in fact recognized only two, the literal and
the 'spiritual'.[6]

Of the two, Erasmus has much less time for the literal or historical
sense although, as we have seen, he recognizes that it has a role to play
in inspiring reflection. Erasmus' mistrust of the literal has much to do
with his scorn for the 'Judaizing' tendencies of some Christian
theologians. St Paul, as Erasmus often reminds us, railed against the
effects of 'the letter which kills' (2 Cor. 3: 6; see, for example, the
Commentary on Psalm 2, 119). Essentially Erasmus treats the psalms as
Christian texts and ignores or underplays their historical context,
despising the Jewish commentators who could see no further. At one
point he belittles the 'contentious and unprofitable speculations' (177)
of the rabbis; at another, he exposes their disagreements with one
another about the mere historical details, and extends his scorn to their
superstition and their prejudice:

> I do not disapprove entirely of looking at what the Hebrew
> commentators have to say, especially the older ones, but I do not
> think that they have very much to offer, since I observe that their
> commentaries are pretty well stuffed with vapourings and old
> wives' tales [*fumis ac fabulis anilibus*], not to mention their desire
> to discredit our interpretations, and their hatred of Christ.
> (*Commentary on Psalm 2*, 80)

Thus Erasmus, like almost all his Christian predecessors, cannot but
focus upon the concealed meaning. In the verse of Psalm 2 under
consideration here, he hastens to apply the psalm not to the historical
King David, but 'to our David, about whom it was unquestionably

---

6 *Ecclesiastes sive de ratione concionandi*, in *Opera omnia* (Leiden, 1703–06), v, col.
1034D.

written'. This typology, so routine and familiar in relation to the Psalms, is authenticated of course by its appearance in the Acts of the Apostles (for instance 4: 24–7 and 13: 32–3). However, Erasmus does not restrict his broad second category of exegesis to the allegory of Christ, as some predecessors had done. His flexible approach enabled him to identify at least five loose allegorical categories, which reflect but do not coincide with the traditional scheme of exegesis; most coincide rather with Erasmus' distinctly pastoral aims in interpreting the psalms. This is evident from a passage in *De copia*:

> Whenever we are endeavouring to turn men towards piety or away from wickedness, we shall find very useful anecdotes drawn from the Old or the New Testament. The hidden meaning of these can be variously handled; it can be explained in terms of human life, or of the body of the Church joined and connected to Christ the head, or of the fellowship of heaven, or of those early days when the faith was new-born, or of our own times.[7]

These categories of exegesis are all present to some extent in the four commentaries under discussion, though when he later constructed a formal *Triple Exposition of Psalm 22* (*Enarratio triplex*) Erasmus confined himself to the tropological and two levels of the allegorical, Christ as head and the Church as Christ's body. In all these commentaries, Erasmus has least to offer on the 'fellowship of heaven', his version of the anagogic or eschatological level, the most abstract of the categories and thus the least relevant to the practical *philosophia Christi*.

Thus, in the *Exposition of Psalm 1*, the eschatological sense is given short shrift; Erasmus merely remarks that sinful Christians, more wicked and goatlike even than the Turks, are threatened with exclusion 'from the company of the blessed souls in the world to come' (60). In this first venture into the genre, Erasmus makes explicit in the subtitle his commitment to an ethical interpretation: *Enarratio primi psalmi, iuxta tropologiam potissimum* (*An Exposition of the First Psalm, principally on the tropological level*). In the introduction he explains that this level of exegesis 'seems both more appropriate to [this psalm] and also more conducive to that reform of morality which is my principal aim' (11). The polemical content and occasionally satirical style do not belie the promise and reflect Erasmus' current activities. The commentary appeared in 1515, the year in which the *Adagia* were republished with long additions on current affairs; at the same time Erasmus was composing the *Institutio principis christiani*, published in 1516 and his most rigorous examination of the role of ethics in public

---

[7] *De copia*, translated as *Foundations of the Abundant Style*, in CWE 24, p. 635.

life. The *Exposition* charts a path for the would-be 'blessed man' through the perils of the world, and its concluding passage underlines Erasmus' relative unconcern at this time with even the allegorical or religious lesson:

> Therefore, if we wish to acquire that most blessed title of 'blessed man', let us ensure that it is not only in our confessions and our acts of worship, but also in our lives and deeds, that we reflect the only source of bliss, Jesus Christ. (79–80)

There was an interval of seven years before the appearance of Erasmus' second commentary on a psalm, and circumstances dictated that this commitment to the ethical was modified if not abandoned henceforth. The *Commentary on Psalm 2* appeared in 1522, when Erasmus was embroiled – along with the rest of Christendom – in doctrinal controversy. Although the commentary avoids direct comment on sectarian dispute, it does much more to highlight the religious lesson and to consider the source of the ills in the Church rather than the position of the individual believer. From this point, Erasmus increasingly treats the psalms principally as a source of spiritual enlightenment and encouragement through typology; nothing could suit his purpose better than the traditional reading of David as a type of Christ. But he also exploits the equally ancient tradition that applied allegorically the struggles depicted in the Old Testament, and often dramatized in the psalms, to the spiritual conflict within the Church as well as within the individual. In this *Commentary* Erasmus analyses what is obviously, in historical terms, a messianic prophecy; he demonstrates comprehensively that the psalm foretells the whole story of the redemption of humanity. Its Christology revolves around the characteristic Erasmian antithesis between the folly of the Cross and the wisdom of the world, with particular warnings concerning spiritual pride and the necessity of humility. Erasmus' attitude towards the Reformers and some of their opponents is implicit in all this.

Although the brief *Paraphrase on Psalm 3* (1524) adopts a new perspective, stylistically, in that Erasmus himself takes on the persona of the psalmist and addresses the Lord directly, his exegesis of the revolt of Absalom evoked by the psalm is similarly religious and diachronic, being applied both to the persecution of Christ and to the spiritual dangers besetting contemporary Christians. Finally, the *Sermon on Psalm 4* (1525), the longest of these pieces, again develops a Christocentric analysis in a dual exegesis. First, Erasmus follows Jerome in attributing the psalmist's words to Christ on the Cross, though here Erasmus makes less of the folly of the Cross than of its redemptive and consolatory function throughout history. He then turns to the individual believer to deliver a homily which mingles spiritual and ethical advice, exhorting the faithful, especially those who have (perhaps symbolically) nodded off (212), to sacrifice their vanity and falsehood in that imitation of Christ in which the religious and the tropological message become intertwined.

It is obvious from these summaries that Erasmus treated each psalm somewhat differently, adopting the genre and the level of exegesis which the material, and his own current preoccupations, seemed to demand. But it is interesting to investigate how the distinctive style of the psalms lent itself to Erasmus' purpose, and indeed how he came to terms with the specific technical problems that they pose. To what extent did the literary criteria expounded by Valla, for example, enable Erasmus to arrive at a preliminary estimate of the psalmist's meaning? It has been argued that Erasmus regarded oratory as more useful, indeed more salutary, than dialectic in the exposition of theology,[8] and in the *Exposition of Psalm 1* he discusses the preacher's choice of language, which must aim to produce a lasting impression on the audience, even at the expense of precision:

> Some words are more impressive than others, some more meaningful, some more impassioned, some more pleasant; no less important [to the preacher] is a knowledge of the rhetorical figures associated with words and phrases. (47)

This principle is illustrated with a remarkably ornate example from the ninth-century hymnist Notker Balbulus; clearly for the author of *De copia* and *Ecclesiastes sive de ratione concionandi* the essential point is to avoid the mind-numbing tediousness of the medieval Scotists, and the imaginative metaphorical diction of the psalmist or of a poetic rhetorician such as Notker is a powerful tool for the preacher and exegete.

Erasmus the satirist and writer of dialogue also found much to admire in the dramatic oral style of the psalms, and he delighted in analysing and sometimes emulating their unexpected twists and turns. His analysis is rhetorical rather than philological. He identifies repetition and antithesis as the basic figures in the psalms; these convey, respectively, the Spirit's desire to reinforce the lesson and the way in which admonition to the wicked frequently alternates with reassurance to the faithful.[9] Erasmus makes liberal if imprecise use of rhetorical terms to underline the technical competence of the poems. He is unsure,

---

[8] See Marjorie O'Rourke Boyle, *Erasmus on Language and Method in Theology* (Toronto, 1977), pp. 55 and 63–7.

[9] Good examples of this kind of analysis will be found in CWE 63, pp. 55–6 and 86.

for example, whether the singular 'leaf' for the plural in Psalm 1: 3 is an example of hypallage or of *emphasis* (in Greek in the text), but by making a parallel with the style of Luke 21: 18 he can confirm in a small way the common inspiration of the psalms and the Gospels. He goes further to suggest the universality and accessibility of the psalms as literature with parallels from Greek lyric poetry (55) and modern poets and rhetoricians (74).

Thus Erasmus the literary critic appreciates the rhetorical qualities of the psalms, amongst which he would doubtless place their tendency to anthropomorphism in the description of God. He mounts a solid defence of what some commentators had reproved as a frivolous and unbecoming usage. There can be no doubt, he agrees, that the divine nature is changeless and unmoving, but he argues that the frequent attribution of human characteristics to God in the psalms is a literary device to assist understanding. In the *Commentary on Psalm 2*, for instance, God's wrath and laughter are evoked; the wrath conveys most vividly the effect on humanity of his threatened vengeance, while the mocking laughter conveys his capacity for irony, here in frustrating the Jews' elaborate but futile plots against Christ (102–3 and 111, where the device is described rather unconvincingly as a synecdoche).

Erasmus the pedagogue always stressed the usefulness of vivid and lifelike imagery. In the *Exposition of Psalm 1* (10) he takes issue with St Hilary, who had objected austerely to the psalm's description of Christ as a tree, or indeed as 'wood', a classic case of Hebrew synecdoche, as Erasmus later explains (33). Would Hilary, he demands, also expunge from Scripture the vine, the palm, the lamb? Later in the same work Erasmus uses literary criteria to assist in expounding the typology of the psalms. He exploits the fact that the range of Hebrew metaphor was very limited, generally to natural phenomena; this meant that it was not difficult to find resonances and reverberations throughout holy writ, most obviously in Christ's parables, and thus to reconcile the Old Testament with the New. In this case, the tree in Psalm 1 recalls dozens of others, from the tree in Eden to the tree by the waters in the Book of Revelation; most importantly for Erasmus' Christology, the list includes Christ's own image of the vine and its branches, and of course the Cross itself (34–6).

As suggested earlier, Erasmus himself found inspiration in the psalms' welcome directness and vivacity. He will occasionally venture to embellish an existing image, for example adding, on the arboreal theme, that a virtuous Christian, when persecuted, is like 'a tree that is pruned [which] grows all the more vigorously and gives more abundant fruit' (77). Developing the psalmist's imagery in another way, he will pun soberly on such antitheses as *angustias dilatare* (Ps. 4: 1), where the literal 'straits' and the metaphorical 'anguish' permit many variations (and, incidentally, create many problems for the translator labouring in a less flexible language!). An impressive original image worthy of the psalmist himself is that of the prophet dwelling in a watchtower halfway between the light of heaven and the impenetrable darkness of earth (212). Again, the commentaries are enlivened by passages of well-paced antithetical dialogue or expostulation, in the style of the originals, when denouncing modern hypocrites (61–2) or evoking the impious plots of the conspirators, both scriptural and contemporary, against Christ (87).

Erasmus' insistence upon the literary qualities of the psalms is explained partly by his inability to comment independently upon the philological issues. Here Erasmus the textual scholar is almost redundant because of his ignorance of Hebrew. He explained to John Colet his reluctance to learn what might seem an essential tongue for a commentator on the psalms: 'I was put off by the strangeness of the language ... the shortness of life and the limitations of human nature will not allow a man to master too many things at once.'[10] For information on the more obscure and controversial readings he turned, naturally, to St Jerome and, more intriguingly, to the fourteenth-century Franciscan scholar Nicholas of Lyra. It is intriguing because Renaissance scholars rarely gave Nicholas his due as one of few medieval scholars accomplished in Hebrew. Erasmus compares his achievements most unfavourably with Valla's in his preface to the latter's *Adnotationes*, and generally lumps him together with the tedious medieval Scotists.[11] Rabelais was merely endorsing a humanist commonplace when he made his slighting pun on the theologian's name: 'si de Lyra ne delyre'.[12] In the *Commentary on Psalm 2*, Erasmus names Nicholas merely in order to chide him for disrespect towards Jerome and Augustine (76–7) – only to profit silently from his erudition a few pages later (79).[13] It must be said that Nicholas's main concern was to expound the literal historical meaning of the Old Testament, an enterprise naturally uncongenial to the Evangelical humanist.

Erasmus' enforced preference for rhetorical effect over textual

---

10 Letter 181 (1504) in *CWE* 2, p. 87.

11 See Letters 182, *CWE* 2, pp. 93–4 and 396, *CWE* 3, p. 258.

12 Rabelais, *Le Tiers Livre*, ch. 1. A contemporary Latin tag put the same pun to different use: 'Si Lyra non lyrasset, Lutherus non delirasset'.

13 Erasmus borrows from his *Postilla super psalterium* (cf. *CWE* 63, p. 79, n. 35), the first commentary on the Hebrew to be printed, and a work much exploited – often surreptitiously – by humanist commentators in Erasmus' day.

accuracy, which shocked some contemporary critics, even led him to conclude, with a touch of bravado, that the Greek and Latin versions of the psalms provided all the information and, especially, all the inspiration required by the exegete. It also made him indifferent to Hebrew itself; considering the different meanings of the word *bar* (a son? purity? wheat?) in Syriac and Hebrew, he cuts discussion short with a dismissive pun: 'There is no need to cudgel our brains with the complexities of these barbaric languages' (142). This is his only contribution to Jerome's erudite discussion of Psalm 2: 12. Similarly, Erasmus later sidesteps a more than usually problematic Hebrew phrase by remarking airily that 'no language is more confusing or more open to misinterpretation and disagreement' (225). Modern Hebrew scholars have demonstrated the coherence of the psalms as songs of praise or prophecy in the Jewish tradition, but Erasmus, along with most contemporaries, was compelled to gloss over what appeared to be logical lapses in the texts as then translated:

> It is not essential that every part of a prophecy should fit perfectly into either a historical or an allegorical reading, because often certain elements are included to ensure chronological coherence while others, which are out of place in the historical context, compel us to have recourse to allegory. (144–5)

Erasmus' uncharacteristically cavalier approach to the text is nowhere clearer than in his comments on a particularly knotty verse of Psalm 4 (verse 2), where the Hebrew, Greek and Latin versions all seem to suggest something different:

> The large number of different readings here should surprise no one. There can be no doubt that what the psalmist wrote, at the behest of the Holy Spirit, was simple and unambiguous; but God allowed these variations, the work of copyists and translators, to appear in the holy books, so that these extra difficulties would rouse us from our torpor. (239)

What appears to be a rationalization is in fact consistent with Erasmus' general view of the function of the psalms as texts dictated by the Holy Spirit. Even in this technical linguistic sphere, their value lies in their capacity to inspire exegesis. The quirky obscurity of some passages is part of the design: 'Very often an unexpected turn of phrase will rouse us from our lethargy, or make us more attentive when we are in danger of nodding off' (226).[14] Erasmus cites the supreme example of this beneficent power: St Augustine's fumbling exposition of Psalm 4, as a

---

14 *Pace* Rabelais's Frere Jan, who lulled himself and his companions to sleep by his recitation of the first psalm: *Gargantua*, ch. 41.

novice, may have been utterly wrong, but it inspired in him the love of
exegesis and helped to establish his vocation, to the inestimable benefit
of all Christians (265).

Thus Erasmus the poet, dramatist and critic found enrichment of
various kinds in the psalms. But it is striking how far Erasmus the
classical scholar was redundant. In these works, the fancier of adages
and editor of secular texts exercised deliberate restraint over his
abundant humanist erudition. At the very outset, considering the duties
of the exegete, he urges a proper reverence: 'Anyone setting out to
expound the sacred psalms of the prophets must remember that he is not
dealing with the hymns of Orpheus or Homer, which relate to a pagan
cult ...' (8). Although willing to adduce the formal techniques of pagan
literature, as we have seen, Erasmus resists even the most obvious
opportunities to deploy its substance. At the point where the 'good
things' evoked in Psalm 4: 6 seem inexorably to demand a discussion of
the Aristotelian categories of the good (familiar enough in Erasmus'
political writings)[15] he remarks primly: 'I think it more fitting to
expound Holy Writ in terms of Holy Writ, lest we substitute mere
human cleverness for the divine Spirit' (261). Only in the *Exposition of
Psalm 1*, written during his 'ethical' period, did Erasmus draw on pagan
philosophers, and even there he carefully reiterated his mistrust of
Aristotle as a source for the theologian. A review of the other three
commentaries produces meagre results: three classical allusions in the
Commentary on Psalm 2, none at all in the *Paraphrase on Psalm 3* and,
in a surprisingly anti-syncretic passage of the *Sermon on Psalm 4*,
Erasmus berates the Greek philosophers for their worldliness and their
hazy notions of the nature of God, grudgingly allowing that 'perhaps a
few did conceive some idea of it but ... did not worship him as the true
God' (182). He goes on to rebuke reputedly pious pagan poets for
failing to believe, still less to practise, what they preached (189). One
exception to the rule of rejection of his more profane self is that Erasmus
continued to embellish his language with his own adages, but in these
commentaries he was unusually careful to label them 'profane' or
'Greek' proverbs, in order no doubt to distinguish them from the biblical
books of Proverbs and Wisdom. Even his exploitation of classical
literary criticism was directed towards stylistic appreciation of the
sacred texts rather than towards the elucidation of their substance; he
calls in Quintilian merely to underline the utility of antithesis (56) and
upbraids 'earlier commentators' for misusing the term hypallage (85).

If Erasmus did not here seek enlightenment from his classical

---

[15] For example in the *Panegyricus* and the *Institutio principis christiani*: see CWE 27,
pp. 32 and 196.

mentors, he also rejected the more relevant contribution of the Jewish commentators, as we have seen. In fact, a deep and (for the modern reader) uncomfortable vein of contempt for the Jews and their traditions runs through these works, reinforced by some uncharitable gloating over their downfall as a result of the failed conspiracy against Christ foretold in both the second and fourth psalms (for example, 110 and 184–8).[16] Ironically, for Erasmus, the Jews had not welcomed the Messiah precisely because they had interpreted these psalms, amongst other prophecies, too literally; the almost gleeful vehemence of Erasmus' invective against the Hebrew traitors may be explained by his conviction that the truth had lain within their grasp but, in their impiety, they had failed to embrace it; in their spiritual blindness, they had failed to see it. It becomes clear, however, that beneath Erasmus' scorn here for Judaism and Pharisaism there lies a thinly veiled attack on the Christian formalism which so disquieted him, and which led him to dismiss those churchmen who encouraged such practices as 'reverend rabbis'.[17] But in these first commentaries, committed essentially to proclaiming a positive message of spiritual hope and an exhortation to moral reform, it is only rarely and cautiously that Erasmus alludes directly to the more controversial issues that he addressed contemporaneously in, for example, the *Colloquia*: the outward observance of pointless ritual, the mania for pilgrimage, the abuse of confession, and so on. There is the occasional echo of these issues, especially in the *Sermon on Psalm 4*, where we find a denunciation of extravagant prayers (219–20), a brief diatribe against monastic self-righteousness (259), and the following skit on the rituals of death, whose use of enumeration and suspense almost qualifies it as satire, though it pales beside such outbursts as the colloquy *Funus*:

> The general run of people try to get everything in, with frequent confession, just as frequent absolution, holy water and holy oil, consecrated candles, bedside confessors, mourners, testaments, funeral feasts, solemn declarations, vows, bulls – and yet they die with unquiet minds. (273)

If there is little scope for such familiar broad satire of superstition, there is still less for Erasmus' waspish portrayals of individual contemporaries. In an unguarded moment in the *Commentary on Psalm 2*, he appears to comment slightingly on the recent death of Pope Leo X: 'His destination is uncertain' (143). But contemporary letters suggest that even this may be an awkwardly expressed refusal to usurp divine

---

16 Dominic Baker-Smith deals at length with this question in his introduction to *CWE* 63, pp. xlix–lvi.

17 See for example Letter 1126, *CWE* 8, p. 17.

privilege and to presume to judge the career of any man (let alone a recent patron).[18]

Little controversy, even less satire: the essential function of these commentaries was to expound Erasmus' *philosophia Christi*. The psalms under discussion are linked by an essential and relevant allegorical theme. If Erasmus exhorts us to approach their portals with due awe and reverence, 'purified by the sacrifice of prayer' (8), it is especially because each psalm in its different way is a prophecy of Christ – as the Fathers agree. Erasmus regarded Christ as the true target and the true centre of all exegesis: 'This level of meaning in particular is almost inexhaustible in the Psalms, and has indeed been shown to be irrefutable, on the authority of Scripture, as I have made clear' (145). If we look at the outline of his commentaries from a different angle, the importance of his contention is plain. According to Erasmus, Psalm 1 teaches that the remedy against temptation is to meditate upon Christ and to imitate him; Psalm 2 describes allegorically the folly and passion of Christ; Psalm 3 exalts him as the exemplar of perseverance, and Psalm 4 foretells his words upon the Cross.

Interestingly, Erasmus' desire to achieve a consistent and comprehensive Christological reading can lead to just the sort of logic-chopping that he despised in his medieval predecessors. Take the problematic verse 9 of Psalm 2: 'You shall rule them with an iron rod; you shall break them like a pot of clay.' This description of a despotic Messiah hardly sits comfortably, as Erasmus admits, with his usual portrayal of the mild and merciful Saviour. He is therefore grateful for St Hilary's suggestion that here the 'rod' may be no more than a sceptre, a mere emblem of authority, like the praetor's rod in ancient Rome; *in extremis*, Erasmus will accept a pagan parallel. Hilary had added, helpfully, that 'iron' might here be read as a symbol of durability rather than harshness, inspiring Erasmus himself to devise a new reading of the 'pot of clay'. He conjectures that the pot has not yet been fired in the oven, that the clay is still damp, and that there is thus a chance of rescuing the material, to be reshaped by the heavenly potter evoked in Romans 9: 20–23 (131–5). Such subtlety is justified by Erasmus on the ground that his aim is to edify, which leads him to a remarkable admission:

> Salvation is not imperilled by a slight departure from the original sense of the Scripture, so long as the new reading conforms to piety and truth; even if our interpretation does not entirely fit into its original context, our labours will have been worthwhile if our reading contributes to moral improvement, and fits in with other scriptural texts. (239–40)

---

18 See Letters 1248 and 1342 in *CWE* 8, pp. 331–2 and *CWE* 9, p. 398.

The last condition is important: the coherence of Scripture was a fundamental tenet of Erasmus' approach to the divine word, which he could not but contrast with the vagaries of human utterance and the inconsistencies of theologians, popes, councils, and even the most respected Fathers of the Church.[19]

The *Exposition of Psalm 1* was Erasmus' first published work of scriptural exegesis, but these four commentaries can hardly be seen as an extension of his contemporary work on the New Testament, since their contribution to textual scholarship is minimal, and their connection with doctrinal dispute is fairly tenuous. Nonetheless, they are part of the same project in the sense that Erasmus presents them as a foreshadowing and to some extent a ratification of the promises of the Gospel. Inspired by the Holy Spirit, the psalms are to be read as an adjunct, poetic and thus occasionally elliptical, to the wisdom of the New Testament. Erasmus places them high in the hierarchy of scripture: 'Despite its extreme brevity, this [first] psalm deals with vital and universal themes' (11); 'Although it is short, this one psalm [the fourth] would enable us to win salvation, if we could manage to understand what we were reading, and put our understanding into practice' (274).

It was still just possible in 1525, when Erasmus published the *Sermon on Psalm 4* alongside his three earlier commentaries, to propose 'slight departures from the original sense', but it is noticeable that Erasmus' later psalm commentaries, while still imbued with pastoral concern, were also reactions to public events, most often to Reformation controversy. Even in the *Sermon on Psalm 4* there is a low-key discussion of justification, part of which was censured later as it seemed to downplay the role of works (219–20). From this moment Erasmus abandoned all pretence of a chronological commentary on the entire Psalter, and the final seven psalms were chosen for what he perceived as their appropriateness to the theme he had chosen. The *Explanation of Psalm 85* (Erasmus' fifth different attempt at a generic title) appeared in 1528 and addressed the justification controversy more directly. In pursuing a synergistic line Erasmus could seem to be clarifying the remarks he had made on the topic three years earlier; he spent much of this decade engaged in controversy with opponents who subjected his amiable pastoral reflections to a hostile dogmatic scrutiny.[20]

---

[19] See, for example, passages in his expositions of Psalms 33 and 38, *Opera omnia* (n. 6 above), v, cols 413 and 423.

[20] A good example is his book on confession, *Exomologesis*, published in 1524 (with the *Paraphrase on Psalm 3* as an appendix) and in revised form in 1530, clearly in response to the unexpectedly rigorous scrutiny of the theologians of Paris and Louvain; see my forthcoming translation in *CWE* 68.

The three most important subsequent commentaries appeared in the 1530s; not only were they among the longest, but each was given a title which partly concealed its status as a psalm commentary; a cynic might suggest that it made good commercial sense for the publisher to embellish a scriptural commentary with some topical title.[21] *On War against the Turks* (*De bello Turcico*, 1530) was only 'incidentally' (*obiter*) an exposition of Psalm 28 (29 in English numbering). In fact the psalm, a more than usually obscure evocation of the might of the Lord, acts simply as a prelude to Erasmus' remarkably detailed discussion of the most urgent geopolitical issue of the day, in which he takes issue both with the pacific Luther and with the firebrands in the Vatican and in the courts; the message of the psalm underlines the impotence of the latter group unless God shall have been placated by a renewal of piety. The last two great commentaries are explicitly devoted to a campaign to douse the fires of the Reformation crisis. *On Repairing the Unity of the Church* (*De sarcienda ecclesiae concordia*, 1533), built round Psalm 83 (84), is a plea for moderation and reconciliation in which yet again Erasmus calls for the abandonment or mitigation of inessential religious practices, while upholding the traditional authority of the Church in certain areas; it includes a characteristically ingenious proposal for compromise on the freedom of the will, a subject on which Erasmus himself had been engaged in dispute with Luther for a decade. The final work, *On the Purity of the Tabernacle or Christian Church* (*De puritate tabernaculi sive ecclesiae christianae*), appeared early in 1536, a few months before Erasmus' death. Initially a commentary on Psalm 14 (15), like the previous psalm a celebration of God's presence among humankind, it continues the campaign of the *De concordia*, giving both a tropological and an anagogical reading of the psalm to reiterate the necessity for an inclusive tabernacle, a common dwelling place for all whose minds are pure; Erasmus yearns for universal recognition of a spiritual membership capable of transcending doctrinal divisions.

Thus Erasmus' career as scriptural exegete began and ended with the psalms. Although his commentaries took different forms and scrutinized the texts with varying degrees of intensity, all contributed to the pastoral project to which Erasmus committed both eloquence and erudition. Himself inspired by the divine rhetoric of the Holy Spirit, speaking through David in the Old Testament, Erasmus presented these poems as a series of bridges to the New Testament, a reinforcement of that Christ-centred piety in which the moral and the spiritual are as closely intertwined as they are in the uniquely powerful metaphors of the Book of Psalms.

---

21 As does Dominic Baker-Smith in *CWE* 63, p. xv. A tally of the various editions gives some support to the theory.

CHAPTER FOUR

Martin Luther's Bible Translation in its German and European Context

John L. Flood

In a letter dated 12 March 1455 to the Spanish Cardinal Juan de Carvajal, the Italian humanist Aeneas Silvius Piccolomini (the later Pope Pius II) casually mentioned how at the Diet of Frankfurt in October 1454 he had met a 'vir mirabilis', a wonderful man, who had been able to supply a Bible which might be read without spectacles and in 158 or 180 identical copies![1] This is undoubtedly a reference to one of the most famous books in history, the Gutenberg Bible, or 42-line Bible (*GW* 4201), printed by Johannes Gutenberg at Mainz, though whether the man in question was Gutenberg himself or one of his associates we do not know for sure. This episode serves as a salutary reminder that the Bible had first been printed in Germany almost thirty years before Martin Luther was even born. By the time of Luther's birth in 1483 Bible printing was already big business there. Of the ninety-four Latin Bibles printed in Europe during the fifteenth century no fewer than fifty-seven were printed in German-speaking towns, while twenty-seven were published in Italy (twenty-two of them at Venice) and ten in France, at Paris and Lyon.[2]

Germany led the way in vernacular Bibles too, long before the Protestant Reformers, in asserting the priesthood of all believers, contended that all Christians had the right and duty to explore scriptural truth for themselves. Eight editions of the Bible in German were already

---

[1] Aeneas Sylvius himself was not sure of the number of copies. For this letter see Erich Meuthen, 'Ein frühes Quellenzeugnis (zu Oktober 1454?) für den ältesten Buchdruck', *Gutenberg-Jahrbuch*, 57 (1982), pp. 108–18, but now especially Martin Davies, 'Juan de Carvajal and Early Printing: The 42-Line Bible and the Sweynheym and Pannartz Aquinas', *The Library*, 6th ser., 18 (1996), pp. 193–215, at pp. 193–201. On the Bible itself see Martin Davies, *The Gutenberg Bible* (London, 1996), and Albert Kapr, *Johann Gutenberg: The Man and his Invention* (Aldershot, 1996).

[2] On the absence of any Vulgate printed in England in the fifteenth century see Kimberly Van Kampen, 'The Bible in Print in England before Tyndale', *Reformation*, 2 (1997), pp. 111–26.

on the market before Luther was born, and indeed two more appeared before 1485 when Berthold von Henneberg, Archbishop of Mainz and one of the mightiest princes of the Empire, attempted to ban the printing of vernacular Bibles on pain of excommunication, confiscation of the books and a fine of 100 gold florins.[3]

The first vernacular Bible ever printed in Europe was the German Bible issued by Johann Mentelin at Strasbourg before 27 June 1466 (*GW* 4295),[4] five years before the first Italian Bible, eleven before the first Dutch Bible, twelve before the first Catalan Bible, twenty-two before the first Czech Bible, thirty-two years before Antoine Vérard's *Bible historiée*, and more than half a century before the first New Testaments in English.[5]

Mentelin's Bible was the first of a long line of pre-Reformation printed Bibles in German.[6] The others were:

[2]   [Strasbourg:] [Heinrich Eggestein], [*c*.1470]; *GW* 4296 (no illustrations)

[3]   [Augsburg:] [Jodocus Pflanzmann], [between 1475 and 20 June 1477]; *GW* 4297 (57 woodcuts)

---

[3] See Hermann Gelhaus, *Der Streit um Luthers Bibelverdeutschung im 16. und 17. Jahrhundert* (Tübingen, 1989), i, pp. 2–5, and ii, pp. 1–6.

[4] Lorna Jane Abray, *The People's Reformation: Magistrates, Clergy, and Commons in Strasbourg 1500–1598* (Oxford, 1985), pp. 22–3, confuses Mentelin's 1466 German Bible with his Latin Bible of 1460/61 (*GW* 4203). Inexplicably – but probably because Mentelin's German Bible is a large book with no illustrations – there is no facsimile of it currently available, but the text is accessible in *Die erste deutsche Bibel*, ed. Wilhelm Kurrelmeyer, 9 vols (Tübingen, 1904–15).

[5] It is worth remembering that the earliest translation of the Bible into any Germanic language was that by the Gothic bishop Wulfila (311–382/3), translated from Greek. Quite how much was translated into Gothic is uncertain: large parts of the Gospels and of the Pauline Epistles (excepting Hebrews) are extant, but of the Old Testament only fragments of Nehemiah 5–7 survive. See Elfriede Stutz, *Gotische Literaturdenkmäler* (Stuttgart, 1966). The standard edition is that by Wilhelm Streitberg, *Die gotische Bibel*, 7th edn (Heidelberg, 2000).

[6] An excellent overview of the pre-Lutheran German Bibles is provided by Walter Eichenberger and Henning Wendland, *Deutsche Bibeln vor Luther* (Hamburg, 1977). See also ch. 3, by Hans Volz, in *The Cambridge History of the Bible*, ii *The West from the Reformation to the Present Day*, ed. S.L. Greenslade (Cambridge, 1963), pp. 94–109, and for an even broader survey see the article 'Bible' in *The Oxford Encyclopedia of the Reformation*, ed. Hans J. Hillerbrand (Oxford, 1996), i, pp. 152–71. The account of the early German Bibles in Mark Greengrass, *The European Reformation c. 1500–1618* (London and New York, 1998), p. 259, is rather misleading. For a study of typographical features of the early German Bibles see John L. Flood, 'Les Premières Bibles allemandes dans le contexte de la typographie européenne des XVe et XVIe siècles', in Betrand Eugène Schwarzbach (ed.), *La Bible imprimée dans l'Europe moderne: XVe–XVIIIe siècle*, Etudes et recherches (Paris, 1999), pp. 144–65.

[4]   Augsburg: [Günther Zainer], [c.1475]; GW 4298 (73 historiated initials)

[5]   [Nuremberg:] [Andreas Frisner and Johann Sensenschmidt], [between 1476 and 1478]; GW 4299 (one woodcut and 73 historiated initials)

[6]   Augsburg: [Günther Zainer], 1477; GW 4300 (73 historiated initials)

[7]   Augsburg: Anton Sorg, 20 June 1477; GW 4301 (77 woodcuts)

[8]   Augsburg: Anton Sorg, 3 January 1480; GW 4302 (73 historiated initials)

[9]   Nuremberg: Anton Koberger, 1483; GW 4303 (109 woodcuts)

[10] Strasbourg: [Johann Grüninger], 2 May 1485; GW 4304 (109 woodcuts)

[11] Augsburg: Johann Schönsperger, 25 May 1487; GW 4305 (109 woodcuts)

[12] Augsburg: Johann Schönsperger, 9 November 1490; GW 4306 (109 woodcuts)

[13] Augsburg: Johann Otmar, 12 February 1507; VD16 B-2675 (109 woodcuts)

[14] Augsburg: Silvan Otmar, 27 January 1518; VD16 B-2676 (109 woodcuts)

In addition to these fourteen editions in High German there were four in various Low German dialects:

Cologne: [Bartholomæus von Unkel or Heinrich Quentell], [1478/9]; GW 4307 (113 woodcuts)

Cologne: [Bartholomæus von Unkel or Heinrich Quentell], [1478/9]; GW 4308 (123 woodcuts)

Lübeck: Steffen Arndes, 19 November 1494; GW 4309 (152 woodcuts)

Halberstadt: Lorenz Stuchs, 8 July 1522; VD16 B-2839 (119 woodcuts)

Of the fourteen High German Bibles the most important after Mentelin's were the fourth, by Zainer, which offered a revised text, and the ninth, by Koberger, which introduced to southern Germany the illustrations from the Cologne Bibles of 1478/79.[7]

Why, then, against this background, was Luther's translation significant? Indeed, we may ask, why did he translate it at all, seeing that German Bibles had already been available in print for more than fifty

---

[7] An indication of the influence of the Cologne Bibles may be seen in the fact that the illustrations in one of the early Italian Bibles, that by Ganglielmus de Cereto, Venice 1493 (GW 4319), are based on them.

years? There are many reasons. The first is that whereas the 1466 Bible
(and its derivatives) had been based on a (now lost) fourteenth-century
manuscript from the Nuremberg area, representing a fairly slavish
translation of the Spanish recension of the Vulgate, and was designed
(initially at least) primarily as an aid to understanding the Latin, Luther
strove to render the Scriptures into natural, idiomatic German,
intending his version to serve as a substitute for the original text – the
contrast was immediately apparent to Luther's biographer Johannes
Mathesius (1504–65) who recalled how, in his youth, he had seen 'an
un-German German Bible, doubtless translated from Latin, which was
dark and obscure'.[8] Furthermore, Lorenzo Valla and, after him, Erasmus
had shown that the Vulgate was textually corrupt, and Luther sought to
translate a more accurate text, using Erasmus' Greek New Testament (in
the second edition of 1519) and the Hebrew text of the Old Testament.
Study of Erasmus' edition (which, ironically, was based on later, inferior
Greek manuscripts than those Jerome had used when working on the
Vulgate!) showed Luther that Greek and Latin might express the same
underlying idea very differently, and he realized that if these classical
languages varied among themselves, then surely there was nothing
inherently wrong in translating the Scriptures using natural German
idiom too. The notion of Latin, Greek and Hebrew being classed as
superior classical and 'Holy' languages – which had its origin in John
19: 20 where Pilate orders that the words 'Jesus of Nazareth King of the
Jews' should be written in Hebrew, Greek and Latin above Jesus' head
on the Cross – was one that had rankled with the Germans at least since
the mid-ninth century when Otfrid of Weissenburg, the first German
poet we know by name, questioned why it was that only the Franks
were not permitted to tell the story of Christ in their native tongue![9]
Luther's great achievement as a translator is to have broken with the
pernicious influence of the classical languages and to have asserted and
championed the equality of German. This emancipation of the
vernacular was of tremendous importance for the emergence of German
as a literary language, and indeed this had an impact on the evaluation
of other vernaculars too – thus Tyndale's translation of the Bible into

    [8] Johannes Mathesius, *Ausgewählte Werke*, iii: *Luthers Leben in Predigten*, ed. Georg
Loesche (Prague, 1906), p. 314: 'Ich hab in meiner jugend auch ein vndeutsche deutsche
Bibel gesehen, one zweiffel auß dem Latein verdeutscht, die war dunckel vnd finster.'
    [9] See the section headed 'Cur scriptor hunc librum theotisce dictaverit' in *Otfrids von
Weissenburg Evangelienbuch*, ed. Johann Kelle (Regensburg, 1856), pp. 17–22. Already in
794 the synod of Frankfurt had defended the use of the vernacular: 'Ut nullus credat, quod
nonnisi in tribus linguis deus orandus sit, quia in omni lingua deus adoratur et homo
exauditur, si iusta petierit.' See Ulrich Ernst, *Der Liber evangeliorum Otfrids von
Weissenburg* (Cologne and Vienna, 1975), pp. 132–7.

English owes much to the force of Luther's example. Furthermore, although much of the debate was carried on in Latin, the regular *lingua franca* of scholars, the Reformation was essentially a vernacular movement: that Luther was writing tracts in German several years before he translated the New Testament was already sufficient to lead Catholics like Johannes Cochlæus and Hieronymus Emser to suspect him of Hussitism.[10]

It was a matter of conviction with Luther and his supporters that the Scriptures must be the foundation of religion.[11] In the preface to *Eyn deutsch Theologia* (1518) Luther had lamented that God's Word had too long 'not only lain under the bench, but was almost destroyed by dust and moths'.[12] Though the Protestant Reformers were not the first to regard Scripture as the prime validator of doctrine, they were the first to place Scripture in direct opposition to the traditions and practices of the medieval church. Whereas, in their view, the church had arrogated unto itself the authority to determine what Scripture said and how it should be interpreted, they held that all practices in the church must be securely underpinned by scriptural authority. And if the Bible was to be the foundation of religion, then it was essential that it should be made available in a form of German ordinary people could understand – idiomatic German, freed from the trammels of Latin. To this end, the Reformers made the best possible use of the printing press. They were fully aware of the potential of the new technology for the propagation of their ideas, Luther himself declaring it to be 'the greatest and latest gift of God, for by this means God seeks to extend the cause of true religion to the ends of the earth and to make it available in all languages',[13] while Sebastian Franck, himself a printer, wrote in his

---

10 See Adolf Laube, 'Das Gespann Cochläus/Dietenberger im Kampf gegen Luther', *Archiv für Reformationsgeschichte*, 87 (1996), pp. 119–35, at p. 121. Emser suspected that, when translating the New Testament, Luther had consulted *ein sonderlich Wickleffisch oder Hussisch exemplar* ('a special Wycliffite or Hussite exemplar'), thus tarring him with the brush of heresy.

11 Cf. Luther's phrase 'solam scripturam regnare' (*Martin Luthers Werke. Kritische Gesamtausgabe. Weimarer Ausgabe* [hereafter *WA*] [Weimar, 1883–], vii, pp. 98–9). Melanchthon credited Erasmus with being the first to lead theology back to its true sources ('qui primus ... Theologiam ad fontes revocavit', *Philippi Melanthonis opera quae supersunt omnia*, ed. Carolus Gottlieb Bretschneider, Corpus Reformatorum, 1 [Halle an der Saale, 1834], i, col. 63).

12 '... das heylig wortt gottis nit allein under der bangk gelegen, sundernn von staub und mutten nahend vorweßet' (*WA*, i, p. 379).

13 'Typographia postremum est donum et idem maximum, per eam enim Deus toti terrarum orbi voluit negotium verae religionis in fine mundi innotescere ac in omnes linguas transfundi' (*WA, Tischreden*, i, p. 523, no. 1038), dating from the early 1530s. On 9 July 1539, speaking of the good fortune of living when he did ('de felicitate huius

Chronica (Strasbourg, 1531): 'By means of the art of printing the long-sealed fount of divine and inexpressible wisdom and knowledge is made accessible to all.'[14]

Though the Wittenberg Reformers first recognized the need for a new translation in November 1520 it was not until December 1521 that Philipp Melanchthon (1497–1560) persuaded Luther to translate the New Testament. The centrality of the Gospels is self-evident, but beyond that, the principal reason for starting with the New Testament was that considerable importance was attached to a reliable and intelligible translation of the Pauline Epistles (whose significance Valla, too, had stressed). In addition, of course, the New Testament was less difficult to translate than the Hebrew Old Testament, for which Luther would need to invoke the assistance of his scholarly friends, notably Matthæus Aurogallus (*c*. 1490–1543), the newly appointed Professor of Hebrew at Wittenberg.

Luther worked on his translation of the New Testament in the remote Wartburg Castle above Eisenach in Thuringia, to which he had been spirited away with the connivance of his protector, Elector Frederick the Wise of Saxony, after being declared an imperial outlaw following his dramatic stand at the Diet of Worms in 1521, immortalized in those humble but memorable words 'Hier stehe ich. Ich kann nicht anders!' ('Here I stand! I can do no other!'), words with which he secured for posterity both academic and spiritual liberty, breaking the stranglehold of the Church over the university as well as the stultifying power of the clergy over the laity.[15] At the Wartburg, within eleven weeks, by the end

---

saeculi'), Luther said that, compared with earlier, learning was flourishing, helped by God's gift of printing whose prime purpose was to exert pressure on the Pope: 'Nam olim tantae erant tenebrae in omnibus facultatibus et artibus, ut nullus usus esset ... Nunc omnes artes illustratae florent. So hatt vns Gott die druckerey dartzu geschenckt, praecipue ad premendum papam' (*WA, Tischreden*, iv, pp. 436–7, no. 4697). Johannes Cochlæus lamented how well the Lutherans but how badly the Catholics were served by the printers: 'Nam quicquid pro Luthero erat, quam diligentissime ac emendatissime imprimebatur: Quicquid uero pro Catholicis, ignauissime ac uitiosissime. Et quae Lutheri aut pro Luthero erant, Chalcographi suis sumptibus imprimebant ...', *Commentaria Ioannis Cochlæi, de actis et scriptis Martini Lutheri Saxonis* (Mainz, 1549; repr. Farnborough, 1968), pp. 58–9; these remarks were doubtless coloured by Cochlæus' own experience of the difficulties of finding a printer (on these see Laube, 'Das Gespann Cochläus/Dietenberger', pp. 125–6). For the role of printing in the Reformation see John L. Flood, 'The Book in Reformation Germany', in Jean-François Gilmont (ed.), *The Reformation and the Book*, English edition and translation by Karin Maag, St Andrews Studies in Reformation History (Aldershot, 1998), pp. 21–103.

14 'Durch dise Kunst der Truckerey wird der lang verschlossen Brunn götlicher und unaußsprechlicher Weißheit unnd Kunst in die Gmeyn außgeteylt.' Cited after Rudolf Hirsch, in *Gutenberg-Jahrbuch*, 37 (1962), p. 116.

15 See James Atkinson, *The Trial of Luther* (London, 1971), p. 9.

of February 1522, Luther had translated the whole New Testament. He sent the first half of the manuscript to Wittenberg around 20 February and travelled there in person on 4 March to deliver the rest for discussion and final revision before handing it over to Melchior Lotter the Younger, who printed it for the publishers Lucas Cranach and Christian Döring.[16] The work was carried out in strict secrecy to avoid the risk of theft and piracy. The first proofs were ready at the beginning of May. Printing took five and a half months in all. Initially a single press was used, but – mindful of the need to have the book, consisting of 222 folio leaves, available for the Leipzig autumn fair which would run from 29 September to 6 October 1522 – from the end of May two, and in the latter stages even three, presses were employed and overtime and night shifts had to be worked. Printing was completed just before 21 September and consequently the book is known as the September Testament (see Figure 4.1). It does not name the translator, the printer or the publisher; the title-page bears only the simple xylographic legend: *Das Newe Testament Deutzsch* and the place of publication, *Wittenberg*.[17] This anonymity can scarcely have been out of circumspection because any mention of Wittenberg gave the game away immediately; more likely it was out of humility, for the Bible was God's book, not Luther's. Estimates of the number of copies printed vary from 3000 to 5000. The price is thought to have been 10½ Groschen in loose sheets, while a bound copy is estimated to have cost 1 Gulden, the value of a pig ready for slaughter.[18]

---

16 On these see John L. Flood, 'Lucas Cranach as Publisher', *German Life and Letters*, new ser. 48 (1995), pp. 241–63. For comprehensive accounts of the genesis of Luther's Bible translation see Hans Volz, *Martin Luthers deutsche Bibel* (Hamburg, 1978) and the two exhibition catalogues by Heimo Reinitzer, *Biblia deutsch: Luthers Bibelübersetzung und ihre Tradition* (Wolfenbüttel, 1983) and by Stefan Strohm and Eberhard Zwink, *Ursprung der Biblia Deutsch von Martin Luther* (Stuttgart, 1983).

17 It was not until later, when the Book of Job was published with a 'Preface of Dr Martin Luther', that the translator's name actually appeared in association with the translation.

18 Whether 10½ Groschen really was about the same as the price of 'two rabbits for the pot', as Abray, *The People's Reformation*, p. 23, claims, seems doubtful. The relation of the Groschen to the Gulden (fl.) fluctuated a great deal but on average 1 fl. = 24 Groschen. Though Bibles were now less expensive than in the fifteenth century, they were not yet really cheap. In 1543 Joachim von Alvensleben paid 5 Gulden for a bound copy of Luther's 1541 Bible, the equivalent of 5 per cent of a pastor's annual income (see Werner Arnold, 'Adelsbildung in Mitteldeutschland', in W. Arnold (ed.), *Bibliotheken und Bücher im Zeitalter der Renaissance*, Wolfenbütteler Abhandlungen zur Renaissanceforschung, 16 (Wiesbaden, 1997), pp. 167–94, at pp. 173–4). Even as late as 1628 only 2 per cent of books owned in Amberg (near Nuremberg) were Bibles, and these tended to be found only in the homes of the wealthier citizens. See Christine Paschen, 'Privatbibliotheken des ausgehenden 16. Jahrhunderts in Amberg/Oberpfalz', in W. Arnold (ed.), *Bibliotheken und Bücher*, pp. 85–112, at p. 101.

4.1 Luther's *New Testament* (Wittenberg, Melchior Lotter, September 1522)

The publishers rightly foresaw that the September Testament would be a great success. It was completely sold out by early December, but steps had already been taken to prepare a second, revised edition, which was ready by 19 December 1522, the December Testament. It has been estimated that during Luther's lifetime 100 000 copies of the New Testament were printed in Wittenberg alone.[19] Another measure of its popularity was the fact that already by the end of the year 1523 more than a dozen reprints had appeared, nine of them in Basle and five in Augsburg. Luther's great adversary Johannes Cochlæus (the man who betrayed Tyndale's printing of the New Testament to the city authorities at Cologne in 1525[20]) lamented that his New Testament was so widely available 'that even tailors and cobblers, even women and other simple folk who had only learnt to read a little German in their lives, were reading it with great enthusiasm as though it were the fount of all truth, while others carried it around, pressed to their bosom, and learned it by heart'.[21] Jacob Schropp (1528–94), who entered the Cistercian house at Maulbronn in 1547 and was sent a copy of Luther's New Testament by his father, had to read it by moonlight since reading anything of Luther's was strictly forbidden.[22]

From the point of view of the History of the Book, too, Luther's New Testament is a milestone. It is the first Bible printed in a single column

---

[19] A summary list of editions down to 1546 may be found in Reinitzer, *Biblia deutsch*, pp. 116–25, with a list of the Low German versions of Luther's translation on pp. 126–7.

[20] For details see David Daniell, *William Tyndale: A Biography* (New Haven, CT, and London, 1994), pp. 108–11. On Cochlæus (1479–1552) see now Monique Samuel-Scheyder, *Johannes Cochlaeus, humaniste et adversaire de Luther* (Nancy, 1993).

[21] 'Antequam uero prodiret labor Emseri, mirum in modum multiplicabatur per Chalcographos nouum Testamentum Lutheri, ut etiam sutores, & mulieres, & quilibet Idiotæ, qui Teuthonicas literas utcunque didicerant, nouum illud Testamentum, tanquam fontem omnis ueritatis, auidissime legerent, quicunque Lutherani erant: illudque sæpe legendo memoriæ commendarent, in sinu secum portantes codicem', *Commentaria Ioannis Cochlæi*, p. 55. Erasmus had expressed a hope that women would read the Scriptures: 'Optarim ut omnes mulierculae legant evangelium, legant Paulinas epistolas'; see *Erasme: Les Préfaces au 'Novum Testamentum'* (1516), eds Yves Delègue and Jean-Paul Gillet, Histoire et société, 20 (Geneva, 1990), p. 74. More generally on women as readers see Susan Wabuda, 'The Woman with the Rock: The Controversy on Women and Bible Reading', in S. Wabuda and Caroline Litzenberger (eds), *Belief and Practice in Reformation England* (Aldershot, 1998), pp. 40–59. Erasmus had spoken of the ploughman, the weaver and the traveller being familiar with the Bible: 'Utinam hinc ad stivam aliquid decantet agricola, hinc nonnihil ad radios suos moduletur textor, huius modi fabulis itineris taedium levet viator' (*Erasme: Les Préfaces*, eds Delègue and Gillet), and a similar notion is found in Tyndale: see Daniell, *William Tyndale*, pp. 1, 18, 44, 92–107 and 317.

[22] See Christian Gottlieb Jöcher, *Allgemeines Gelehrten-Lexicon* (Leipzig, 1750–51), iv, col. 363. Schropp became abbot of Maulbronn in 1578.

of text, instead of the traditional two columns. This not only made it look more spacious but, more importantly, it made it much easier to accommodate Luther's copious interpretative marginal notes. The presentation of the lineage of Joseph, the husband of Mary, detailed in Matthew 1: 1–16, is a model of lucidity which was imitated by Tyndale in his English New Testaments.[23] Luther reordered the last nine books of the New Testament (1 and 2 Peter, 1, 2 and 3 John, Hebrews, James, Jude and Revelation, instead of Hebrews, James, 1 and 2 Peter, 1, 2 and 3 John, Jude, Revelation, as in the Vulgate and the King James Bible), reflecting his view that Hebrews, James, Jude and Revelation were all quasi-deuterocanonical: whereas the canonical books from Matthew to 3 John are numbered from 1 to 23 in the table of contents, Hebrews to Revelation are distinguished by being unnumbered, and in this too Luther served as a model for Tyndale.[24] Tyndale also owes a debt to Luther's prefaces.[25]

The September Testament also contains a number of pictures, though it can hardly be called an illustrated Bible. Several of the pre-Lutheran printed German Bibles – the Cologne Bibles of 1478/79, as well as the Lübeck and Halberstadt Low German editions, and among the High German ones notably those by Koberger, Grüninger, Schönsperger, and Johann and Silvan Otmar – contained illustrations, in the Old rather than in the New Testament. In Luther's September Testament, though the Gospels and Epistles are ornamented with historiated initials, only the Book of Revelation is fully illustrated, with a cycle of twenty-one full-page woodcuts, executed by Luther's close friend, the Wittenberg court artist Lucas Cranach (1472–1553) and his assistants. The illustrations, deriving from the (fifteen) pictures in Dürer's *Apocalypse* of 1498, constitute one of the book's chief glories. Some of the woodcuts

23 See Daniell, *William Tyndale*, pl. 5 (between pp. 214 and 215), and the plates in Eberhard Zwink, 'Confusion about Tyndale: The Stuttgart Copy of the 1526 New Testament in English', *Reformation*, 3 (1998), pp. 28–48, at pp. 46–7.

24 Zwink, 'Confusion about Tyndale', pp. 46–8. That, for example, James must be of lesser status was evident to Luther since James 2 appears to contradict Romans 3: 28, the passage on which Luther's fundamental doctrine of Justification by Faith is based. In fact, Paul and James hark back to Gen. 15: 6, and are simply approaching the same problem from different angles.

25 For Luther's prefaces see *Martin Luthers Vorreden zur Bibel*, ed. Heinrich Bornkamm, Furche-Bücherei, 238 (Hamburg, 1967), and Jürgen Quack, *Evangelische Bibelvorreden von der Reformation bis zur Aufklärung*, Quellen und Forschungen zur Reformationsgeschichte, 43 (Gütersloh, 1975). For Tyndale's debt to Luther see L.J. Trinterud, 'A Reappraisal of William Tyndale's Debt to Martin Luther', *Church History*, 31 (1962), pp. 24–45; Gerald Hammond, 'William Tyndale's Pentateuch: Its Relation to Luther's German Bible and the Hebrew Original', *Renaissance Quarterly*, 33 (1980), pp. 351–85.

are noted for their anti-papal features. For instance, there was the picture allegedly depicting the destruction of Babylon which is all too recognizably based on the picture of Rome from the famous Nuremberg Chronicle of 1493 (Figures 4.2 and 4.3). It was probably not least on account of these pictures that Henry VIII, King of England, wrote to Duke George of Saxony on 20 January 1523 to urge that Luther be restrained.[26] The Duke ordered his subjects to hand in every available copy in exchange for payment so that they might be destroyed, but the plan met with little success. However, his opposition did result in the toning down of some of the most offensive features in the December edition, especially the picture of the Whore of Babylon (in Revelation 17) wearing the papal tiara, which was one of the features most vehemently criticized by Duke George (Figures 4.4 and 4.5).[27] But the Duke was not satisfied merely by banning the translation in his own territory: he commissioned his secretary and chaplain Hieronymus Emser (1478–1527) to undertake a critical examination of the 'heretical' translation and then to prepare an acceptable Catholic version.[28] That the Catholics were now forced to counter with rival versions was tacit admission that Luther had been victorious in his campaign for a generally accessible vernacular Bible.

With the New Testament published, Luther now embarked on the Old Testament.[29] If translation of Erasmus's Greek New Testament had

---

26 See *Serenissimi ac potentissimi regis Anglie … ad … Saxonie principes, de coercenda abigendaque Lutherana factione, & Luthero ipso Epistola. Item Illustrissmi principis Ducis Georgii ad eundem Regem rescriptio* (Leipzig, [1523]) (British Library: C.175.c.4). To understand the political background, it is necessary to know that in 1485 the Saxon lands had been divided into the 'Albertine' territory (over which Luther's opponent Duke George (1471–1539) ruled) and the 'Ernestine' territory (ruled over by Luther's protector Frederick the Wise (1463–1525)). For details see 'Saxony' in *The Oxford Encyclopedia of the Reformation*, iii, pp. 489–90.

27 For the duke's ban see Otto Vossler, 'Herzog Georg der Bärtige und seine Ablehnung Luthers', *Historische Zeitschrift*, 184 (1957), pp. 272–91. On the illustrations see Peter Martin, *Martin Luther und die Bilder zur Apokalypse: Die Ikonographie der Illustrationen zur Offenbarung des Johannes in der Lutherbibel 1522 bis 1546*, Vestigia Bibliae, 5 (Hamburg, 1983). Despite the ban, the offending picture nevertheless reappeared later on, as may be seen from Figure 4.6.

28 For a detailed comparison of part of Emser's version with Luther's see Heinz Bluhm, 'Emser's "Emendation" of Luther's New Testament: Galatians 1', *Modern Language Notes*, 81 (1966), pp. 370–97. For other contemporary reactions to Luther's New Testament see Otto Reichert, 'D. M. Luther's September-Testament in seinen und seiner Zeitgenossen Zeugnissen', *Luther: Mitteilungen der Luther-Gesellschaft*, 4 (1922), pp. 49–64 (also separately published in the series 'Flugschriften der Luther-Gesellschaft').

29 For Luther's Hebrew sources see Strohm and Zwink, *Ursprung der Biblia Deutsch*, pp. 13–15, and Siegfried Raeder, *Die Benutzung des masoretischen Textes bei Luther* (Tübingen, 1967).

4.2 Lucas Cranach, 'The Destruction of Babylon' [= Rome], in Luther's *New Testament*, September 1522

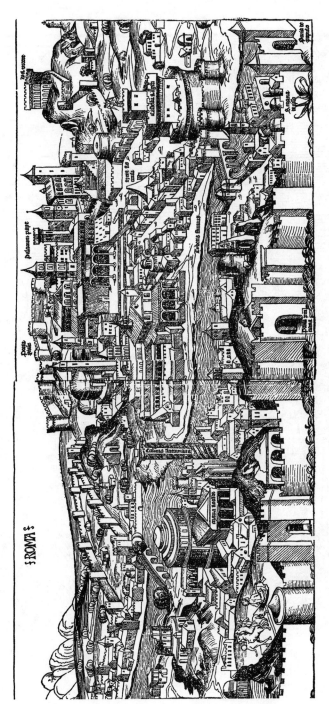

4.3 'Rome', in Hartmann Schedel, *Buch der Croniken und Geschichten* ['The Nuremberg Chronicle'] (Nuremberg, Anton Koberger, 1493)

Jobannis.

4.4 'The Whore of Babylon', in Luther's *New Testament*, September 1522

Die offinbarung

4.5 'The Whore of Babylon', in Luther's *New Testament*, December 1522

occupied him for eleven weeks, rendering the Old Testament out of Hebrew kept him busy, on and off, for twelve years. From the outset he was acutely aware not only of the immensity of the task but also of the desirability of not publishing such a large and necessarily expensive work as a single volume. Accordingly he announced on 3 November 1522 that he would begin by translating the Pentateuch, which would then be followed by the historical books and finally by the Prophets and the poetical books. The Pentateuch and the historical and poetical books were all completed by October 1524, but the remainder was to take ten years, not least because of the extreme difficulty of translating Job and the prophets. In a letter to Wenceslaus Linck, dated 14 June 1528, Luther sighed:

> We are now sweating blood to put the Prophets into the vernacular. Dear God, it is such hard work and so difficult to make the Hebrew writers speak German! Just as they refuse to abandon their Hebrew style, they balk at following the native habits of German. It is as though the nightingale, having lost its sweet melody, had to imitate the cuckoo and its monotonous call.[30]

As with the New Testament, piracy was a problem, and in an attempt to safeguard the position of Wittenberg printers Luther inserted his own copyright mark – consisting of a lamb and flag device, a medallion showing the 'Luther rose', and the initials M L[31] – in the third part (comprising some of the prophets and the poetical books) published in 1524. Almost simultaneously there appeared a separate edition of the Psalter, with a number of textual improvements. Thereafter, until 1532, Luther had little time for his translating, though Jonah, Habakkuk, Zechariah and Isaiah came out between 1526 and 1528, Proverbs in 1529, and Daniel in 1530, and at the same time he was constantly revising and improving the translation of the Psalms and the New Testament. By spring 1532 he was able to publish the final part of the Old Testament, comprising Jeremiah, Ezekiel and the remaining minor prophets.

Luther's slow progress with the prophets only served to encourage others to try to expedite matters by publishing their own rival versions. By 1529 Peter Schöffer at Worms was able to publish his 'combined' Bible (VD16 B-2681), made up of the first three parts of Luther's

---

30 'Nos iam in prophetis vernacule donandis sudamus. Deus, quantum et quam molestum opus, Hebraicos scriptores cogere Germanice loqui, qui resistunt, quam suam Hebraicitatem relinquere nolunt, et barbariem Germanicam imitari, tanquam si philomela cuculum cogatur, deserta elegantissima melodia, unisonam illius vocem detestans, imitari' (WA, Briefwechsel, iv, p. 484).

31 Reproduced in Reinitzer, Biblia deutsch, p. 146.

translation of the Old Testament, the Prophets translated by Ludwig Hetzer (or Hätzer, *c.* 1500–29) and the anabaptist Hans Denck (*c.* 1500–27), the Apocrypha by Leo Jud (1482–1542) and Luther's New Testament. Christoph Froschauer's Zurich Bible of 1530 (*VD16* B-2687) and Wolfgang Köpfel's Strasbourg one of 1529/30 (*VD16* B-2686) were of a similar nature.

Such competition made it imperative for Luther to complete his prophets and the Apocrypha. He had Philipp Melanchthon, Caspar Cruciger and Justus Jonas help him with the latter, and the manuscript, complete with Luther's prefaces, was ready in the spring of 1534. At last the Wittenberg Bible, printed by Hans Lufft, was finished.[32] It cost 2 Gulden 8 Groschen, whereas Koberger's Nuremberg Bible of 1483 had cost 6 Gulden and an unbound copy of Mentelin's Strasbourg Bible of 1466 had been sold to a customer in Augsburg for 12 Gulden, while a rich Augsburg patrician even paid 16 Gulden for one,[33] though even that had been relatively inexpensive compared with Gutenberg's 42-line Bible which, unbound and not illuminated, is thought to have cost 90 Rhenish Gulden in vellum and 40 on paper, while the splendid illuminated copy in the Huntington Library, the only surviving copy with a contemporary note of the price, cost 100 Rhenish Gulden – the price of a decent town house or a craftsman's wages for five years.[34]

One should not fail to notice that even the typographical appearance of the German Bible proclaimed a manifesto. This is nowhere more obvious than in the editions of the 1540s, where Hans Lufft's principal compositor Georg Rörer introduced a device intended to help the reader interpret the text correctly. Though the text is basically set in gothic type throughout, Rörer arranged for certain words to be picked out with initial letters in roman type. This 'symbolic typography' is intended to imply that these words have negative connotations; in the sample shown as Figure 4.6, virtually all the nouns associated with the Whore of Babylon are given a roman capital.[35] The underlying typographical

---

[32] Before it appeared in print at Wittenberg the Apocrypha, recast in Low German by Johannes Bugenhagen, was first published on 1 April 1534 by the Lübeck printer Ludwig Dietz.

[33] In 1461 Mentelin had also charged 12 Gulden, payable in three instalments, for a copy of his Latin Bible (*GW* 4203). See Leonhard Hoffmann, 'Gutenberg und die Folgen: Zur Entwicklung des Bücherpreises im 15. und 16. Jahrhundert', *Bibliothek und Wissenschaft*, **29** (1996), pp. 5–23, at pp. 7–8.

[34] Leonhard Hoffmann, 'Die Gutenberg-Bibel: Eine Kosten- und Gewinnschätzung auf der Grundlage zeitgenössischer Quellen', *Archiv für Geschichte des Buchwesens*, **39** (1993), pp. 255–319; and Hoffmann, 'Gutenberg und die Folgen', p. 6.

[35] A notable exception is the word *Weib* ('woman'), the reason being that the roman font did not contain the letter W.

S. Johannis. CXVII. CCCCVIII.

x.

Hurerey. Vnd er bracht mich im Geist in die wüsten. Vnd ich sahe das Weib sitzen auff einem rosinfarben Thier / das war vol Namen der lesterung / vnd hatte zehen Hörner. Vnd das Weib war bekleidet mit Scharlacken vnd Rosinfarb / vnd vbergüldet mit Gold vnd Edlensteinen vnd Perlen / vnd hatte einen gülden Becher in der Hand / vol Grewels vnd vnsauberkeit jrer Hurerey. Vnd an jrer Stirn geschrieben den Namen / Das Geheimnis / Die grosse Babylon / die Mutter der hurerey vnd aller grewel auff Erden. Vnd ich sahe das Weib truncken von dem Blut der Heiligen / vnd von dem blut der zeugen Jhesu. Vnd ich verwundert mich seer / da ich sie sahe.

(Geheimnis)
Das ist / die geistliche grosse Babylon etc.

4.6 Georg Rörer's 'symbolic typography', from the Wittenberg Bible of 1545

principle, reflecting an already traditional tension between German and Italian typographers, is that gothic type is used for German text and for Lutheran truth, and roman type for Roman lies.[36]

For all its importance in the History of the Book, the real significance of Luther's Bible lies in its success in propagating the Gospel, for which in large measure the quality of the translation was responsible. It is vital to see Luther in the broader context of contemporary translation theory and practice in Germany. There were some among late fifteenth-century German humanists who believed that the only way to improve the quality of German writing was to model it closely on the style of Latin, the idea being that if one followed the example of Cicero, the result would perforce be elegant Ciceronian German. Others took the view that the paramount aim was to render the sense of the original accurately while the style was incidental if not immaterial.[37] Luther struck a happy balance between these approaches: he asserted that fidelity to the sense of the original was paramount – especially in the case of Holy Scripture – and that it was essential to ensure that it was rendered into natural, idiomatic German. Defending his method in his *Sendbrief von Dolmetschen* ('Open letter on translating') of 1530, one of several programmatic statements on his approach to translation, he says Latin, Greek or Hebrew idiom is irrelevant; the important thing is naturalness of expression in the target language.[38] 'One must not be guided by the literal Latin text to find out how to express things in German, as these [Popish] asses do, but one should consult the mother in the house, the children in the street, the common man in the market

36 For German antagonism towards foreign, especially Italianate, features in printing see John L. Flood 'Nationalistic Currents in Early German Typography', *The Library*, 6th ser., **15** (1993), pp. 125–41. This had long-lasting consequences for German printing, right down to the early 1940s: see Christine Killius, *Die Antiqua-Fraktur-Debatte um 1800 und ihre historische Herleitung* (Wiesbaden, 1999), and Silvia Hartmann, *Fraktur oder Antiqua: Der Schriftstreit von 1881 bis 1941* (Frankfurt am Main, 1998).

37 For these contrasting approaches see my articles 'Niklas von Wyle' and 'Albrecht von Eyb', in *German Writers of the Renaissance 1280–1580*, eds James Hardin and Max Reinhart, Dictionary of Literary Biography, 179 (Detroit, Washington, DC, and London, 1997), pp. 332–7 and 48–54 respectively.

38 In addition to the edition in WA xxx/2, pp. 627–46, there are many modern separate editions of Luther's short tract on his approach to translation, but the most useful are: Martin Luther, *Sendbrief vom Dolmetschen*, ed. Karl Bischoff, 2nd edn (Tübingen, 1965) and Martin Luther, *Sendbrief vom Dolmetschen und Summarien über die Psalmen und Ursachen des Dolmetschens, mit einem Anhang ausgewählter Selbstzeugnisse und Übersetzungsproben*, ed. Erwin Arndt (Halle an der Saale, 1968). An English translation, by Charles M. Jacobs, revised by E. Theodore Bachmann, entitled 'On Translating: An Open Letter', may be found in *Luther's Works*, ed. Jaroslav Pelikan, American Edition, 54 vols (St Louis, MO, and Philadelphia, PA, 1958–67), xxxv, pp. 175–202.

place and listen to how they speak and translate accordingly; then they will understand it and recognize that you are talking German to them.'[39] In the same way Tyndale's English translation would reflect 'the language spoken in the Vale of Berkeley by his parents, brothers, friends, neighbours, by officials and labourers, priests and ploughboys'.[40] Luther takes as an example Gabriel's salutation of Mary, 'Hail Mary, full of Grace: "Gegrüsset seistu Maria vol gnaden". Is that German?', he asks;

> What does it mean 'full of grace'? A German hearing that will think of a barrel full of beer or a purse full of money. But I have translated it 'Du holdselige', even though it would be more natural to say 'Du liebe Maria' ('Dear Mary'), but if I had done that the Papists would have gone berserk and have accused me of ruining the angel's greeting.[41]

Indeed, as it was, he was accused of making it sound as though Gabriel were addressing his girlfriend when he had the angel address her as 'Du holdselige' ('Fair lady'). Duke George's secretary, Hieronymus Emser, had charged Luther with perpetrating 1400 'heretical' errors in translating the New Testament, one of which was to have rendered the opening words of the Lord's Prayer 'Pater noster' as 'Unser Vater' ('Our Father') using normal German word order (adjective before the noun), instead of 'Vater unser', the Latinate word order that had been standard in Germany for nearly a thousand years.[42] It is evident that, despite their pettifogging criticisms, the Catholics secretly admired Luther's translation: the version which Emser published at Dresden in 1527 was, as Luther immediately recognized, in reality nothing but Luther's own translation with Emser's name on the title-page and a few minor changes to the text.[43] Not surprisingly, Luther was not best pleased. People just

---

[39] '... den man mus nicht die buchstaben inn der lateinischen sprachen fragen / wie man sol Deutsch reden / wie diese esel thun / sondern / man mus die mutter jhm hause / die kinder auff der gassen / den gemeinen man auff dem marckt drumb fragen / vnd den selbigen auff das maul sehen / wie sie reden / vnd darnach dolmetzschen so verstehen sie es den / vnd mercken / das man Deutsch mit jn redet' (WA, xxx/2, p. 637).

[40] Thus Daniell, *William Tyndale*, p. 18.

[41] For the passage in question, in the *Sendbrief von Dolmetschen*, see WA, xxx/2, p. 638.

[42] Emser's criticisms are set out in his *Auß was gründ vnnd vrsach Luthers dolmatschung / vber das nawe testament / dem gemeinen man billich vorbotten worden sey* (Leipzig, 1523). Urbanus Rhegius sprang to Luther's defence with his *Ob das new testament ytz recht verteutscht sey* ([Augsburg], 1524).

[43] In the *Sendbrief von Dolmetschen* Luther writes that Emser admitted 'das mein deutsch susse vnd gut sey / vnd sahe wol / das ers nicht besser machen kundt / vnd wolt es doch zu schanden machen / fur zu / vnd nam fur sich mein New Testament / fast von wort zu wort / wie ichs gemacht hab / vnd thet meine vorrhede / gloß vnd namen dauon / schreib seinen namen / vorrhede vnd gloß dazu / verkaufft also mein New Testament vnter seinem

did not realize how much hard work had gone into the translation: 'Ploughing is easy once the obstacles have been removed. But nobody wants to remove the trees and the stumps and prepare the ground. There is no gratitude in the world ...'. [44]

Luther's German was modelled on living speech, not on written literary style. 'Written text is dead language, speech is living language', he famously said,[45] and he is known to have spoken his translation aloud to test its qualities. Natural German idiom, homely proverbial expressions, alliterative phrases, and above all outstanding rhythmic quality make Luther's Bible language what it is, every bit as influential in German literary history as the language of the King James Bible and the Book of Common Prayer have been in English; Luther already did for German what Tyndale later did for the English Bible. The naturalness of Luther's language deserves particular emphasis given the current vogue for claiming that this quality was essentially Tyndale's contribution to Bible translation. David Daniell has drawn attention to how, in Tyndale's translation of Luke 2: 16 we find a succession of *a*-sounds: 'Mary and Joseph and the babe laid in a manger'; but Luther's version 'Maria und Joseph, dazu das Kind in der Krippe liegen' is no less effective with its succession of long and short *i*-sounds and alliteration of *Kind* and *Krippe*. Again, Daniell draws attention to the fact that Tyndale translates the Greek as 'wonder' (rather than 'were astonished', 'marvelled' and so on) which is then echoed as 'pondered' in Luke 2: 18–19. But Luther too has 'wunderten sich der Rede' and though he does not have the echo 'wonder'/'ponder', he does have 'behielt'/'bewegte' in Luke 2: 19. Consider also the woodenness of Matthew 6: 26 in Anton Koberger's Nuremberg Bible of 1483, the year of Luther's birth:

> Seht an die vögel des hymels. wann sy seen noch schneyden nit. noch sameln in den kasten. und ewer hymlischer vater füret sy.

compared with the rhythm and melody of Luther's final version of 1545:

---

namen' (*WA*, xxx/2, p. 634). At least eighteen editions of Emser's version were published (predominantly in Catholic towns) between 1527 and 1589: Dresden (*VD16* B-4374), Leipzig (*VD16* B-4384, B-4392), Cologne (*VD16* B-4382, B-4383, B-4391, B-4406, B-4465, B-4472, B-4478, B-4485, B-4486), Augsburg (VD16 B-4389), Freiburg im Breisgau (*VD16* B-4411, B-4424, B-4425, B-4446), and Neisse (*VD16* B-4470). The first edition of Emser's version follows Luther's page layout and reproduces Cranach's woodcuts from the December Testament.

44 'Es ist gut pflugen / wenn der acker gereinigt ist. Aber den wald vnd die stöcke aus rotten / vnd den acker zu richten / da will niemand an. Es ist bey der welt kein danck zu verdienen ...' (*WA*, xxx/2, p. 636).

45 'Die buchstaben sind todte wörter, die mundliche rede sind lebendige wörter' (*WA*, liv, p. 74).

> Sehet die Vogel unter dem Himel an / Sie seen nicht / sie erndten
> nicht / sie samlen nicht in die Schewnen / Und ewer himlischer Vater
> neeret sie doch.

And can there be anything finer than the ultimate outcome of Luther's
constant wrestling with the poetry of the Psalms, especially Psalm 23,
which in the first complete Bible of 1534 reads:

> Der HERR ist mein Hirte / mir wird nichts mangeln.
> Er weidet mich auff einer grünen awen / Vnd füret mich zum
>   frisschen Wasser.
> Er erquicket meine Seele / er füret mich auff rechter strasse / vmb
>   seines namens willen.
> Vnd ob ich schon wandert im finstern tal / fürchte ich kein vnglück /
>   Denn du bist bey mir / Dein stecken vnd stab trösten mich.
> Du bereitest fur mir einen tisch gegen meine feinde / Du salbest mein
>   heubt mit öle / vnd schenkest mir vol ein.
> Gutes vnd barmherzigkeit werden mir folgen mein lebenlang / Vnd
>   werde bleiben im Hause des HERRN jmer dar.

If anything, the passage of time has made this rendering ever more
beautiful, with its now rather archaic vocabulary (*awen, erquicket, ob
... schon, stecken vnd stab, salbest*), antiquated morphology (especially
the rhythmically important unstressed syllables: *füret, erquicket, salbest,
schenkest*) and quaint word order (*ob ich schon wandert im finstern tal,
werden mir folgen mein lebenlang*), and its rich alliterative patterning.
Unfortunately, in general, modern revisions of Luther's Bible have
sacrificed some of the beauties of his original.[46] These days we normally
read silently to ourselves whereas in Luther's time people generally read
aloud, in a group, in the family, or even when alone. In particular the
musical qualities inherent in the patterning of the stressed and
unstressed syllables tend to have been sacrificed. Just as English has lost
disyllabic present-tense forms like *goeth, keepeth, loveth,* so too German
has meanwhile lost many of the unstressed syllables that once
characterized it. A purple passage in Luther is 1 Corinthians 13, which
in his original version from the 1520s possesses an amazing rhythmical
quality but which is now largely lost. In the Wittenberg Bible of 1545,
the last edition to appear in Luther's lifetime, 1 Corinthians 13: 1–8
read:

> Wenn ich mit Menschen vnd mit Engel zungen redet / vnd hette der
> Liebe nicht / So were ich ein donend Ertz oder eine klingende

---

[46] Revised versions of the Luther Bible were published in 1973 and, even more
thoroughly revised, in 1976. See Samuel Brügger, *Die deutschen Bibelübersetzungen des
20. Jahrhunderts im sprachwissenschaftlichen Vergleich*, Europäische Hochschulschriften,
ser. I, vol. 707 (Berne, 1983).

Schelle. Vnd wenn ich weissagen kündte / vnd wüste alle Geheimnis / vnd alle Erkentnis / vnd hette allen Glauben / also / daß ich Berge versetzte / vnd hette der Liebe nicht / So were ich nichts. Vnd wenn ich alle meine Habe den Armen gebe / vnd liesse meinen Leib brennen / So were mirs nichts nütze.

Die Liebe ist langmütig vnd freundlich / die liebe eiuert nicht / die liebe treibt nicht mutwillen / sie blehet sich nicht / sie stellet nicht vngeberdig / sie süchet nicht das jre / sie lesset sich nicht erbittern / sie trachtet nicht nach schaden / sie frewet sich nicht der vngerechtigkeit / sie frewet sich aber der warheit / Sie vertreget alles / sie gleubet alles / sie hoffet alles / sie duldet alles. Die Liebe wird nicht müde / Es müssen auffhören die Weissagungen / vnd auffhören die Sprachen / vnd das Erkentnis wird auch auffhören.[47]

The quality of Luther's translation was recognized even by contemporary publishers: to cite just one instance, when the Basle printer Adam Petri brought out a pirated edition of the New Testament in March 1523 he refrained from replacing Luther's Central German vocabulary with the Upper German words more familiar to his book-buying clientele, supplying instead a comprehensive glossary to help them, rather than risking spoiling Luther's excellent translation.[48] This example neatly illustrates the linguistic problem which confronted Luther: as yet there was no standard German language. As he himself remarked,

---

[47] The beauty of this passage is well brought out if one compares it with the halting style in the corresponding passage in the Mentelin Bible of 1466 (see *Die erste deutsche Bibel*, ed. Kurrelmeyer, ii, 94 f.; also reprinted in Martin Luther, *Sendbrief vom Dolmetschen*, ed. Bischoff, p. 53). There is an excellent facsimile of the entire 1545 text: *Biblia Germanica 1545. Die Bibel in der deutschen Übersetzung Martin Luthers. Ausgabe letzter Hand* (Stuttgart, 1967). *D. Martin Luther, Die gantze Heilige Schrifft Deudsch. Wittenberg 1545*, ed. Hans Volz, 3 vols (Munich, 1972), is a reprint in roman type, with useful supplementary material. An inexpensive scholarly edition of the New Testament only is *Das Neue Testament in der deutschen Übersetzung von Martin Luther nach dem Bibeldruck von 1545 mit sämtlichen Holzschnitten. Studienausgabe*, i: *Text in der Fassung des Bibeldrucks von 1545*; ii: *Entstehungsvarianten, Glossar, Bibliographie, Nachwort*, ed. Hans-Gert Roloff, Reclams Universal-Bibliothek, 3741, 3742 (Stuttgart, 1989).

[48] The glossary, part of which is reproduced in facsimile in Strohm and Zwink, *Ursprung der Biblia Deutsch*, p. 47, is prefaced with the words: 'Lieber Christlicher Leser / So ich gemerckt hab / das nitt yederman verston mag ettliche wörtter im yetzt gründtlichen verteutschten neuwen testament / doch die selbigen wörtter nit on schaden hetten mögen verwandlet werden / hab ich lassen dieselbigen auff vnser hoch teutsch außlegen vnd ordenlich in ein klein register ... fleißlich verordnet.' ('Dear Christian Reader, having noticed that not everyone can understand certain words in this New Testament which has been translated into German properly, and yet these words could not have been altered without spoiling it, I have had them turned into our Upper German and have arranged them diligently in a little alphabetical list.') One may suspect that it was easier for Petri to compile the glossary than to go to the length of revising the whole text of the New Testament.

> Germany has many dialects, different ways of speaking, so that
> people living thirty miles apart cannot understand one another very
> well. The Austrians and the Bavarians do not understand the
> Thuringians and the Saxons, not to mention the Low German
> speakers.[49]

He believed he had solved the problem for himself by adopting what he
imagined to be the language of the Saxon chancery as a kind of
compromise language, intelligible to both northerners and southerners:

> I do not have any particular form of German of my own, rather I
> use the common German language so that people from Upper
> Germany and Lowlanders too can understand me. My language is
> that of the Saxon chancery which all the princes and kings of
> Germany follow; all imperial cities and the courts of princes follow
> the practice of the Saxon chancery of our Elector,[50] wherefore it
> really is the most generally accepted form of German. Emperor
> Maximilian and Elector Frederick, Duke of Saxony etc. have
> moulded the German languages in the Roman Empire into one.[51]

The problems that this passage has posed for linguistic historians need
not detain us here.

One of many glowing testimonies to the quality of Luther's Bible
translation came from Friedrich Nietzsche who, as a Professor of
Classics, was well able to assess Luther's linguistic achievement:
recognizing Luther's complete mastery of oratory and noting how
appropriate it was that the masterpiece of German prose should be the
masterpiece of Germany's greatest preacher, Nietzsche simply declared
Luther's Bible to be 'the best German book thus far'.[52]

In the *Sendbrief von Dolmetschen* Luther said of his translation, 'I
can assert with a good conscience that I have faithfully invested my

---

[49] 'Deutschland hat mancherley Dialectos, Art zu reden, also, daß die Leute in 30
Meilen Weges einander nicht wol können verstehen. Die Oesterreicher und Bayern
verstehen die Thüringer und Sachsen nicht, sonderlich die Niderländer' (*WA, Tischreden*,
v, p. 512, no. 6146).

[50] That is, Elector Frederick the Wise.

[51] 'Nullam certam linguam Germanice habeo, sed communem, ut me intelligere
possint ex superiori et inferiori Germania. Ich rede nach der Sechsischen cantzley, quam
imitantur omnes duces et reges Germaniae: alle reichstette, fürsten höfe schreiben nach der
Sechsischen cantzeleien vnser churfürsten. Ideo est communissima lingua Germaniae.
Maximilianus imperator et elector Fridericus imperium ita ad certam linguam definierunt,
haben also alle sprachen in eine getzogen' (*WA, Tischreden*, ii, pp. 639–40). Another
version of the same utterance, this time in German throughout, is given in *WA, Tischreden*,
i, pp. 524–5, no. 1040. Luther probably made this statement around 1532.

[52] 'Das Meisterstück der deutschen Prosa ist ... billigerweise das Meisterstück ihres
größten Predigers: die Bibel war bisher das beste deutsche Buch.' Friedrich Nietzsche,
Jenseits von Gut und Böse, § 247, in Friedrich Nietzsche, *Werke in drei Bänden*, ed. Karl
Schlechta, 7th edn (Munich, 1973), p. 715.

4.7 Studio of Lucas Cranach the Elder, 'Luther on his deathbed', 1546

energies in it, have had no unworthy thoughts, for I have neither taken, sought nor accepted a single penny for it, and God knows that I did not seek to advance my reputation by it, but I did it as a service to my dear Christians and to the honour of One who thrones above …'.[53] Luther's serene countenance in this propagandistic deathbed picture (Figure 4.7), made in the studio of Lucas Cranach in 1546, indeed shows him dying with a good conscience. His adversaries had predicted that he would die a terrible death as retribution for his vitriolic attacks on the papacy – but clearly they were mistaken about this too.

---

[53] 'Das kan ich mit gutem gewissen zeugen / das ich meine höchste trew vnd vleis darinnen erzeigt / vnd nye kein falsche gedancken gehabt habe / denn ich habe keinen heller dafur genommen noch gesücht / noch damit gewonnen / So hab ich meine ehre drinnen nicht gemeinet / das weis Gott mein Herr / sondern habs zu dienst gethan den lieben Christen vnnd zu ehren einem der droben sitzet …' (WA, xxx/2, p. 640). It has been estimated that, by the time of Luther's death, no fewer than 600 000 copies of his Bible or parts of it had been published in authorized or pirated editions: see Heimo Reinitzer, 'Bibeldruck', in Lexikon des gesamten Buchwesens, ed. Severin Corsten et al., 2nd edn (Stuttgart, 1987–   ), i, pp. 349–53.

CHAPTER FIVE

A Neglected Facet of Cardinal Cajetan: Biblical Reform in High Renaissance Rome

Michael O'Connor

The Dominican theologian and cardinal Tommaso de Vio (1469–1534), known as Cajetan after Gaeta, his birthplace, is best remembered for his encounter with Martin Luther in October 1518. On that occasion, Cajetan sought to persuade Luther to withdraw a number of theological opinions on account of their alleged unorthodoxy. Several years later, Cajetan was involved, albeit peripherally, with the Roman commission that drew up the formal condemnation of Luther's teaching. It is widely and plausibly assumed that the rest of Cajetan's work is to be understood in this light, especially his commentaries on biblical texts, which he worked on from 1524 until his death in 1534. Jerry Bentley's remarks in the *Oxford Companion to the Bible* sum up the conventional view: 'In long commentaries on the Gospels and the Pauline letters, Cajetan depended upon the methods of humanist scholarship to argue that the New Testament proved the truth of Roman Catholic doctrine and confuted the Protestant alternative.'[1] This view, promoted in T.H.L. Parker's recent study of sixteenth-century commentaries on *Romans*, can be traced back at least to Richard Simon (1638–1712), the French biblical scholar and historian of biblical criticism.[2] Nor is it totally wrong. In the 1520s, there were writers who approached scriptural exegesis with precisely this aim in mind and there is some justification

---

[1] Bruce M. Metzger and Michael D. Coogan (eds), *The Oxford Companion to the Bible* (Oxford, 1993), p. 318. For a more detailed account of the argument of this chapter, see my unpublished doctoral thesis, 'Exegesis, Doctrine and Reform in the Biblical Commentaries of Cardinal Cajetan, 1469–1534' (Oxford University, 1997). A rare dissenter from the conventional view, to whom I am greatly indebted, is A.F. von Gunten, especially his 'La Contribution des "Hebreux" à l'œuvre exégétique de Cajétan', in Olivier Fatio and Pierre Fraenkel (eds), *Histoire de l'exégèse au XVIᵉ siècle* (Geneva, 1978), pp. 46–83.

[2] Richard Simon (1638–1712), *Histoire critique des principaux commentateurs du Nouveau Testament* (Rotterdam, 1693), pp. 538–9. T.H.L. Parker, *Commentaries on the Epistle to the Romans 1532–1542* (Edinburgh, 1986), p. 8 and *passim*.

for including Cajetan among them. It was clearly expected of him, in some quarters.[3] Cajetan himself appears to provide just this explanation in one of his polemical works: his 1531 controversial treatise, *De sacrificio missae et ritu adversus Lutheranos*. Here he explains that the Gospels show Christ refuting the Sadducees by arguing solely from the books of Moses, the only books of Scripture they recognized (Matt. 22: 23–33).[4] Heretics likewise, Cajetan argues, must be countered with arguments from the authorities to which they themselves appeal. For this reason, Cajetan declares that he will present the case in support of the sacrifice of the mass exclusively from Scripture.[5] The conventional view assumes that this was the rationale behind all of Cajetan's biblical exegesis; it is the aim of this chapter to argue otherwise.

Error and heresy in Cajetan's biblical commentaries

There are about two dozen mentions of unspecified 'heretics' in the biblical commentaries. Many of these are general comments about the heretics' selective use of Scripture[6] and their moral turpitude,[7] or arguments that heresy is the work of the devil,[8] and that heretics, like the Samaritans before them, are often hated more than pagans.[9] Cajetan gives some indication of the kinds of false teachers he has in mind. They are the sort who deny divine providence or the immortality of the soul.

---

[3] 'Quis autem adversus Lutheri pestem aut verius scribere potuit, aut doctius, aut etiam confidentius?', *Epistola theologorum Parisiensium ad Cardinalem Caietanum reprehensoria* (Berlin, Staatsbibliothek zu Berlin – Preußischer Kulturbesitz MS Dg 2920), cited in M.-H. Laurent, 'Quelques documents des archives Vaticanes (1517–1534)', *Revue Thomiste*, **17** (1934–35), pp. 50–148, at p. 116, n. 17.

[4] See Aquinas, *Catena aurea in quatuor evangelia* (Turin and Rome, 1953), i, p. 324b.

[5] 'Unicus magister omnium Dominus Iesus Sadducaeos (qui ex sacris libris solos libros Moysi recepiebant) confutando ex libris Moysi, docuit nos, ut adversus haereticos abstineamus a testimoniis quae non recipiunt, sed illis utamur sacris testibus quos non refutant. Quocirca adversus haereticos qui Lutherani vocantur, innitentes solis testimoniis sacrarum scripturarum, scripturus de sacrificio missae ex solis sacris scripturis disputationem doctrinamque omnem perficere intendo.' *Opuscula omnia* (Antwerp, 1576), iii, 164^{va-b}.

[6] 'Vere amica est veritas veritati. Remittit se Iesus ad scripturas, nullam sacrarum scripturam refutans, nullam mendosam, falsam aut suspectam dicens. Cuius oppositum faciunt haeretici, cuius oppositum fecit Mahomet.' On John 5: 39, iv, 323b–324a. Cajetan's commentaries and *Ientacula* are cited according to the complete five-volume edition, *Opera omnia quotquot in sacrae scripturae expositionem reperiuntur* (Lyons, 1639); references are to scripture verse, volume, page and column.

[7] On Rom. 8: 1, v, 40a–b.

[8] On 1 Tim. 4: 1, v, 299b.

[9] On John 4: 9, iv, 311a.

Among Christians, they are those who deny the Trinity and other doctrines professed by the Catholic Church.[10] The list of specifically named heresies or heretics is extensive: Arius and Arianism (fifteen times confuted from Scripture), Sabellius, Valentinus, Nestorius, Eutyches, Helvidius, the Nicolaitans, the Manichees and the Ebionites. The passages that are most peppered with an awareness of heresy are those concerned with the incarnation.[11]

But what of the contemporary threat to Catholic truth? Areas of doctrine and practice contested by the reformers are certainly covered by Cajetan. There are, however, in the course of over half a million words, only four explicit references to 'Lutherans'. Moreover, these are the only instances in which Cajetan actually names contemporaries as opponents. In the first case, the Lutherans are said to level against the pastors of the Church the accusation Christ levelled against the Pharisees, namely, that they teach the traditions of men as the law of God. Cajetan is far from dismissive of this charge; he examines the text with care and calmly appeals to the Lutherans to obey these laws not as divine commands but, in a second position, 'post divina'.[12] In the second case, the Lutherans are criticized for having lifted every burden from the shoulders of Christian people; Cajetan's comments on this verse, however, are directed primarily at confessors who multiply the burdens laid on the people.[13] The third text concerns Paul's teaching on the eucharist and will be discussed below. These three remarks, from commentaries on New Testament books, date from the period Cajetan spent in Gaeta, between May 1527 and August 1529.

The fourth case, from the early months of 1533, conveys an unmistakable sense of alarm. The Lutherans are seen to be in the throes

---

10 On Prov. 6: 17, iii, 522b.

11 For example, on Luke 1: 31, iv, 177b; on Luke 1: 35, iv, 178b; on Luke 1: 42, iv, 179b.

12 'Quia Lutherani ex hoc textu exauthorant ecclesiam, et super hunc textum fundant nullitatem mandatorum ecclesiae, utpote reprobatorum ub utroque testamento, veteri scilicet apud Esaiam, et novo hic a Domino Iesu, ideo diligentius textum hunc discutere oportet, ut illius veritas non commentum elucescat. ... Venerare igitur Lutherane ecclesiae mandata non ut divina, sed secundo loco, scilicet post divina. Quoniam sic oportet nos implere omnem iustitiam.' On Matt. 15: 9, iv, 72b.

13 'Utinam haec verba Domini Iesu in sedentibus super cathedram Moysi finem habuissent; utinam hodie non verificarentur. Tot iam onera sunt super utriusque testamenti honestissima praecepta, imposita super humeros hominum ut Christiani facile se servire Christo credant, si tot laqueis non subiicerentur, et confessores felices se arbitrarentur si de solis divinis praeceptis soliciti esse deberent. Cum his tamen omnibus parendum est Iesu dicenti, omnia quae dixerint servare, servate et facite. Et ipsi quidem sedentes super cathedram Iesu Christi damnationem suam cognoscant multiplicando onera; et tu Lutherane damnationem tuam abiiciendo illa.' On Matt 23: 4, iv, 101b.

of a dramatic and scandalous act of schism. For Cajetan, Leviathan's
serried teeth are the teeth of the devil, effortlessly ripping apart anything
that is good, whether in the moral life of individual Christians or the
unity of the Church as a whole. Cajetan warns his readers to look on
and wonder at the swiftness and the licentiousness with which this
schism has taken place, and to fear further divisions amongst other
nations.[14]

In only one of these texts does Cajetan touch on a doctrinal issue,
namely, the teaching of Paul concerning the words to be used in the
celebration of the eucharist (1 Cor. 11: 23–6). 'Lutherans', according to
Cajetan, would try to discount the authenticity of this tradition
regarding the eucharist, were it not the case that Paul not only 'handed
it on' in his preaching to the Corinthians, but providentially put it in
writing too. Two things should be noted about Cajetan's remarks.
Firstly, he inaccurately attributes to the 'Lutherans' a position in fact
closer to that of Zwingli; it was precisely this issue that passionately
divided Zwingli and Luther and their followers.[15] Secondly, Cajetan
minimizes the nature of the objection: although it concerns Paul's
teaching ('doctrina'), Cajetan considers it chiefly as a liturgical
objection ('de ritu et usu'). In support of his reading of this text he
appeals to a liturgical source, to the liturgy of the Greeks, who still use
the Pauline formula of consecration when celebrating the sacrifice of
the mass.[16]

Cajetan's most prolonged discussion of eucharistic controversies, his
commentary on John 6, proceeds on two fronts. Against the 'sect of the
Bohemians', he defends the Catholic practices of not communicating
infants and not offering the chalice to the laity. But against the ancient
error, 'recently revived', which interpreted John 6: 64 as a denial of the
real presence of Christ in the eucharist, he offers a convoluted

---

[14] 'Et huiusmodi dentium circumitus, quoad mores quidem, tu videris, et cave; quoad
ecclesiae vero unitatem, videmus nostra aetate Lutheranos tam magnam scissuram cum
tanta peccandi licentia effecisse tam cito, ut mirum incredibileque sit et formidandum ne
nationes alias scindant.' On Job 41: 8, ii, 551b.

[15] Bernard M.G. Reardon, *Religious Thought in the Reformation*, 2nd edn (London
and New York, 1995), pp. 100–105; Heiko A. Oberman, *Luther: Man between God and
the Devil*, trans. Eileen Walliser-Schwarzbart (London, 1993), pp. 232–45. For fluidity in
the use of the term 'Lutherans' in the 1520s, see Cornelis Augustijn, *Erasmus: His Life,
Works, and Influence*, trans. J.C. Grayson (Toronto, 1991), p. 147.

[16] 'Nota ex isto textu clare habere Paulum docuisse Corinthios de ritu et usu
eucharistiae antequam scriberet eis hanc epistolam. Et nisi Paulus hoc testificaretur, non
crederent Lutherani doctrinam Pauli fuisse, et tamen in rei veritate fuisset doctrina Pauli.
Et usque adeo haec Pauli traditio apud Graecos perseverat, ut usque in hodiernum diem in
sacrificio missae Graeci utantur his Pauli verbis consecrando corpus Christi, *hoc est corpus
meum, quod pro vobis frangitur*.' On 1 Cor. 11: 23, v, 125a.

Augustinian reading of the whole chapter which steers clear of the eucharist altogether: eating and drinking the flesh and blood of Jesus Christ, the bread of life, is a complex metaphor for believing in his incarnation and saving death.[17]

At other points, Cajetan is ready to bring the accusation of heresy. But in the handful of cases where he does so, he stops short of naming the alleged heretics. Those who say that the eucharist is nothing but a sign of the body and blood of the Lord are called heretics,[18] whilst Cajetan defines as a 'recent error' ('errorem noviter exortum') the claim that, at the time of the apostles, the eucharist was not considered a sacrifice but only a sacrament.[19] In an unusual tone of considerable pessimism (or the stylized pessimism not uncommon in medieval and Renaissance rhetoric), he laments that the small part of the world that is still in Christian hands is riven with heresy, schism and immorality and that the number of genuine Christians is minuscule.[20]

On the one hand, then, Cajetan is not slow to condemn views he considers erroneous or heretical, without naming heretics other than those formally recognized and long dead. On the other hand, he has no qualms in naming the Lutherans, but never calls them heretics. If there is a heresiarch before Cajetan's eyes as he writes, it is far more likely to be Arius than Luther. In each of the four cases considered above, the scope of the criticisms is narrow and discrete, largely confined to the perceived pastoral damage caused by schism and ineffective moral leadership. For Cajetan, the substantive 'Lutheran problem' would seem to be that of ecclesial discipline and unity.

Apart from these texts, Cajetan says very little about specifically 'reformation' doctrine and disputes. The very issue that he will defend as scriptural against both Zwingli in 1525 and the Lutherans in 1531 (the sacrifice of the mass), he is content, in March 1529, to allude to casually (and inconsistently) amongst those things passed on by oral, non-scriptural tradition (together with the sign of the cross, the

---

[17] See 'Exegesis, Doctrine and Reform', ch. 11, 'Is John 6 about the eucharist?'

[18] 'Et confutentur haeretici dicentes non esse nisi signum corporis et sanguinis Domini. Iniuria itaque irrogatur corpori et sanguini Domini indigne sumendo.' On 1 Cor. 11: 27, v, 125b–126a.

[19] 'Adverte hic, prudens lector, errorem noviter exortum dicentium quod tempore apostolorum eucharistia non erat sacrificium, sed tantum sacramentum, ex hoc loco manifeste confutari: nam hic clare de eucharistia quatenus sacrificium est, est sermo.' On 1 Cor. 10: 21, v, 120a. (This is anticipated in the *Instructio* of 1525, *Opuscula*, ii, 105[r]b.)

[20] 'Magna siquidem mundi pars Mahumetana est; et parva pars Christianis relicta, tot haeresibus et schismatibus ac pravis usibus repleta est, ut exiguus vere fidelium numerus iam apparere videatur.' On Luke 18: 8, iv, 251b.

Apostles' Creed and Sunday observance).[21] It is possible that here Cajetan has the liturgical form of eucharistic sacrifice in mind.

The only other apparently 'reformation' doctrine strenuously to be refuted is that concerning the priesthood of all believers. Cajetan opposes the view that all Christians are properly ('proprie') priests and that there is no other mode of priesthood. The two disputed texts are both in the First Letter of Peter.[22] In the first, Cajetan argues from the context. Peter brings together, in the same sentence, two expressions: you are 'living stones built into a spiritual house', and 'a holy priesthood' (1 Pet. 2: 5). For Cajetan, since the first of these is clearly a metaphor (the 'spiritual house'), the second, which is set in the same context, must also be taken metaphorically ('holy priesthood').[23] Peter goes on to say that the 'holy priesthood' must offer a 'spiritual sacrifice'. For Cajetan, this expression reinforces his conclusion. To offer a spiritual sacrifice, in prayer and meditation and spiritual instruction, is common to all Christians and this activity is correctly but metaphorically described as a holy priesthood. This metaphorical priesthood is quite distinct from the priesthood that offers the eucharist, which, according to Cajetan, is not under consideration in this text.[24] If this use of metaphor is not understood, the reader risks being caught in the trap of the heretics, who say that all Christians are, properly speaking, priests.[25]

The second text occurs just a few verses later in the same chapter, when Peter quotes from Exodus 19: 6, 'You are a chosen race, a royal priesthood, a holy nation' (1 Pet. 2: 9). Cajetan refers to the mindless logic that would conclude from this that every individual Jew was a king and a priest. These things were said then of Israel, and now of the Church, not in reference to every individual, but to the people as a

---

[21] 'Ubi et nota prudens lector, adversus exigentes scripturam de omnibus traditionibus apostolicis. Ecce Paulus aperte dicit *traditiones per sermonem*. Tali enim modo habemus Symbolum Apostolorum, habemus signare nos signo crucis, habemus festivitatem diei Dominicae, sacrificium altaris, &c.' On 2 Thess. 2: 14, v, 288b.

[22] These texts, alongside two similar texts from Revelation (Rev. 1: 6, 5: 10), are discussed in greater detail in *Ientacula*, III.1–3, v, 425a–427b.

[23] 'Deprehende caecitatem istorum ex hoc quod eodem contextu utrumque dicit, *aedificamini domus spiritualis, sacerdotium sanctum*. Quemadmodum metaphora est, *aedificamini domus spiritualis*, ita metaphora est, *sacerdotium sanctum*.' On 1 Pet. 2: 5, v, 374a.

[24] 'Offerre siquidem spirituales hostias orationum sanctarumque meditationum ac spiritualium instructionum, commune est omnibus, sicut offerre seipsum Deo in hostiam suavitatis. Nullus est itaque hic sermo de sacerdotio quo offertur eucharistia.' On 1 Pet. 2: 5, v, 374a.

[25] 'Adverte hic prudens lector, ne in haereticorum laqueum incidas, dicentium ex hoc loco Christianos omnes esse proprie sacerdotes.' On 1 Pet. 2: 5, v, 374a.

whole. It is because there were priests and kings within the people of Israel, that the people as a whole enjoyed a royal and priestly dignity. Likewise in the Church: it is because there are some who are priests and because the spiritual kingdom of God is amongst them, that the Christian people as a whole enjoy a royal and priestly dignity. At the same time, the royal priesthood of the whole people could be said to be particularly present in the Pope, who ranks above all temporal kings, presiding over them in spiritual matters.[26]

In these texts, Cajetan quite clearly denounces as heresy a view held by the Protestant reformers. But as with his treatment of eucharistic doctrine, accusations of heresy are never coupled with specific names. Cajetan could quite easily be thinking of the followers of Wyclif and Hus, rather than of Luther or Zwingli. Indeed, Cajetan's text could be read as a solicitous warning to the Lutherans, to Zwingli and even to Erasmus, to steer clear of a trap before them.

Elsewhere in his commentaries, and perhaps contrary to the expectations that these remarks might arouse, Cajetan appears somewhat agnostic about the terminology of ministry in the New Testament. He recognizes that certain Greek words have straightforward meanings that do not necessarily transfer to sacramental and hierarchical distinctions. Commenting on the words 'episcopos' and 'presbyteros', he denies that they are used to designate hierarchical or sacramental categories. Neither term stands for the name of an order, but for a general kind of official function. An 'episcopos' is an overseer, a 'presbyteros', an elder and, therefore, by extension, also a supervisor.[27] More significantly, Cajetan acknowledges, but then avoids addressing, one of the very points that would be so problematic for the reformers: how did the Greek term 'presbyteros' (elder) come to be translated into Latin as 'sacerdos' (priest) and can this translation be justified? This, he says in a telling remark, is not his business at present.[28] Were he

---

[26] 'Ubi et adverte contra haereticos fingentes ex similibus authoritatibus scripturae Christianos omnes esse sacerdotes. Convincit eos hic textus, quo ad universum populum dictum est, *eritis mihi regnum sacerdotale* [Exod. 19: 6]. Constat enim amentis esse intelligere universum populum Israel fuisse reges et sacerdotes. Sed haec et tunc dicta sunt, et nunc dicuntur, ut significetur utraque dignitas collata populo non ut singulis sed ut universis, hoc est, quod esset in universitate et dignitas sacerdotii et dignitas regalis. ... Modo autem verificatur in universo populo Christiano, sacerdotium quidem secundum quosdam consecratos, regnum autem spiritualiter. Quamvis etiam universus populus Christianus habeat regale sacerdotium in summo Pontifice, cui suapte natura convenit praeesse regibus omnibus et relative ad spiritualia de eis disponere.' On 1 Pet. 2: 9, v, 374b.

[27] On Titus 1: 7, v, 321a.

[28] 'Quomodo autem nomen *presbyterii* translatum sit ad significandum *sacerdotem*, non est praesentis negotii.' On Titus 1: 7, v, 321a.

concerned in these commentaries with defending Catholic terminology and discipline, this question would be very much his business.

Further arguments from silence undermine the conventional view of Cajetan's biblical commentaries. His discussion of the role of Peter, and the consequences of this for his view of the papacy, is a case in point. Firstly, in his comments on Matthew 16: 18–19, there is barely an attempt to justify the existence of a Petrine office or its continued exercise by the Bishop of Rome; on the other hand, there is a constant effort to deny any scriptural warrant for the abuse of this office. With his preoccupations seemingly elsewhere than with the doubts of the reformers, Cajetan is repeatedly setting limits and laying down qualifications. His anticipated audience for these remarks would seem to be somewhat closer to hand.[29]

Secondly, Cajetan refers the reader to one of his apologetic works on the subject of the papacy. After explaining briefly the pun on the name 'Rock', he asks the reader to consult his *De institutione pontificatus a Iesu Christo* (against Luther, 1521) for further detail, in order to avoid repetition.[30] In itself, this remark is inconclusive; Cajetan is either saying that the polemical work is complementary to his present commentaries, continuing their purpose in greater detail, or, conversely, that the reader must always look outside of these commentaries for Cajetan's refutation of Luther. Nonetheless, it is suggestive of a reluctance to engage at length, in the biblical commentaries, with matters of a controversial nature.

This initial look at the commentaries themselves shows that the conventional view, that Cajetan's biblical commentaries are examples of early Counter-Reformation polemical writing, is supported by very little evidence. There are far more references to ancient errors, heresies and heretics than to Cajetan's contemporaries and these latter are mentioned rarely and with discretion. Cajetan disappoints the reader who is looking for ammunition to use against the reformers; contested issues, such as the Petrine office, the sacrifice of the mass and the terminology of priesthood, are passed over without robust defence. Cajetan takes for granted that his reader accepts certain doctrines and practices, even if they are under attack. Furthermore, on a number of issues (notably polygamy, divorce and the authorship of biblical books) Cajetan's revisionism led some in Paris to the alarming conclusion that he himself was complicit with the attack.[31]

---

[29] See 'Exegesis, Doctrine and Reform', ch. 5, 'Reform of pastors, prelates and preachers'.

[30] On Matt. 16: 18, iv, 76a.

[31] See 'Exegesis , Doctrine and Reform', ch. 8, 'Authorship and canonicity' and ch. 10, 'The literal sense: the harmony and sufficiency of scripture'.

Cajetan's stated reasons

Cajetan himself says very little explicitly about his reasons for embarking on this work; what he does say, however briefly, points to a consistent and intelligible purpose. In the dedication of the commentary on the Psalms, Cajetan speaks of the importance of the Psalms in the life of the Church. They are the best known and most widely used of the books of the Bible. Some books of the Bible are used now and then, even daily, but the Psalms are used at all hours of the day (if no longer of the night). He goes on to note that, although many commentaries on Scripture have appeared, none has given the literal meaning of the Psalter.[32] And yet it is this sense, the sense that is most frequently at issue in the liturgy, which should be better and more transparently known by those who sing and read the Psalms.[33] Cajetan is thus offering to provide a commentary on the literal sense of the Psalms to help clergy and religious with their prayers.

A second, more general reason is given in the preface to the commentary on the Pentateuch: now advanced in years, and driven only by a love of the truth, he has begun this work, in order to stir up the minds of others towards the sacred Scriptures.[34]

After completing his commentary on the Pentateuch, Cajetan begins explaining the historical books of the Old Testament, beginning with Joshua. He gives three reasons for this commentary. Firstly, some things in these books are obscure and need to be made clear. Cajetan attributes the obscurity either to the text itself or to the translation. Secondly, there are unusual things said and done by holy men in these books. By implication, the ambiguities evident in their words and deeds need to be clarified in

---

[32] Beryl Smalley has remarked that Cajetan was clearly unaware of the medieval English tradition of commentaries on the Psalms; *The Study of the Bible in the Middle Ages*, 3rd edn (Oxford, 1983), pp. 351–2.

[33] 'Inter omnes sacrae scripturae libros beatissime Pater, psalmi quum maxime familiares cuique aetati ecclesiae fuerint et esse non desinant, mirum quod minus cogniti ac minus intellecti perseverant. Et alios quidem sacrae legis libros interdum legimus, alios quotidie, sed tamen certo diei tempore inter sacrificii solemnia audimus: a psalmis vero nulla omnino diei hora (ut nocturnas nunc psalmodias taceamus) eximitur. Ad haec, novi et veteris testamenti mysteria, multi multis commentariis aperuerunt: solus psalterii sensus quem literalem vocant, nulli est adhuc pervius, sed abstrusus: quum fere omnes qui commentarios in illud ediderunt, mysticos tantum sensus attulerint. Et tamen literalis, quo crebrius psalmi leguntur in ecclesia vel cantantur, eo deberet esse lucidior et apertior.' *Psalmi Davidici ad Hebraicam veritatem castigati et iuxta sensum quem literalem dicunt ennarati* (Venice, 1530), Dedication, vii^v.

[34] 'Ego iam senex non novitatis sed veritatis solius amore allectus, opus hoc aggredior in holocaustum omnipotenti Deo ad accendendum aliorum mentes erga Sacras Scripturas.' Preface to Pentateuch, i, facing 1.

order to prevent others being led astray. Thirdly, those who read and study the Bible are not always equal to the task of understanding the text. A commentary is provided to make the meaning of the text clearer.[35]

His purpose can be seen to emerge from these brief hints: namely, to explain the ambiguities and obscurities of the Scriptures to those who prayed, studied and preached them. They cannot but benefit from a better knowledge, and less confusion, about the meaning of sacred Scripture. Cajetan's work is offered to religious, clerics and literate laypeople, as a tool to give accurate access to the Bible, to help them to pray, and to give moral guidance in the light of the holy men and women of Scripture. Concerns about heresies may not be far from his mind, but only in so far as heresy adds to an already existing and widespread confusion.

A new hypothesis, based on Cajetan's own statements of intention, would be as follows: Cajetan's voice, as raised in the biblical commentaries, should be heard alongside the voices of those addressing the whole Church in the first decades of the sixteenth century, and calling for reform: for a renewal of fidelity to the words and commands of Christ, as contained in the Gospels and the teachings of the apostles; for reform of liturgical and devotional life, of theology and of patterns of leadership.[36] If this hypothesis is correct, then it should be possible to detect signs of these twin interests, Scripture and reform, in Cajetan's thought prior to the biblical commentaries themselves.

Scripture in Cajetan's thought before 1518

Key texts in the evolution of Cajetan's approach to Scripture are the encyclical letters he wrote as Master General to his fellow Dominicans, on the occasion of a General Chapter. In 1508, following the Chapter held in Rome during which he was elected Master General, he wrote briefly but firmly of the need to adhere to the order's traditions of poverty and study.[37]

---

[35] 'Tria me movent post expositos libros Mosis ad scribendum super libros historiales Veteris Testamenti. Primum, difficultas rei gestae, vel quia obscure traditur, vel quia secus interpretes eam reddiderunt. Secundum, ratio, tum verborum, tum factorum, quae ambigua videntur, virorum praesertim sanctorum. Tertium, imbecilitas multitudinis legentium studiose sacram scripturam, ut quae illis minus clara sunt, manifesta fiant.' On Josh. 1: 1, ii, 1a.

[36] 'En abordant son œuvre exégétique il pensait simplement donner à l'Ecriture la place qu'elle méritait dans l'Eglise et, grâce aux moyens les plus adéquats, aider ceux qui la lisaient à en pénétrer le contenu.' Von Gunten, 'La Contribution', p. 58.

[37] Monumenta Ordinis Praedicatorum Historiae, 9 [hereafter MOPH 9] = *Acta Capitulorum Generalium Ordinis Praedicatorum*, iv, 1501–53, ed. Benedict Maria Reichert (Rome, 1901), p. 83.

The more expansive encyclical that followed the General Chapter of 1513 (Genoa), reinforces these concerns: the common life must be carried out without compromise, trusting in the one who cares for the lilies of the field and the birds of the air. This is the root of religious life, the key to reform, without which no reform is worthy of the name.[38] Turning to study, reading and preaching, and taking his cue from Psalm 48, Cajetan urges the brethren to go up on high and proclaim divine 'doctrina' from the towers of Sion by their exemplary lives and teaching, rather than squander it in the ditches of ignorance, hypocrisy and scandal.[39]

The letter goes on to give detailed indications of the kind of studies the friars should be undertaking: first grammar, then logic and philosophy, moral and speculative theology, and finally Scripture. In this way, the order will be provided with able confessors, preachers, lectors, teachers and pastors.[40]

Using again the imagery of Sion, Cajetan identifies 'those who hate Sion' as those who usurp the name of teacher or preacher, those who wish neither to learn for themselves nor to see others learn. Let other religious orders, he concludes, glory in their prerogatives; if the Order of Preachers is not commended by its 'sacra doctrina', it is finished.[41]

Following the Chapter of May 1515 (Naples), Cajetan again writes of the two things most urgently needed for the reform of the order: common life and study. The former touches the salvation of the friars themselves, whilst the latter concerns the salvation of their neighbours. Whilst community is the 'nerve' of religious life, the study of sacred letters illuminates, inflames and saves the souls of others.[42] After exhorting the brethren to renew their commitment to a genuine style of common life, Cajetan reminds them that they are bound by their constitutions to nourish the people by example and word. He puts the

---

[38] 'Haec siquidem est religionis radix, haec reformationis clavis, absque hac omnis reformatio reformationis nomine indigna est.' MOPH 9, p. 94.

[39] MOPH 9, p. 94.

[40] 'Ponite siquidem non voces tantum, sed corda vestra in eius virtute expulsiva vitiorum, genitrice virtutum, duceque certissima ad caelestem patriam, et distribuite domos eius, ut quasi in quibusdam habitaculis distributi, alii grammaticae, alii logicae, alii philosophiae, alii casibus conscientiae, alii subtilibus theologiae quaestionibus, alii sacrae bibliae lectioni, studii sui praecipuas partes impendendo discant, ut in distributis domibus confessorum, praedicatorum, lectorum, doctorum, pastorumque praeesse et prodesse possint.' MOPH 9, p. 94.

[41] 'Gaudeant alii, fratres charissimi, suis praerogativis, nos nisi sacra doctrina commendet, de nostro ordine actum est.' MOPH 9, p. 94.

[42] 'Profitemur quippe inter cetera duo, quorum alterum nostra, alterum proximorum salus est. In rerum communitate religionis nervus consistit, sacrarum litterarum studium proximorum animos illustrat, accendit, salvat.' MOPH 9, p. 124.

focus squarely on Scripture, stressing the vital importance for evangelization of the study of sacred letters.[43] Once again, he expects this kind of work to be seen as typical of Dominican life: for other orders it is a bonus if they are able to put forward learned preachers and teachers; the Order of Preachers, however, whose calling is to study and to evangelization, has no choice. Together with a genuine common life, study will accomplish a much-needed reform of the order and its work.[44]

As Master General, then, Cajetan strongly exhorted his confrères to study. In 1508, this general requirement is linked to effective pastoral ministry, especially confession and preaching. In 1513, a variety of studies, culminating in the reading of Scripture, is linked to the different ministries exercised within the order. In 1515, the bond between study and mission is clearer still: without the study of sacred letters, there is no evangelization. In other words, those who do not study the Gospel, cannot preach the Gospel. Nearly ten years before he embarked on his own exegetical project, and three years before he met Luther, Cajetan had declared Scripture to be the centre of the intellectual life, reform and mission of his order.

By implication, this principle applied to anyone who held pastoral responsibility in the Church. Towards the end of his commentary on the *Secunda secundae*, which was completed in February 1517, Cajetan is led to reflect on the nature of the episcopate. One very practical question that arises is this: should a bishop be 'doctus et doctor' in canon law or in theology? Some, he comments, argue in favour of the former: in earlier times bishops had to fight against heresy with the sword of theology, but now a bishop's task is more administrative and requires primarily a knowledge of canon law. For Cajetan, this is far wide of the mark: the office of a bishop is to preach, and the subject of his preaching is not the law but the Gospel; and the Gospel is to be found in the Scriptures, the study of which is truly and properly the science of theology. For Cajetan, the office of preaching is a permanent feature of the episcopate; it is imposed on today's bishops at their consecration no

---

[43] Mortier's translation of this phrase, 'l'étude des sciences sacrées', is surely inexact. R.P. Mortier, *Histoire des Maîtres Généraux de l'Ordre des Frères Prêcheurs*, v, 1487–1589 (Paris, 1911), p. 149. For the scriptural focus of 'sacrae litterae', see Augustijn, *Erasmus: His Life, Works, and Influence*, pp. 104–6.

[44] 'Iungite, quaeso, communitati sacrarum studia litterarum, ut exemplo et verbo pascere populos, ut tenemini constitutione ordinis, possitis. Aliarum siquidem religionum professores quidquid impendunt doctrinae gratis erogant, nobis autem vix imminet, nisi studeamus ut evangelizemus. Haec duo sunt, quibus servatis, ordo noster facile reformabitur.' MOPH 9, p. 125. See G.M. Lohr, 'De Caietano Reformatore Ordinis Praedicatorum', *Angelicum*, 11 (1934), pp. 593–602.

less than on those of old – even though, he complains, there is none who actually fulfils it.[45]

Scripture scholarship, 1505–17

In an important sense, there is nothing novel in Cajetan's appeal to Scripture. By any measure, the Bible occupies a privileged place in Christian theology. Furthermore, as a Dominican and a disciple of Aquinas, Cajetan would not have surprised anyone by making scriptural studies central to the life of his order. As Denis Janz observes, 'In this respect at least, it can be said that Cajetan was more true to the spirit of St. Thomas than his predecessors in the Thomist school.'[46]

Nevertheless, in the first two decades of the sixteenth century, remarkable developments took place which were greatly to influence approaches to the text, the translation and the interpretation of Scripture. The textual skills developed by the humanists and hitherto used mainly to retrieve and understand the texts of classical authors were now applied to the Bible.[47] The call for a return 'ad fontes', when applied to the sources of Christian theology, bore remarkable fruit during these years in a 'series of publishing milestones' in Scripture studies.[48] Any list must include at least the following: Johannes Reuchlin's pioneering manual of the Hebrew language (1506) together with his appropriation of the cabbala (1517);[49] Erasmus' publication of Lorenzo Valla's *Adnotationes* on the New Testament (1506) and his own edition of the Greek New Testament

---

[45] 'Sed hi longe aberrant. Tum quia officium episcoporum, quod eis in consecratione imponitur, est praedicare. Materia autem praedicationis non est ius, sed evangelium, dicente Domino, *Praedicate evangelium* [Mark 16: 15], sub quo sacra scriptura comprehenditur, quae est vere et proprie scientia theologiae. Nec minus tenentur hodie quam olim episcopi ad praedicandum. Quia non minus hodie quam olim eis officium hoc imponitur, quamvis hodie tanti sit abusio quod, *non est qui faciat*, fere, *usque ad unum.* [Ps. 14: 1, 3]'. On *Summa theologiae* II-II, 185, 4 [IV]. Cajetan's commentary on Aquinas's *Summa theologiae* is quoted from the the Leonine edition, Thomas Aquinas, *Opera omnia iussu impensaque Leonis XIII P. M. edita* (Rome, 1882–); references are to part, question and article, with the paragraph of Cajetan's commentary in square brackets.

[46] Denis R. Janz, *Luther and Late-Medieval Thomism: A Study in Theological Anthropology* (Waterloo, 1983), p. 141–2.

[47] Euan Cameron, *The European Reformation* (Oxford, 1991), p. 141.

[48] Ibid., p. 68.

[49] Johannes Reuchlin (1455–1522), *De rudimentis hebraicis* (Pforzheim, 1506); *De arte cabalistica* (Hagenau, 1517). The *De rudimentis*, heavily influenced by the work of medieval rabbis, for example, David Kimchi (*c.* 1160–1235), is probably the first Latin work to be printed in Hebrew fashion, that is, from right to left.

with a new and annotated Latin translation (1516);[50] Lefèvre d'Etaples's edition of five different Latin versions of the Psalter (1508) and his commentaries on, and new Latin translation of, the Epistles of St Paul (1512);[51] the compilation, under the patronage of Cardinal Francisco Ximénes de Cisneros, of the polyglot Bible at the Spanish university of Alcalà (1514–17, published 1521–22);[52] Felix de Prato's polyglot Psalter (1515) and his celebrated collation of rabbinic commentaries and glosses (c. 1516–17), produced by the pioneering printer Daniel Bomberg.[53]

In the mid-fifteenth century, Valla had found New Testament scholarship dominated by those who used faulty translations, knew no Greek and relied heavily on the hermeneutical framework provided by scholastic versions of Aristotle's logic. In order to disencumber the sacred text from so much that obscured its meaning, Valla proposed a change of direction that turned on a few basic prescriptions: read the New Testament in Greek, study philology, learn from history.[54] For Ximénes, the best translator can only capture a part of the sublime truth of Scripture; the whole cannot be understood in any language other than the original.[55] For Erasmus, the purpose of all his meticulous scholarship is reform and renewal: the best hope for the restoration and rebuilding of Christianity is for those who profess the Christian faith to absorb the principles laid down by Christ in the New Testament. Christ, the Word of God incarnate, lives and breathes and acts and speaks in the New Testament, and with more immediacy than in any other way. Furthermore, the teaching which leads to salvation is at its

---

[50] Lorenzo Valla (1407–57), *Adnotationes in Novum Testamentum*, ed. Erasmus (Paris, 1505). Desiderius Erasmus (c. 1469–1536), *Novum instrumentum omne* (Basle, 1516).

[51] Jacques Lefèvre d'Etaples (c. 1460–1536), *Quincuplex Psalterium* (Paris, 1509, 2nd edn, Paris, 1513). The second edition is reprinted in Travaux d'Humanisme et Renaissance 170 (Geneva, 1979); *Commentarii D. Pauli epistolarum* (Paris, 1512, 2nd edn, Paris, 1515).

[52] *Biblia polyglotta*, ed. Diego López Zuñiga et al., 6 vols. (Alcalá, printed 1514–17, published 1521–22). Although the New Testament was printed by 1514 and the Old Testament by 1517, papal permission to publish was not finally obtained until 1521–22. This edition is known as the Complutensian Polyglot (Alcalá is known as Complutum in Latin).

[53] Felix de Prato, *Psalterium ex Hebraeo diligentissime ad verbum fere traslatum* (Venice, 1515). *Biblia sacra hebraea cum utraque Masora et Targum item cum commentariis rabbinorum*, or *Biblia rabbinica* (Venice, c. 1516–17).

[54] Jerry H. Bentley, *Humanists and Holy Writ* (Princeton, NJ, 1983), p. 68.

[55] '... quae nequeant aliunde quam ex ipso archetypae linguae fonte cognosci', Dedicatory Prologue to *Biblia polyglotta*, i, fol. *3ʳ. An English translation of this Prologue is included in John C. Olin (ed.), *Catholic Reform from Cardinal Ximenes to the Council of Trent 1495–1563* (New York, 1990), pp. 61–4.

purest and most life-giving at the fountainhead of the original language sources.[56]

By the 1520s, these principles, embraced by many, heatedly rejected by others, had become part of a wide and lively debate.[57] 'Trilingual' colleges or university faculties, institutionalizing the teaching of Greek and Hebrew alongside Latin, were established across Europe: at Alcalá (1508), Wittenberg (1518) and Louvain (the eponymous *Collegium Trilingue*, 1518).[58]

A striking feature of works mentioned above is the number of them dedicated to Pope Leo X: Reuchlin's introduction to the cabbala, Erasmus' New Testament, the Complutensian Polyglot, Felix de Prato's Psalter (as well as works by Pagnini and Giustiniani, to be considered below). This fact testifies both to the anxieties of scholars, who sought the highest approval for work they knew might be contested, and to the willingness of the Medici Pope to promote such scholarship. Leo consistently supported such work; for example, in 1513, he established a Greek 'gymnasium' in Rome and he boosted the provision for Greek teaching at Rome's university.[59]

The Pope was not the only patron of biblical studies in the Italian peninsula. Giles of Viterbo stated his fundamental reform principle in his oration to the Fifth Lateran Council: 'Men must be changed by religion, not religion by men' (1512).[60] One implementation of this principle was the exhaustive, if at times esoteric, scrutiny of the Word of God in Scripture. In 1515 Giles welcomed the Jewish scholar Elias Levita (1469–1549) into his home, trading hospitality and Greek lessons for lessons in Hebrew. During this time, Levita taught and published works on Hebrew grammar, until he was forced to leave the city (and his library) when Rome was sacked in May 1527. From Rome, Levita went to Venice, assisting Bomberg with further editions of the *Biblia rabbinica* (the second edition, published in 1523, included texts of the Babylonian and Jerusalem Talmud) and editions of the works of Kimchi.[61]

---

[56] Dedicatory letter to Leo X, in *Erasmi epistolae*, ed. P.S. Allen (Oxford, 1906–58), ii, p. 185.

[57] Erika Rummel, *The Humanist–Scholastic Debate in the Renaissance and Reformation* (Cambridge, MA, 1995), pp. 96–125.

[58] Basil Hall, 'The Trilingual College of San Ildefonso and the Making of the Complutensian Polyglot Bible', in G.J. Cuming (ed.), *Studies in Church History*, v: *The Church and Academic Learning* (Leiden, 1969), pp. 114–46.

[59] See Charles Stinger, *The Renaissance in Rome* (Bloomington, IN, 1985), p. 187.

[60] See John W. O'Malley, *Giles of Viterbo on Church and Reform* (Leiden, 1968), pp. 127–9.

[61] On Levita, see G. Weil, *Elie Levita: humaniste et massorète (1469–1549)* (Leiden, 1963).

Gian Matteo Giberti corresponded with Giles in 1517 about his *Libellus de litteris Hebraicis*; he employed and encouraged Hebrew scholarship, Jewish and Christian alike.[62] In 1515, Agacio Guidacerio dedicated his work on the Psalter to Giberti.[63] The dedication alludes to an intended revision of the Vulgate, by a team of Greek, Latin and Hebrew experts, Christian and Jewish, a project seemingly of Giberti's instigation.[64] In later life, Giberti would stress the importance of Scripture for the life of the Church, praising those who devote their studies to explaining Scripture.[65] As the reforming bishop of Verona, he described the kind of priests he would like to work in his diocese, saying that they will be more acceptable to him the more they have a grasp of Greek, Latin, style, and a 'non-disputatious' (presumably, non-scholastic) knowledge of sacred letters.[66]

Two Dominican scholars are of considerable significance in the field of the new biblical studies. The Genoese Agostino Giustiniani (1470–1536) edited an ambitious polyglot Psalter which was published in November 1516. This work, he says, was done at the urging of princes and prelates.[67] Although never assigned to any of his order's

---

[62] Adriano Prosperi, *Tra evangelismo e controriforma: G. M. Giberti (1495–1543)* (Rome, 1969), p. 103.

[63] Agacio Guidacerio, *In Omnes Davidicos Psalmos Argumentum et in primum interpretatio* (Rome, 1515). Little is known of Guidacerio; he taught at the Sapienza, wrote a Hebrew grammar which was dedicated to Leo X, and he taught Hebrew to Eck. In 1527, losing his library in the Sack, he fled to Sadoleto in Avignon and thereafter to Paris. See Prosperi, *Tra evangelismo e controriforma*, p. 103; H. Galliner, 'Agathius Guidacerius: An Early Hebrew Grammarian in Rome and Paris', *Historia judaica*, 2 (October 1940), pp. 85–101.

[64] '... ac veterem ecclesiasticam translationem, quae, ut ingenue fatear, tum interpretis, tum dormitantium librariorum incuria, in multis perquam depravata est, cum ipsis archetypis hebraicis, graecisque exemplaribus conferendam, ac recognoscendam, e plerisque trium linguarum peritissimis viris Christianis, et hebrais ... summopere procuras'. *In Omnes Davidicos Psalmos*, sig. A. II[r], quoted in Prosperi, *Tra evangelismo e controriforma*, pp. 103–4, n. 24. Compare this to Clement VII's 1524 team of twelve Hebraists (six Jews and six Christians) commissioned to revise the Vulgate Old Testament (Von Gunten, 'La Contribution', pp. 60–62).

[65] '... a discacciar le tenebre che occupano la più bella parte della sacra scrittura'. Letter to Sadoleto, Lodi. 8 November 1524, quoted in Prosperi, *Tra evangelismo e controriforma*, p. 106.

[66] 'L'altra [conditione] che quanto più buone lettere havesseno, e greche, e latine, e stilo, e cognitione di letere sacre, et non disputative, tanto più mi aggradariano.' Letter to Romolo Amaseo, Verona, 13 August 1528, quoted in Prosperi, *Tra evangelismo e controriforma*, p. 93.

[67] Agostino Giustiniani, *Psalterium Hebraeum, Graecum, Arabicum, et Chaldaeum, cum tribus latinis interpretationibus et glossis* (Genoa, 1516). Pelikan reproduces the exquisite title-page, noting also the pride of the Genoans in a native son: at Ps. 19: 4, 'et in fines mundi verba eorum', there is what amounts to the first life of Christopher Columbus (1451–1506); Jaroslav Pelikan, *The Reformation of the Bible. The Bible of the Reformation* (New Haven, CT, 1996), pp. 112–13.

houses in Rome, as Bishop of Nebbio (in Corsica) Giustiniani attended sessions of the Fifth Lateran Council just weeks after his Psalter, dedicated to Pope Leo X, was published.[68]

Santi Pagnini (1470–1536) came to Rome to produce a new translation and commentary on the Psalter, seemingly on the promise of financial assistance from Pope Leo. That money never materialized, possibly as a result of the Reuchlin affair, and the commentary halts abruptly before the last verse of Psalm 29. Pagnini also produced a new translation of both the Old Testament and New Testament from Hebrew and Greek. The influence of Erasmus on Pagnini is evident both in the use of the title *Instrumentum* and in the translation given of the opening words of John's gospel, 'In principio erat sermo ille'.[69]

These are not isolated occurrences. The City's university, the Sapienza, which had provided teaching in Greek and Hebrew sporadically since the 1480s, began to make more regular provision for both.[70] One distinctive and extreme voice within Renaissance Roman humanism is that of Adriano Castellesi, Vice Cardinal-Protector of the Order of Preachers (*c.* 1507–17).[71] His position, which has been described as 'scriptural skepticism',[72] is marked by a general denigration of all philosophy and secular learning. Sharing with others an interest in Hebrew and the cabbala, he makes selective use of the Latin Fathers, to

---

68 Sessions IX (19 December 1516) and XII (27 February 1517). Between 1517 and 1522, he taught Hebrew in Paris and made an important visit to England. On Giustiniani, see *Erasmi epistolae*, iii, p. 278.

69 Santi Pagnini, *Psalterium nuper translatum ex Hebraeo, Chaldaeo et Graeco cum commentariis Hebraeorum translatis, et scholiis cum orthodoxa atque catholica expositione* (Rome, 1520); *Biblia. Habes in hoc libro utriusque instrumenti novam translationem* (Lyons, 1527–28). On Pagnini, see T.M. Centi, 'L'attività letteraria di Santi Pagnini (1470-1536) nel campo delle scienze bibliche', *Archivum Fratrum Praedicatorum*, 15 (1945), pp. 5–51; Anna Morisi Guerra, 'Santi Pagnini traducteur de la Bible', in I. Backus and F. Higman (eds), *Théorie et pratique de l'exégèse*, Etudes de Philosophie et d'Histoire, 43 (Geneva, 1990), pp. 191–8; *eadem*, 'Incontri ebraico-cristiani: il Salterio poliglotta di Santi Pagnini', *Itinerari ebraico-cristiani* (Fasano, 1987), pp. 11–37.

70 See D.S. Chambers, '*Studium Urbis* and *gabella studii*: The University of Rome in the Fifteenth Century', in Cecil H. Clough (ed.), *Cultural Aspects of the Italian Renaissance: Essays in Honour of Paul Oskar Kristeller* (Manchester, 1976), pp. 68–110. Teachers included Pietro Colonna, known also as Galatino, who taught Greek, and Guidacerio who taught Hebrew (see n. 63 above). Galatino was an observant Franciscan who lived in Rome for many years, serving as papal penitentiary to Leo X and Adrian VI. He belonged to the Hebrew circle of Giles of Viterbo and his works show an enduring interest in Hebrew, Joachimism, the mystical metaphysics of Bonaventure and the cabbala; see John D'Amico, *Renaissance Humanism in Papal Rome* (Baltimore, MD, 1983), p. 219.

71 On Castellesi, see D'Amico, *Renaissance Humanism*, pp. 16–19, 169–88; Stephen L. Forte, *The Cardinal Protector of the Dominican Order* (Rome, 1959), p. 67.

72 D'Amico, *Renaissance Humanism*, pp. 169–88.

show that all non-scriptural learning is to be shunned. The only source of truth and light is in Scripture.

Castellesi was an unusual, but not a peripheral figure in Renaissance Rome. His views were expressed chiefly in *De vera philosophia* (1507). A letter in support of these views, written by a Spanish Dominican, Cyprianus Benetus (d. 1522), became a second introduction to the book in a later edition (published in 1514).[73] Benetus echoes Castellesi's view that only the true philosophy, that is, Scripture, can lead to grace and salvation. Benetus writes that he has demonstrated the usefulness of Castellesi's work in his courses at the Sapienza, where he used it to attack Plato, Aristotle and other philosophers; the success of his teaching, he says, led to the request for the new edition.[74] Castellesi's views may not have enjoyed wide popularity, but the support of Benetus, not least in the classrooms of the Sapienza, indicates that an audience was available.

The views of Castellesi and Benetus found echoes outside Rome, most significantly in the reform programme submitted to Leo X in 1513 by the two Venetian Camaldolese hermits, Pietro Quirini and Paolo Giustiniani. In their *Libellus ad Leonem Decimum*, they view secular learning as dangerous, to be studied only under the close control of religion. Classical languages are useful for the study of Scripture and the fathers, but should not be pursued for their own sake. They urge that a new official translation of the Bible be prepared and that study of Scripture replace the poets and orators of antiquity.[75] Even the more moderate Paolo Cortesi criticized the excessive concern for philosophy and natural science amongst the preaching orders; their efforts yielded doubt and misinformation. Preachers, he insisted, should direct their attention towards sacred Scripture, which contains certitude and truth.[76]

By the second half of the second decade of the sixteenth century, something of a consensus can be seen to be emerging concerning the study of Scripture. At the risk of over-simplification, the elements in this consensus can be summarized as follows: firstly, the current Latin

---

[73] Adriano Castellesi, *De vera philosophia ex quatuor doctoribus ecclesiae* (Bologna, 1507, 2nd edn, Rome, 1514).

[74] On Benetus, see D'Amico, *Renaissance Humanism*, p. 173.

[75] The text is discussed in Nelson Minnich, 'Concepts of Reform Proposed at the Fifth Lateran Council', *Archivum Historiae Pontificiae*, 7 (1969), pp. 163–251, repr., with new appendices, in Minnich, *The Fifth Lateran Council (1512–1517)* (Aldershot, 1993), ch. IV, pp. 163–251, 252*–253*; John O'Malley, 'The Discovery of America and Reform Thought at the Papal Court in the Early Cinquecento', in Fredi Chiapelli (ed.), *First Images of America: The Impact of the New World on the Old* (Berkeley and Los Angeles, CA, 1976), i, pp. 185–200; D'Amico, *Renaissance Humanism*, p. 186.

[76] D'Amico, *Renaissance Humanism*, p. 153.

version, the Vulgate, was acknowledged as less than desirably accurate; it was marred by errors introduced by translators, editors and copyists; it suffered from omissions and interpolations; the Latin was inelegant and misleading. The Vulgate, therefore, needed revising.

Secondly, precedence is to be given to the original language sources; the inspired books were written in Greek and Hebrew not Latin. The scholar must seek out and evaluate all available manuscripts and must master Greek and Hebrew. Grammatical and philological learning is central to biblical exegesis.

Thirdly, the value of non-Catholic witnesses was acknowledged. The practice of conferring with the Greeks in order to ascertain correct readings in the New Testament was defended, likewise the consultation of the commentaries and glosses of rabbis on the Hebrew Bible. (A considerable number of Christian Hebraists were former Jews themselves, including Felix de Prato and most of the Complutensian Old Testament scholars, facilitating the absorption by Christians of Jewish sources.) In addition to Catholic philosophy and speculative theology, exegetes may profitably avail themselves of a wide range of historical, geographical and liturgical sources.

Fourthly, the underlying reason for such scholarly labour is the renewal of Christian life: the education of the clergy, the improvement of preaching and teaching, the better knowledge and understanding of the faith among Christians, the evangelization and conversion of non-Christians. The Word of God must be allowed to nourish every Christian life and the Word of God must be preached to the ends of the world. For some, this aim was accompanied by a sceptical attitude to the abilities of human reason; the Word of God, as handed on and interpreted by the saints of the early Church, was the only word that could be trusted.

Cajetan cannot have been unaware of this consensus. He was active in the Roman curia throughout the period under consideration; he taught at the Sapienza from 1501 to 1508; he preached at the Fifth Lateran Council during which he worked alongside Giles; he knew both Giles and Giberti well; he was Master General in the same order as Giustiniani and Pagnini, living in the same priory in Rome as Pagnini for a number of years; nor can he have been unaware of the views of Castellesi and Benetus: one was a Dominican Cardinal Protector during his generalate and the other a Dominican teaching theology and philosophy at the Sapienza. When he met Luther in October 1518, Cajetan did not need convincing of the need for biblical preaching and a solid scriptural foundation for theology. Luther's appeal to Cajetan cannot have fallen on deaf ears; both men, notwithstanding the diversity in their theological training and personal experience, had come under the influence of the same developments in Scripture studies.

Scripture and reform in Cajetan's works between 1518 and 1524

If it is true that the motivation for Cajetan's later Scripture commentaries owed much to the inspiration of the 'biblical movement' of the early sixteenth century, then it should be possible to trace some signs of this influence in the works that immediately preceded the commentaries themselves.

The works of this period fall into three groups: firstly, the commentary on Aquinas's *Summa theologiae*; secondly, treatises occasioned by the case of Luther, particularly as this was being viewed in Rome; and thirdly, the two substantial works completed in Hungary, the *Summula peccatorum* and *Ientacula Novi Testamenti*. In works in each group, the appeal to Scripture is conspicuous.

Cajetan had completed his commentary on Aquinas's *Secunda secundae* in February 1517 and he seems to have begun work on *Tertia pars* soon after. By July 1517, he had reached ST III, 7, 11.[77] By the beginning of 1519, he was commenting on ST III, 48, 5.[78] On returning to Rome he commented on the last parts of Aquinas's unfinished work, adding a further eleven sets of questions to complete the treatment of sacramental theology. It has been argued that the commentary on the Tertia pars reflects a new awareness of Scripture which was absent in the earlier parts.[79] However, even when the statistical evidence is clear, conclusions need to be drawn with care. About half of the *Tertia pars* is directly concerned with Christology and Aquinas himself makes much greater use of New Testament material in these questions than he does in other sections, for understandable reasons.

In the dedication of his commentary to the *Tertia pars* (March 1522), Cajetan reveals his view of the task facing the newly elected Pope Adrian VI. Although Luther is not named, Cajetan speaks of the agitation caused by new heresy; but heresy is not the sole worry. Cajetan's list of concerns begins with the moral corruption, spiritual bankruptcy and wilful ignorance he sees in the Church of his day; and he names the lack

---

[77] Cajetan departs from his text to mention the Pope's decision to create him a cardinal, on ST III, 7, 11, [I].

[78] Where he quotes the 'very recently' issued bull *Cum postquam*, on ST III, 48, 5, [III].

[79] Jared Wicks, *Cajetan und die Anfänge der Reformation* (Münster, 1983), p. 122; E. Stöve, 'De Vio, Tommaso', in *Dizionario biografico degli italiani* (Rome, 1960–   ), xxxix, p. 571.

of peace amongst Christian princes and the threat of the Turks as major causes of decline.[80]

In addition to the fifteen treatises composed in Augsburg in 1518, Luther's case occasioned three more works from Cajetan in the following years. The first of these is a defence of the use of Scripture in canon law (1519).[81] The second is the long *De divina institutione* (1521), most of which consists of detailed exegesis of Matthew 16 and John 20.[82] The third is an explanation of the condemnation of some aspects of Luther's theology.[83] This brief treatise (1521) is written for home consumption; Cajetan refers to certain 'eminent persons' who are uneasy with some of the points that have been condemned and he seeks to justify and qualify the bull on these questions.

At this point, Cajetan's involvement in Luther's case appears to cease. After completing this work, Cajetan wrote nothing more against Luther or the Lutherans for a decade. The *Instructio* for the nuntio, written to combat Zwingli's *Eucharistic Theology* (1525), is the only explicitly Counter-Reformation work to be written until Cajetan receives a copy of the *Augsburg Confession* in 1530. The conventional view would see Cajetan's Scripture commentaries as the continuation, in less explicit mode, of an evolving campaign against Luther. Internal evidence has already been examined which questions this view. External evidence encourages further doubts. His influence on the handling of Luther's case was not dominant; his attempts to propose more moderate censures of Luther's teaching were frustrated by absence through illness.[84] His subsequent explanation of the condemnation of Luther's teaching is deliberately measured, commenting on just five of the condemned articles.[85] Furthermore, throughout this period, Sylvester Prierias was the

---

[80] '... turpissimis moribus foedata, bonis spiritalibus destituta, ignorantiae tenebris obsessa, novis haeresum tempestatibus agitata, bellorum tumultibus inter Christianos principes concussa, Turcarum impietate labefacta ac diminuta existit'. Leonine, XI, p. 2. The vernacular document attributed to Cajetan in *Concilium Tridentinum: diariorum, actorum, epistularum, tractatuum nova collectio*, Societas Gorresiana (Freiburg, 1901–38, repr. 1963–67), xii, pp. 32–9, 'Consilium datum summo pontifici super reformatione ecclesiae Christianae', will not be considered here; Tavuzzi doubts the accuracy of the attribution, which dates only from this century, and is researching a more plausible alternative (see Michael Tavuzzi, *Prierias: The Life and Works of Silvestro Mazzolini da Prierio, 1456–1527* (Durham, NC, 1997), pp. 115–19).

[81] *De usu sacrarum scripturarum ab ecclesia, Opuscula*, i, fols. 89ᵛ–90ᵛ.

[82] *De divina institutione pontificatus Romani pontificis super totam Ecclesiam a Christo in Petro*, ed. F. Lauchert, Corpus catholicorum, 10 (Münster, 1925).

[83] *Super quinque Martini Lutheri articulos, Opuscula*, i, fols. 90ᵛ–92ʳ.

[84] Stöve, 'De Vio, Tommaso', p. 471. See also 'Haec sunt pater beatissime quae inter tot adversas corporis valetudines obedientiae tuae gratia ex prompto animo sub apostolatus tui censura protuli', *Super quinque Martini Lutheri articulos, Opuscula*, iii, fol. 92ʳ.

[85] Wicks, *Cajetan und die Anfänge der Reformation*, pp. 125–7.

Master of the Sacred Palace, the Pope's official theologian. Intellectual differences between Prierias and Cajetan seem to have had an adverse effect on their ability to collaborate. Just at the point when they should have been working closely together, there were considerable personal and professional tensions between them.[86] Cajetan's involvement in the Roman process against Luther must therefore be interpreted with care, particularly in so far as this involvement might be said to influence the character of later works.

Cajetan was sent to Hungary by Pope Adrian VI in July 1523 to discuss defences against the Turks. After the death of the Pope, which annulled his mission, Cajetan found himself potentially idle. Not wishing to waste time, he worked on two projects until he returned to Italy in the summer of 1524. The first was the completion of a work he had begun earlier in Rome, a handbook for confessors, the *Summula peccatorum*. At first sight, this book is in the solid alphabetic tradition of the manualists and canonists, providing advice for priests on almost every conceivable sin from A to Z. In the prologue, however, Cajetan distances himself from that tradition, lamenting the all too frequent presentation of a stifling multiplication of authorities and the lack of common sense.[87]

The second work is the *Ientacula Novi Testamenti, literalis expositio*. This work is really a collection of independent articles, each one nibbling at a problematic text or group of texts from the New Testament ('ientacula' are 'snacks'!). Although one of the discussions touches a matter of Reformation controversy (that on the royal priesthood),[88] others are clearly prompted by other concerns. Enduring questions of exegesis are represented (Who was the young man who ran away naked from Gethsemane? Did the apostle Thomas actually touch the risen Lord?);[89] Cajetan alludes implicitly to disputes in the published writings of his contemporaries (Who was the woman who anointed Jesus at Bethany?);[90] questions of translation are discussed;[91] and, writing on the beatitudes, Cajetan plugs a gap in his own *Summa* commentary.[92] He

---

[86] See Michael Tavuzzi, 'Capreolus dans les écrits de Silvestro da Prierio, o. p. (1456–1527)', *Mémoire Dominicaine*, Numéro spécial No. 1, *Jean Capreolus et son temps 1380–1444* (Paris, 1997), pp. 239–58, esp. pp. 249–52.

[87] *Summula peccatorum* (Lyons, 1551).

[88] *Ientacula* III.1–3, v, 425a–429a.

[89] *Ientacula* VI.4, v, 444b; *Ientacula* VII.2, v, 448a.

[90] *Ientacula* I.1, v, 405a–408a; *Ientacula* XII.1–2, v, 466a–467a.

[91] *Ientacula* II.1, v, 416a–419b.

[92] *Ientacula* IV.1–5, v, 429a–439a. Over a decade earlier, he had advised, 'Quaestio sexagesimanona et septuagesima lectione frequenti, meditationeque iugi egent, non expositione.' On I-II, 69–70 [I].

writes in the dedication that texts were chosen at random, as they took his fancy ('Absque ordine siquidem et delectu occurrentes').[93] Some of the texts were evidently suggested by the liturgical celebrations of the day.[94] Regarding the style and format, a movement can be seen from the 'quaestio' of a scholastic treatise towards the 'annotatio' typical of the humanists. This hybrid form will be typical of Cajetan's later biblical commentaries and is a warning against too neat a division between scholastics and humanists in this period.

Conclusion

Cajetan's works prior to 1524 show an increasing use of Scripture and an increasing willingness to depend predominantly on scriptural sources. Controversy alone, if understood in a narrowly Counter-Reformation sense, fails to provide a satisfactory explanation of this phenomenon. When left with time on his hands, Cajetan dedicated himself to two works, the *Summula peccatorum* and the *Ientacula*. These two works correspond to the two areas of pastoral importance he had singled out some years before as Dominican Master General: confession and preaching. If it is difficult to explain the biblical commentaries as evidence of a continued wrestling with nascent Protestantism, it is next to impossible in the case of the *Ientacula*. Perhaps most clearly of all, the *Ientacula* demonstrates that Cajetan came to exegesis with a wide range of interests (speculative, controversial and above all pastoral). That this same breadth of interest and stimulus informs the biblical commentaries is suggested in the dedication of the *Ientacula* to Clement VII: the snacks had to be set aside when the possibility arose of embarking on the more substantial banquet of a commentary on the Psalms.[95]

In turning to Scripture commentary, Cajetan was using newly acquired methods in pursuit of an established aim. His commentaries are best understood as a 'return to the sources', in search of truth for the mind and guidance for the conscience – principles fundamental to any reform programme, however un-programmatic. As a member of the

---

[93] *Ientacula Novi Testamenti* (Lyons, 1551), title-page verso.

[94] For example, 'Occurrunt septimo in hac solemnitate Paschali tria ... tertium, quod in his diebus legitur ex Apoc. cap. 5, *Dignus est agnus qui occisus est accipere divinitatem*', *Ientacula* VII, v, 446a.

[95] 'Nec propterea finem feci, quod omnes declaratione dignas arbitrarer me complexum esse; sed ubi obtulit se commoditas inchoandi commentaria Psalmorum iuxta literalem sensum, omissis Ientaculis, convivio apparando vacandum credidi.' *Ientacula Novi Testamenti* (Lyons, 1551), title-page verso.

Order of Preachers, Cajetan intended his mature biblical humanism eventually for the pulpit and the confessional; and he expected his readers to include those who would be in a position to disseminate this teaching – friars and bishops, for example. While the theologian writes, the preacher of the gospel is always in the background: the preacher who expounds the Word of God, the preacher who corrects error and encourages virtue, the preacher who delights in praising the mighty deeds of God.

CHAPTER SIX

Strategies of Biblical Exemplarity in Gil Vicente

Paulo Cardoso Pereira

Though there were endeavours in drama in Portugal previous to Gil Vicente's production, particularly those of Anrique da Mota and Garcia de Resende, it is Vicente who has above all been hailed as the pioneer of the Portuguese theatrical tradition. Not much is known about his biography. He was born probably between 1460 and 1470, and worked under the patronage of King João II and Queen Leonor. His dramatic career started in 1502 with the performance of *Monólogo do Vaqueiro* (*The Herdsman's Monologue*) for Queen Maria, to celebrate Prince João's birth. Between this date and 1536 Vicente wrote forty-four plays as a court official, under the tutelage of Queen Leonor and Kings D. Manuel I and D. João III. His dramatic career is thus inseparable from the constrictions of royal patronage, as has been stressed by Laurence Keates,[1] for Vicente's theatre is essentially aulic as far as its context and dramatic function are concerned. He combines the traditional dramatic heritage represented by late medieval liturgical plays, mysteries and moralities with a new humanistic approach, and at the same time reflects the social and ideological agenda created by Portuguese overseas expansion. He wrote in a complex period of social history. The maritime expansion, and especially the discovery of the sea route to India, generated not only wealth but also an inevitable exodus from the countryside, and a growing mercantile bourgeoisie. The now obsolete lesser nobility, composed of *escudeiros* (squires), sought refuge in the court in order to carry on an idle and parasitic lifestyle. Vicente's playlets give voice to a multiplicity of characters who epitomize the multiple social and professional strata of the period: the gentry, the clergy, the professionals, the common people. The complex and often hybrid typology of his plays incessantly mirrors the ambivalence between the a-historical dogmas of Christian faith (as in the *moralidades* and *autos de devoção*) and the transience of contextual imperatives, as is made clear by the registers of satire and humour (*farsas*). According to Celso Lafer,

---

[1] Laurence Keates, *O Teatro de Gil Vicente na Corte* (Lisbon, 1962).

Vicente gives proof of a dualism reflected in the literary genres he adopted: on the one hand, man's realm, transitory and imperfect; on the other, the sacred universe defined by perfection and eternity. This *Weltanschauung* generated both *farsas* and *obras de devoçam*.[2]

Although there is no undisputed material evidence that Vicente received academic training, the philosophical and theological knowledge to be found in his plays, expressed as it is by an array of classical *auctoritates* and the use of some of the technical procedures prescribed by the *artes praedicandi*, allows us to infer that he received some formal instruction, probably at a convent school.[3] Religious texts were certainly a primary source for Vicente's work, particularly for his devotional plays. Constant references to the Old and New Testaments, the breviary, or the book of hours engender an intertextual structure and a plurality of registers ranging from the reverential *sententia* to the lyrical overtones of the Psalms, or to the burlesque sermon based on the subversion of sacred texts. The parable of the Good Samaritan is one of the sources of *Auto da Alma*; the *Auto dos Quatro Tempos* constitutes a dramatic expansion of the *Laudate* and the *Benedicite*; the *Auto da Cananeia* dramatizes a passage from St Mark's Gospel; one could multiply the examples.[4] Vicente also produced a paraphrase of the biblical psalm *Miserere mei Deus*, included in the fifth book of *Compilaçam*, which was largely based on Savonarola's meditation on the same penitential psalm. Many of the religious *topoi* that reverberate in this text, such as the overwhelming strife between human conscience and man's inborn sinful nature, the daunting prospect of irrevocable damnation, the need for contrition and an overall eschatological pessimism, were to be given dramatic reality in several devotional plays, particularly the *Auto da Alma*.

The creative, at times almost carnivalized, exposition of religious themes in Vicente's plays clothed open attacks on the clergy and on the abuses committed either by the Church itself or by its representatives. In plays such as *Frágoa de Amor*, *Barca do Inferno*, *Clérigo da Beira* or *Romagem dos Agravados*, Vicente mercilessly condemns certain religious tendencies, criticizing the dubious ethics of priests and friars (seen as particularly prone to the temporal excesses of drink and fornication), and the hypocritical hollowness of worship and prayer

---

[2] Celso Lafer, 'O Judeu em Gil Vicente', in *Gil Vicente e Camões* (São Paulo, 1978), pp. 30–31.

[3] On the literary culture of Vicente, see Joaquim de Carvalho, 'Os sermões de Gil Vicente e a Arte de Pregar', in *Estudos sobre a cultura portuguesa do século XVI*, 2 vols (Coimbra, 1948), ii, 205–30.

[4] On this subject, see Paul Teyssier, *Gil Vicente – o homem e a obra* (Lisbon, 1985).

when not based on inner conviction; he accuses simoniac popes and, in short, denounces the inexorable decline of an institutionalized system of belief. In the *Auto da Feira*, Rome, who, adhering to the mercantile dynamic of the secular realm, goes to the fair hoping to buy peace, truth and faith, is tempted by the Devil into purchasing something more in tune with the ethical dissolution of the present time; the Devil's argumentative speech evokes the rhetoric of the *adynaton*:

> A verdade pera quê?
> Cousa que não aproveita,
> e aborrece, pera que é?
> Não trazeis bons fundamentos
> pera o que haveis mister;
> e a segundo são os tempos,
> assim hão-de ser os tentos,
> pera saberdes viver.
>
> E pois agora à verdade
> chamam Maria Peçonha,
> e parvoice à vergonha,
> e aviso à ruindade,
> peitai a quem vo-la ponha,
> a ruindade digo eu:
> e aconselho-vos mui bem,
> porque quem bondade tem
> nunca o mundo será seu,
> e mil canseiras lhe vem.[5]

What is truth for? It serves no purpose and is displeasing; what is it for? You provide no reasons for what you need, and you must take care, so that you know how to live according to the times. For nowadays truth is called Mary Poison, while shame is called folly and depravity is called prudence. Pay tribute to whomever you may, I say it is depravity and strongly warn you, because whoever possesses goodness will never possess the world, and a thousand troubles will come to him.

As has been remarked by Maria João Almeida, Rome here has a hybrid rhetorical status: 'Besides being a spiritual and religious entity … it is also a human and secular reality'.[6] This sums up Vicente's attitude. While acknowledging the ecclesiastical institution's formal dignity, he stresses the fact that it is made up of men whose morals are not above reproach.

This violent criticism unashamedly directed towards the Church as an ecclesiastical institution has caused some critics to consider Vicente to

---

[5] *Auto de Feira*, in Maria Leonor Carvalhão Buescu, *Compilaçam de Todalas Obras de Gil Vicente*, 2 vols (Lisbon, 1989), i, p. 156.

[6] Maria João Almeida, *Feira* (Lisbon, 1989), p. 9.

have been a follower of Erasmus.[7] It is true that the playwright participated enthusiastically in the pre-Reformation ideology prevalent in his time. His work bears witness to the debate on such controversial subjects as confession, purgatory and indulgences, and he does defend an essentialist experience of Christian faith. In this sense he may, in fact, be considered 'proto-Erasmian',[8] owing to his condemnation of ecclesiastical ceremonial and mechanical cult, and also because he seems to share an analogous evangelical attitude purporting to return to the scriptural sources of faith. But the advocacy of the value of inner piety, and the renewal of interest in the literal authority of biblical texts, are not necessarily proof of an Erasmian influence, but are part of the broader complexity of the religious experience of the time. As Marcel Bataillon has pointed out, these characteristics were in no way a monopoly of Erasmus.[9] Moreover, in spite of his explicitly anticlerical attitude, Vicente never directs his criticism towards the foundations of Catholic orthodoxy. He was therefore able to reconcile a critical perspective on the ecclesial structure, and personal practices of faith, with the strictest observance of orthodox Catholic practice. This same opinion has already been expounded by Marcel Bataillon, according to whom Vicente was not directly influenced by Erasmus: 'This was no Christian humanist, but rather the spokesman of an anticlericalism long since rooted in the people. This anticlericalism had no need of Luther and Erasmus in order to mock the bulls, the jubilees, the graces and good works which Rome traded.'[10] Even the alleged similarities between Erasmus and Vicente, which have been underlined by Marques Braga as existing in the *Barcas* trilogy, are unlikely. The trilogy was written during 1517–19, at a time when Erasmus' influence was restricted to a cultured minority.[11]

It was not until around 1530 that we find a number of Portuguese intellectuals adhering to Erasmus' anti-scholastic and evangelical doctrines; naturally the Hispanic peninsula was not immune to the influence of his Christian humanism. In the same period, which coincided with the final years of Vicente's career, King João III promoted a comprehensive cultural programme which involved the reform of the

---

[7] This view has been defended by, among other scholars, Carolina Michaëlis and Júlio Dantas.

[8] The term is used by Hendrik Houwens Post in his article 'Gil Vicente proto-érasmien', *Caravelle*, **9** (1967), pp. 97–108.

[9] Marcel Bataillon, *Erasmo y el Erasmismo* (Barcelona, 1978), p. 147.

[10] Marcel Bataillon, *Erasmo y España: estudios sobre la historia espiritual del siglo XVI* (Mexico and Buenos Aires, 1966), p. 613. João Mendes defends Vicente's orthodoxy in 'Do erasmismo de Gil Vicente', *Brotéria*, **23** (1936), pp. 303–19.

[11] Marcel Bataillon, *Erasmo y España*, p. 612.

University and an invitation addressed to Erasmus to teach there in 1533
– subsequently refused by him. In the same year Clenardo, a Flemish
humanist, arrived in Évora, destined to become the tutor of Infante D.
Henrique who, somewhat ironically, was to become the future Inquisitor
General. André de Resende returned to Portugal in 1533, after having
attended the most prestigious Renaissance schools in Europe and having
written the *Erasmi Encomium* (1531). In 1532, João de Barros's *Ropica
Pnefma* (Spiritual Merchandise) was published, in which four allegorical
entities (the Will, Understanding, Reason and Time) engage in a
dialogue, in which Catholic Reason exalts the ethical and spiritual
values of an evangelical message clearly influenced by the teachings of
Erasmus. The things that are condemned include useless scholasticism,
the theological *disputatio*, the obscurity of sermons, false devotion to
the saints and, naturally, clerical corruption.

Vicente's paradigm of the spiritual life, however, appears fairly typical of
the pre-Reformation period, reflecting as it does the three major themes
which François Vadenbroucke has identified in the spirituality of that
period: pessimism, an obsession with the devil and popular piety. There was,
says Vadenbroucke, a generalized pessimistic attitude about the state of the
Church, the morals of the clergy, and the capacity of the Church to meet the
needs of the new nationalisms. On the other hand, a powerful fascination
with the devil and his works, which pervaded the popular imagination, was
noticeable from the fifteenth to the seventeenth centuries. Popular piety
produced a humanized experience of Christian life, which grew
progressively more detached from the formal Divine Office and, in the spirit
of the *devotio moderna*, became more centred on its own prayerbooks and
books of hours. The cult of the Virgin, the rosary and the Angelus
contributed to what Vadenbroucke calls the 'individualistic tendency' in
spirituality.[12] Even though we are here dealing with a generalization which
certainly does not account for the whole of Christian spirituality of the
period, it is easy to see how compatible Vicente's work is with it.

The *Auto da Alma* is a Passion morality composed in 1518, and
performed before Manuel I's court. The theme is the struggle between
Angel and Devil for the possession of the human soul in the course of its
existential pilgrimage, culminating in a holy supper (the Communion).[13]

---

[12] J. Leclerq, F. Vadenbroucke and L. Bouyer, *The Spirituality of the Middle Ages (A
History of Christian Spirituality)* (London, 1968), pp. 481–505.

[13] Maria Jorge emphasizes the similarities between Vicente's *Auto da Alma* and the
English morality play *Wisdom* (c. 1465–70) with regard to the action, the doctrine of the
three powers of the soul, the temptation and the references to Easter. Maria Jorge, *Alma*
(Lisbon, 1933), p. 33.

The structure is bipartite, and the dramatic substance of the play is announced in the Argument that precedes it, and which establishes a fundamental allegory: that of the *homo viator*, and of the Church as the inn/innkeeper of souls:

> Assi como foi cousa muito necessária haver nos caminhos estalagens, pera repouso e refeição dos cansados caminhantes, assi foi cousa conveniente que nesta caminhante vida houvesse ua estalajadeira, pera refeição e descanso das almas que vão caminhantes pera a eternal morada de Deus. Esta estalajedeira das almas é a Madre Santa Igreja; a mesa é o altar, os manjares as insígnias da Paixão. E desta prefiguração trata a obra seguinte.[14]

> Just as it was a most necessary thing to have lodgings along the routes, rest and food for the tired travellers, so it was right that in this wandering life there should be a resting place for food and rest for souls travelling towards God's eternal home. This resting place of souls is our Holy Mother the Church; the table is the altar, the delicacies the symbols of the Passion. The work which follows deals with the prefiguration of all this.

The keyword 'prefiguração' immediately evokes a specific point-by-point allegorical strategy commonly associated with exemplarity, as in sermon techniques. As a mode of writing and reading, allegory is founded on the homology between the dramatic structure and the ideal conduct that should be stimulated in the audience. When applied to the Book, allegorical reading resorts to relationships of analogy that ensure revelation and reinforce the dogmatic tradition. As a narrative or dramatic strategy, however, it follows the opposite procedure: 'partant d'une vérité, elle engendre, des éléments de celle-ci, une *littera*'.[15] The dramatic *exempla* selected to illustrate theological points (in this case, the power of free will and the endless rewards of the soul after its sacrificial journey) are univocally constructed so as to eradicate the possibility of ambiguous readings. Therefore, the interpretative freedom of the audience is restricted by constant authorial guidance.

In the first sequence, Holy Mother Church is surrounded by her four doctors: Thomas Aquinas, Jerome, Ambrose and Augustine. Augustine's initial prologue textualizes the topic of the wandering mortal, his soul ceaselessly in transit in search of salvation, and that of earthly life as an endless exhausting *peregrinatio*:

> Necessário foi, amigos,
> que nesta triste carreira
> desta vida,

---

[14] *Auto da Alma*, in *Compilaçam de Todalas Obras de Gil Vicente*, i, 175.
[15] Paul Zumthor, *Le Masque et la lumière: la poétique des grands rhétoriqueurs* (Paris, 1978), p. 80.

pera os mui perigosos perigos
dos imigos,
houvesse algua maneira
de guarida.
Porque a humana transitória
natureza vai cansada
em várias calmas,
nesta carreira da glória
meritória,
foi necessário pousada
pera as almas.[16]

My friends, it was necessary that on this, life's sad journey, there
should be some form of shelter from the great dangers of the enemy.
For human, transitory nature becomes tired during moments of
calm, and a resting place was necessary for souls on this journey of
meritorious glory.

Augustine lays the foundations for the hermeneutic procedures to be
followed by the audience throughout the performance and, at the same
time, codifies the allegorical terms according to which the theatrical
content should be deciphered, by reiterating the *similitudo* Mother
Church/Inn.

Angel and Soul are the next characters to enter the stage. Their initial
dialogue depicts a debilitated soul, on the verge of falling into worldly
temptation, and an angel that, through theological authority and
doctrinal injunction, attempts to strengthen her willpower. The structure
of the dialogue, used as a vehicle for evangelical didacticism, is
frequently reminiscent of the theological *disputatio*. When
characterizing the soul, the angel introduces the major theme of the play,
free will, and exhorts the soul to avoid Satan's cunning traps:

Vosso Livre alvedrio,
Isento, forro, poderoso,
Vos é dado
Polo divinal poderio
E senhorio,
Que possais fazer glorioso
Vosso estado.
Deu-vos livre entendimento,
E vontade libertada
E a memória,
Que tenhais em vosso tento
Fundamento,
Que sois por ele criada
Pera a glória.[17]

---

[16] *Auto da Alma*, p. 176.
[17] Ibid., p.179.

> Your free will is unfettered, independent, powerful, and given to
> you by the divine power, by the Lord, so that you may glorify your
> being. He gave you free understanding, free will and memory so
> that you may succeed in your endeavours, for you were made by
> Him for glory.

Stephen Reckert has demonstrated that this conception of free will is
indebted to Augustine's theory of the three powers of the soul (memory,
understanding and will), which shape the dramatic itinerary of the Soul;
late medieval typologies of sin were intimately dependent on these
faculties. In the typology adopted by Isidore of Seville, for instance, the
modalities of knowledge, ability and will constitute the criteria for an
assessment of the gravity of the fault committed. A paraphrase of this
concept is included in the *Virgeu de Consolaçon*, a Portuguese
translation of the Castilian version (1497) of the *Viridarium
Consolationis* of Jacob of Benavente:

> E diz sancto ysidoro en tres maneyras he o pecado geerado: a
> primeyra por o nõ saber, a segunda per nõ poder, a terceyra per
> querer. Da primeyra avemus exemplo dos primeyros padres.
> Primeyramente pecou eva nõ saber. Da segunda avemos exemplo de
> Adam que pecou per querer. Ca Adam nõ foy enganado mais cõ
> toda sua sabedoria peccou. Eva foy enganada. E sã pedro pecou per
> migua de fortaleza e per nõ poder quando por medo dhua manceba
> que o preguntou negou seu senhor. E assi parece que mais grave
> cousa he peccar per nõ poder ca per nõ saber. E mais grave cousa he
> peccar per querer ca per nõ poder ou nõ saber.[18]

> Saint Isidore said that sin is created in three ways: the first is
> through lack of knowledge, the second through lack of ability, and
> the third through desire. Of the first we have the example of the first
> fathers. Firstly Eve sinned through lack of knowledge. Of the
> second we have the example of Adam, who sinned through desire.
> For Adam was not ignorant, but sinned in full knowledge. Eve was
> ignorant. And Saint Peter sinned for lack of strength, and because
> he was not able, when, through his fear of a young girl when she
> asked him, he denied his Lord. So it would seem a more grave thing
> to sin through lack of ability than through lack of knowledge. And
> it is more grave to sin through desire than through lack of ability or
> lack of knowledge.

The idea of man's loneliness and complete freedom of judgement when
resisting temptation can be found in the angel's speech in *Auto da Alma*:

> *Alma*:   Tende sempre mão em mim,
> porque he medo de empeçar,
> e de cair.

---

[18] Albino B. Veiga (ed.), *Virgeu de Consolaçon* (Porto Alegre, 1959), pp. 36–7.

Anjo: Pera isso são e a isso vim;
        mas em fim,
        cumpre-vos de me adjudar
        a resistir.
        Não vos ocupem vaidades,
        riquezas, nem seus debates.
        Olhai por vós,
        que pompas, honras, herdades
        e vaidades,
        são embates e combates
        pera vós.[19]

Soul: Always keep a hand on me, for I am frightened of stumbling and falling.
Angel: That is why I am here and why I came, but really you should help me to resist. Do not allow vanities, riches, or their arguments to occupy you. Look to yourself; for pomp, honour, wealth and vanity are campaigns and battles against you.

The Devil's discourse is filled with signs of the secular, and therefore contrasts vividly with the doctrinal subtleties voiced by the Angel:

Tempo há i pera folgar
e caminhar:
vivei à vossa vontade,
e havei prazer.
Gozai, gozai dos bens da terra,
procurai por senhorios
e haveres.
Quem da vida vos desterra
à triste serra?[20]

This is a time to enjoy and to travel; live as you wish and have fun. Enjoy, enjoy the good things of the earth, seek out dominions and possessions. Who is there who will remove you from life and take you to the bleak mountains?

The Devil insists on the irresistible seduction of sensual pleasures, through the exposition of a kind of inverted didacticism, and appeals to the soul's vanity by offering her luxurious garments, and praising her femininity.

In the second section of the play, the soul reaches the 'pousada verdadeira e mui segura' [truthful and safe inn], and is welcomed by the Church, not without first having declared her vehement contrition. The functional relevance of this conversion section lies in the fact that it closes the temptation cycle. The moments of Fall and Redemption have to be dramatized to be believed:

---

[19] *Auto da Alma*, p. 178.
[20] Ibid., p. 180.

Cada passo me perdi;
em lugar de merecer:
eu sou culpada.
Havei piedade de mi,
que não me vi;
perdi meu inocente ser,
e sou danada. ...
Conheço-me por culpada,
e digo diante de vós
minha culpa.[21]

I became lost at each step. Instead of being worthy I am guilty. Have mercy on me, for I did not see myself. I lost my innocent self, I am damned. ... I know myself to be guilty, and tell you to your face of my guilt.

The Heavenly Supper is the allegorical confirmation of redemption. Once again Augustine instructs the soul (and the audience) to unveil hidden meanings in the banquet, not apprehended through visual perception[22] but rather by the obliteration of physical longings:

Cerrai os olhos corporais,
deitai ferros aos danados
apetitos,
caminheiros infernais,
pois buscais
os caminhos bem guiados
dos contritos.[23]

Close your bodily eyes, fetter your harmful desires, those routes to hell, then search for the well-mapped routes of the penitent.

The *pathos* of Augustine's prayer that follows the procession of divine nourishment turns it into a *planctus* where the Incarnation plays a central role. The Virgin is referred to as Daughter, Mother and Wife and also as *advocata*, an allusion to the mediating relationship between the supreme Judge and His mother which seems to have been influenced by the literary tradition of the Passion lamentations and the *Salve Regina*. Ambrose's commentary on the Passion evokes Jeremiah's lamentations and the prophecy of Christ's death:

---

[21] Ibid., pp. 189–90.

[22] The substitution of spiritual or magical sight for the bodily eyes explains why the praise of blindness is so frequent in devotional treatises and *exempla* collections. Mário Martins calls this phenomenon perceptive de-temporalization, and states that the suppression of sight leads to the enhancement of contemplative insight. See Mário Martins, 'Experiência religiosa e analogia sensorial', in *Estudos de Cultura Medieval* (Lisbon, 1969), p. 73.

[23] *Auto da Alma*, p. 193.

Isto chorou Jeremias
sobre o monte de Sião
há já dias;
porque sentiu que o Messias
era nossa redenção.
E chorava a sem ventura,
triste de Jerusalém
homicida,
matando, contra natura,
seu Deus nascido em Belém
nesta vida.[24]

Jeremiah wept over this on Mount Zion, for he realized that the
Messiah was our redemption. And hapless, sad, murderous
Jerusalem wept too as, against nature, it killed its God, born to this
life in Bethlehem.

All nourishment presented before the soul recreates Christ's Passion
which is now going to be re-enacted by the soul before the audience.
The soul is served the lashes, the crown of thorns, the nails and the
crucifix and, though each moment is confined to the transience of
theatrical representation (Time), it is also given the transcendence of
sacred history (Eternity) by the figural coincidence of the soul and
Christ. A sacramental view of history which reconciles cyclic and linear
time becomes clear, since God's project of eternity is materialized
through a succession of earthly events. Marie-Louise von Franz has
pointed out the place of the cyclic conception of time in the Jewish-
Christian tradition:

> It [the Christian notion of time] included certain cyclic elements, as
> well as the idea of a Divine design – a teleological linearity of time
> – periodized in terms of the seven days of creation. In the Old
> Testament there are *typoi* – images or prefigurations of events and
> things which were later revealed more fully in the New Testament.
> ... Thus an eternal pattern interacted with the linear course of
> history.[25]

The *Breve Sumário da História de Deus* was composed during the last
years of Vicente's career, probably in 1526 or 1528.[26] It has been
categorized as either a morality or a mystery play, since both its
inspiration and its conception reveal undeniable similarity with those

---

[24] Ibid., pp. 195–6.

[25] Marie-Louise von Franz, *Time – Rhythm and Repose* (London, 1992), p. 16.

[26] The date indicated in the compilation is 1527. Braamcamp Freire, however, has
pointed out that in Easter 1527 the Court was not in Almeirim, where the play was first
performed. On the subject see José Moreira, *História de Deus* (Lisbon, 1990), p. 3.

theatrical genres, which had enjoyed extreme popularity all over Europe, especially in France. The theme of the play is the history of Redemption, from the Fall to the Resurrection. It is particularly true that this play responds to 'the desire to elaborate and to combine, to establish in visible and popular shape, the revealed pattern of redemption'[27] that produced the mystery cycles, in which the story of man extended from the fall of Lucifer to the Last Judgement. Vicente's dramatic project, however, was much more modest; in order to sketch a summary, he merely retained a selection of episodes excerpted from the sacred history he intended to narrate. The urge for brevity frequently dictated the playwright's preference for ellipsis or allusion.

The structural model of the play follows a triple temporal pattern and is organized according to the Law of Nature (which comprises the Fall of Adam and Eve, Abel and Job), the Law of Scripture (the Prophets represented by Abraham, Moses, David and Isaiah) and the Law of Grace (John the Baptist and Christ). As the Angel announces in the prologue:

> Agora vereis
> que por diversos doctores lereis
> d'*ab initio mundi* até à resurreição.[28]

> Now you will see what you will read by several doctors of letters *ab initio mundi* until the Resurrection.

The dichotomy read/see contrasts the tradition of systematic theological reflection epitomized by the *doctores* and the visual perception of biblical exemplarity associated with performance. The exemplary *auctoritas* is not based on the assertive power of abstract truth but rather appeals 'to something that diverts the audience from a direct affirmation and says "see for yourself"'.[29] Moreover, time is presented in its biblical dimension, as the history of Redemption is conceived as a chronological stream. This temporal *continuum* has been crystallized by Christianity into three distinct moments: the moment before Creation, the moment between Creation and the coming of the Messiah, and the time after Christ until the end of the world. The strategy of periodization used by Vicente was, of course, a theological commonplace. St Paul distinguished three periods: from Adam to Moses (the natural law), from Moses to Christ (the written law), and lastly, after Christ (the law of Grace). Similar conceptions of sacred time were produced by St

---

[27] Robert Speaight, *The Christian Theatre* (London, 1960), p. 23.

[28] *Auto da História de Deus*, in *Compilaçam de Todalas Obras de Gil Vicente*, i, 281.

[29] John Lyons, *Exemplum: The Rhetoric of Example in Early Modern France and Italy* (Princeton, NJ, 1989), p. 28.

Augustine and Gregory the Great.[30] The theological concept of Time is here expounded by World:

> Agora estes quatro bem abastarão
> quanto aos padres da lei de natura;
> logo virão, de lei da Escritura,
> Moisés, Isaias, David, Abraão.[31]

> Now these four will supply enough natural law for the fathers; in the law of the Scriptures Moses, Isaiah, David and Abraham will all come at once.

All the characters since the Fall are destined to die. When Time so decides, they are taken away by Death to the darkness of Limbo. Only by the end of the performance will the prisoners be released by the crucified Christ. The iterative dramatic syntax chosen by Vicente is materialized in the symmetric stage movements of the characters.[32] The prophetic structure of the play is based on, and authorized by, the theological principle that the Old Testament prefigures the revelation of the New Testament, and that correspondences are to be sought for. The figural interpretation applied to the biblical text is therefore the *modus legendi* required by Vicente's play. In Timothy Hampton's words, figural interpretation is founded on the principle that 'both present and past take their respective places as moments in the great master narrative of Christian salvation history, which stretches from time's beginning to its end'.[33]

As Pinto Ribeiro has noted, the New Testament conception of time is centred on Christ, since he bestows meaning on the time that both precedes and follows him. Therefore, if the Law of Nature includes every man, the Law of Scripture, on the other hand, is only applicable to the people of Israel, and the Law of Grace to Christ.

The procession of characters starts with Adam and Eve, and dramatizes the moments of the Fall and Repentance. When they appear on stage, Adam and Eve express their amazement at the other characters, in an intertextual reminder of the pastoral *naïveté* present in Vicente's work since *Monólogo do Vaqueiro*. Telling prevails over showing, and the episode of the Temptation is merely narrated. Adam

---

[30] On the concept of biblical time in *Breve Sumário*, see José António Pinto Ribeiro, 'Breve Sumário de História de Deus: uma visão agustiniana da História?', *Revista da Universidade de Aveiro/Letras*, 1 (1984), pp. 249–85.

[31] *Auto da História de Deus*, p. 298.

[32] With a few exceptions, the characters' trajectory comprises the following moments: introduction, entrance, temptation, intervention of Death and access to Limbo.

[33] Timothy Hampton, *Writing from History: The Rhetoric of Exemplarity in Renaissance Literature* (Ithaca, NY, and London, 1990).

repents, accepts the regenerating punishment and persuades Eve to emulate him. Prophetic hope of redemption is granted by contrition, and Adam praises God's omnipotence:

> Poderoso é o Padre na glória dos Céus,
> poderoso é o Padre no nosso paraiso,
> poderoso é o Padre neste triste abiso,
> em todo lugar poderoso é Deus;
> e não vos mateis.[34]

> The Father is powerful in the glory of the heavens, the Father is powerful in our paradise, the Father is powerful in this sad abyss, God is powerful everywhere, and you shall not kill Him.

This hope in future redemption, legitimized by the biblical text, is further enhanced by a system of analogies between Adam and Christ.[35] Abel is introduced by Vicente as a handsome young man, resilient and hardworking and able to exercise virtuous justice. The prophetic link uniting Abel and Christ is their common sacrificial character.

The next character is Job who, in *Breve Sumário*, epitomizes the *bem mudável* (changeable fortune), the redeeming power of suffering and the cathartic virtues of pain:

> Se os bens do mundo nos dá a ventura,
> também em ventura está quem os tem.
> O bem que é mudável não pode ser bem,
> mas mal, pois é a causa de tanta tristura;
> e se Deus os dá,
> como eu creio mui bem que será,
> e a fortuna tem tanto poder,
> que os tira logo cada vez que quer,
> o segredo disto, oh! quem m'o dirá,
> pera eu o saber?[36]

> If Fortune gives us the goods of the world, than those who possess such goods are fortunate. Goods that are mutable cannot be good, but bad, since they are the cause of so much misery; if it is God who gives them, as I truly believe will be the case, and if Fortune holds such power that it can remove them whenever it wishes, oh, who will tell me the secret of this so that I may know it?

Changeable Fortune subsumes the process of making History exemplary, for it represents through Job cyclic renewal, but also the

---

[34] *Auto da História de Deus*, p. 288.

[35] St Paul (Rom. 5: 12–15) states that Adam was the prefiguration of the one that was yet to come, and Christ, the second Adam, would annihilate the destructive effects of the sin perpetrated by the first Adam. On this subject, see Pinto Ribeiro, 'Breve Sumário da História de Deus', p. 263.

[36] *Auto da História de Deus*, pp. 296–7.

inevitability of man's Fall and the principle of immanent justice implicit in history, in short, a theodicy. Among the Christian writers on Job, one of the most influential was certainly Gregory the Great with his *Morals on the Book of Job*. In the *Moralia* Gregory, following the parameters of medieval exegesis, expounded the threefold sense of the book: 'A literal sense (Job is afflicted by God in order to increase his merit), an allegorical sense (Job is the suffering Redeemer and the Church in its earthly sufferings), and a moral sense (Job transcends the temporal realm and ascends to the eternal).'[37] Vicente's Job was certainly inspired by a similar exegetic legacy. Vicente paraphrases and dramatically remodels Job's words when, after having been told about the death of his children, he is touched by Satan and covered with leprosy:

> Oh Deus meu! e porque me persegues?
> Responde-me, quantas maldades te fiz
> contra a folha prove,
> que ligeiramente o vento revolve
> mostras as forças que tu tens contigo? ...
> Senhor, homem de mulher nascido
> muito breve tempo vive miserando,
> e como flor se vai acabando,
> e como a sombra será consumido.[38]

> Oh my God, why do you persecute me? Tell me, how many sins have I committed against you, against the leaf which the wind spins slowly as you show the powers which you possess? Lord, man born of woman, living unhappily for a short time, dies like a flower to be consumed like a shadow.

Vicente draws on the Bible or on the liturgy of the Office of the Dead, focusing on the similes about the brevity or inanity of life.[39] In Job 13: 25 we find: 'Wilt thou break a leaf driven to and fro?', and in 14: 1–2: 'Man that is born of a woman is of few days, and full of trouble. He cometh forth like a flower, and is cut down: he fleeth also as a shadow, and continueth not.'

Job's paradigmatic dimension makes it clear that 'the history of exemplarity is ... also, on one level, a history of the figurations of the self'.[40] The evocation of an *exemplar* meets with the requirements of a hermeneutic procedure by means of which the *auctoritas* of the past is

---

[37] David J.A. Clines, 'Job and the Spirituality of the Reformation', in W.P. Stephens (ed.), *The Bible, the Reformation and the Church: Essays in Honour of James Atkinson* (Sheffield, 1995), p. 52.

[38] *Auto da História de Deus*, pp. 296–7.

[39] Maria Aliete Galhoz, '*Topoi* da inanidade e brevidade da vida na fala de *Job* do "Breve Sumário da História de Deus" de Gil Vicente – Similes comparativos', in *Temas Vicentinos: Actas do colóquio em torno da obra de Gil Vicente* (Lisbon, 1992), pp. 73–80.

[40] Timothy Hampton, *Writing from History*, p. xi.

transferred onto the present of the audience, thus playing a sacramental function. As has been pointed out by Alan Bernstein about the function assigned to the *exemplum* by medieval authors, 'This act of making wisdom concrete by first becoming flesh, then preaching by comparisons and parables, was not to disguise the hidden truth, but to make it knowable. Thus the exterior faithfully represents the inner truth, the nature and the teaching of Christ.'[41]

In the section of the play dealing with the Law of Scripture, Vicente selects four biblical figures to represent the Hebrew people according to the specific functions they were assigned in the Old Testament: Abraham, Moses, David and Isaiah. Vicente depicts Abraham as *justo verdadeiro* [just and truthful], a faithful servant of God surrounded by the perversion and decay of Sodom and Gomorrah, and associates him with the Holy Trinity (*pregoeiro da Santa Trindade*/messenger of the Holy Trinity), following the reference in Genesis (18: 1–3). His opening speech is clearly prophetic:

> O Deus mui alto, ignoto, escondido,
> demonstra-te às gentes, que já tempo é
> que daquele tempo do justo Noé
> está o teu nome na terra perdido,
> e está sonegado
> o tributo do mundo, que é teu de morgado.[42]

> O God so high, unknown, concealed, show yourself to men, for now, ever since the time of honest Noah, your name has been lost on earth, and the tribute of the world, which is yours by right, is denied you.

As, in Vicente's time, Moses was believed to have written the five books of the Pentateuch, this act of divine revelation is central to the text:

> E assentarei
> mistérios profundos no livro da lei,
> tudo figuras da Santa Trindade,
> tudo mistérios da eternidade,
> que Deus me dirá e eu escreverei
> à sua vontade.
> E ele estará em pessoa comigo
> aos cinco livros, quando os escrever.[43]

> I shall write profound mysteries in the book of Law, all the figures

---

[41] Alan E. Bernstein, 'The Exemplum as "Incorporation" of Abstract Truth in the Thought of Humbert of Romans and Stephen of Bourbon', in Laurent Mayali and Stephanie A.J. Tibbetts (eds), *The Two Laws: Studies in Medieval Legal History Dedicated to Stephan Kuttner* (Washington, DC, 1990), p. 93.

[42] *Auto da História de Deus*, p. 299.

[43] Ibid., p. 299.

of the Holy Trinity, all the mysteries of eternity which God will tell me, and I shall write according to His will. And He will be with me in the five books when I write them.

The reference to the testimonial presence of God during Moses's 'theography' is used by Vicente to argue in favour of the inspiration of the sacred Books, while emphasizing the double meaning of the scriptural texts:

Tu, homem, penetra,
e dos sacrifícios não tomes a letra:
que outro sacrifício figuram em si,
que matar bezerros, nem aves ali:
outra mais alta oferta soletra,
e outro Genesi.[44]

You, man, must understand, and must not accept sacrifices as right;
for they mean sacrifices other than those of killing cattle or birds;
they spell out another, higher gift and another Genesis.

This excerpt reveals a clear didactic aim, by proposing a method of scriptural hermeneutics. Vicente transposes and simplifies, with a pedagogical purpose, the medieval distinction between the *simplicitas litterae* and the *altitudo prophetiae*,[45] between the literal and the spiritual sense. This sense of indecipherable mysteries which need to be retold and constantly reflected upon had already been referred to in the angel's prologue ('Even though all matters of the past may be well known to Your Highness, the story of God has such depth that nothing is ever lost in retelling it'), and by the World when he commented on Abel's tragic fate: 'They are deep secrets that the Lord has kept to Himself'. The absolute and transcendent truth communicated by the biblical text awakens and stimulates knowledge while appealing to the rational faculty of interpretation, so that the literal and spiritual meaning may be illuminated. This is by no means original; but it does prove that Vicente was most certainly influenced by late medieval vernacular devotional works and sermons, in which this distinction was recurrent. In the *Orto do Esposo*, a late fourteenth-century anonymous *exemplum* collection, it is said that:

A Sancta Escriptura he huu liuro que conte em si os segredos de Deus e he cuberto e çarrado cõ a cubertura da letera, ca defora, quanto ao sinplez ssiso de letera, he descuberto, e dentro he cuberto e çarrado segundo o entendimento espiritual. ... Ca muytos ouue a

---

[44] Ibid., p. 300.
[45] See Henri de Lubac, *Exégèse médiévale: les quatre sens de l'Ecriture* (Paris, 1959), p. 482.

Sancta Escriptura com a orelha de fora e nõ a rrecebem cõ a orelha de dentro do coracõ ne a ecorporõ e ssy.[46]

Holy Scripture is a book which contains the secrets of God and is covered and concealed within the cover of the word on the outside, and however simple the knowledge of the word is, it is uncovered, while inside it is covered and concealed according to spiritual understanding. ... For many hear Holy Scripture with their outside ear and do not receive it with the inside ear of the heart, and take it to themselves.

Vicente's *Breve Sumário* reflects this simplified hermeneutic circle, frequent in medieval interpretative theories, according to which belief was inextricably linked with intelligible access to the Christian truth embedded in the biblical text, and consequently with the understanding of *another Genesis*.

David is represented as priest, prophet and sacred writer, the paradigmatic embodiment of the Messianic king. He is the one who prophetically voices Christ's martyrdom:

Eu também o sei, mui certo sabido;
serão suas mãos e pés mui furados,
e todos seus ossos lhe serão contados.[47]

I always know it, it is very well known, his hands and feet will be pierced deeply and all his bones will be broken.

In Isaiah's intervention we find a laudatory evocation of the Virgin. Christ is a sacrificial victim offered to God's justice, and the narration of some of the torments of Christ's Passion establishes a link between his martyrdom and Adam's sin. This procedure of foretelling will ultimately be demonstrated by Christ himself, who will embody, by turning Word into Flesh, what is now being narrated.

The third section of the play dramatizes the Law of Grace. The first character, John the Baptist, announces the earthly return of Christ both in terms of the sacred history being summarized, and in those of the entrance of a new character:

O mortais de terra, em terra tornados,
pois são vossas almas de tão fina lei,
abri vossas olhos, que *ecce agnus* Dei,
que veio ao mundo tirar os peccados.[48]

O mortals of earth, made of earth, your souls are so fine; so open your eyes, for *ecce agnus Dei*, who came into the world to save sins.

---

[46] *Orto de Esposo*, ed. Bertil Maler (Rio de Janeiro, 1956), p. 77.
[47] *Auto da História de Deus*, p. 301.
[48] Ibid., p. 304.

The dramatic apex of the play, repeatedly suggested through prophetic discourse, is the apparition of Christ. Besides affirming his contempt for worldly matters, he declares himself subject to the relentless and universal laws of Time and Death. The advent of Christ as Word made Flesh thus embodies a dramatization of doctrine, since all the prophecies are to be fulfilled in him: the tortures (Job), the crucifixion (Adam and Eve, Isaiah), the immolation (Abraham) and the death (Abel). As has been noted by Pinto Ribeiro, both doctrinal and dramatic closures are ensured by the fulfilment of the *prophetiae verbi and prophetiae facti*.[49] His appearance after the Resurrection confirms its significance according to the theological conception of History. Founded as it is upon the recurrent pattern of history, prophetic discourse is somewhat paradoxically based on reification through memory. Reminiscing and re-enacting central moments of sacred history, extracting a moral precept from them, appears to be the predominant hermeneutic role which both characters and audience are expected to play. In the prologue, for instance, the angel refers to the Tree of Knowledge, stating that it is necessary to recollect Adam's original sin. After the Expulsion, Eve nostalgically evokes the memories of the ephemeral edenic idyll.

The solemnity of the Christian allegorical tradition, to which the *Breve Sumário* is so clearly indebted, would seem to preclude all signs of humour. This is not the case. The play opens with an explicitly humorous dialogue between Belial, a devil, and Lucifer, who has commissioned Satan, and not him, to tempt Eve and cause her and Adam's fall from grace. In the concluding sequence of the play, when Christ enumerates the different parts of his body that will be submitted to torture, Belial announces his sudden illness, and parodies Christ's torments by describing in humorously crude phraseology his own martyrdom. These examples of 'Carnival anatomy'[50] are not incompatible with biblical exemplarity. The example as a rhetorical device attempted to make the opacity of abstract truth and the mysteries of faith accessible to the *simplices* by constant reference to the *palpabilia* or *facta*. Comic relief can thus be regarded as a reconciliation of *docere* and *delectatio*. This is not after all an innovative procedure. There was a fertile medieval tradition of anticlerical satire based on carnivalized discourse and the parody of biblical texts.

---

[49] Pinto Ribeiro, 'Breve Sumário da História de Deus', p. 249.

[50] The expression is used by José I. Suárez, *The Carnival Stage: Vicentine Comedy within the Serio-comic Mode* (London and Toronto, 1993), p. 75.

To a considerable extent, Vicente appears to have been influenced by the medieval exemplary tradition. In the *Breve Sumário* the selection and combination of biblical narratives aim to indoctrinate a lay court audience through visual and verbal manifestation. Underlying Vicente's use of biblical material is the belief that figurative *exempla* are powerful didactic instruments suitable for shedding some light on the mysteries of the Book. After an in-depth analysis of Vicente's sermons, Joaquim de Carvalho concludes that he mastered the techniques of composition involved in sacred eloquence, namely the strategies of *divisio* and *amplificatio* by means of *sententiae* and *exempla*. Furthermore, Vicente certainly had access to the copies of Alain de Lille's and Jean de la Rochelle's *artes praedicandi* which were to be found in the monastic libraries of Alcobaça and Santa Cruz de Coimbra.[51]

Above all, Vicente, imbued with medieval monastic writings, certainly believed that 'no passage of Scripture ... should be regarded as valueless ... for its all-perfect author could inspire nothing untrue, trivial or degraded. It would seem that, behind the great diversity and range of styles found in the Bible, lies the singleness and security of divine authority.'[52] However, his work indubitably contains some expression of the religious crisis of his time. Specific historical circumstances certainly stimulated a longing for radical change, pervasive throughout the fifteenth and sixteenth centuries. While, on the one hand, it is undeniable that Vicente's perspective on Christian history and biblical authority was clearly medieval, his plays also reveal obvious affinities with the humanist renewal: he criticizes formalized cult rituals such as indulgences, mechanical prayer, obscure preaching rhetoric and scholastic subtleties. When King João III began negotiations in Rome to establish the Inquisition in Portugal, Vicente vehemently criticized the violent conversion being forced upon Jews.

As a whole, Vicente's work reflects the theoretical eclecticism or ambivalence which is the hallmark of transitional periods. Anticipating, partly because of personal insight, partly owing to the appeal of historical transformation, the new spirit of the Renaissance *devotio moderna*, he still partook in the belief in an ideal unity of Christian faith embodied in the completeness and closure of the biblical text. As the allegory of Faith epigrammatically expounds in *Auto da Fé*:

---

[51] Carvalho, 'Os sermões de Gil Vicente', ii, 255. For a substantially different opinion, see I.S. Révah's comments in *Les Sermons de Gil Vicente (en marge d'un opuscule du professeur Joaquim de Carvalho)* (Lisbon, 1948).

[52] A.J. Minnis, *Medieval Theory of Authorship: Scholastic Literary Attitudes in the Later Middle Ages* (London, 1984), p. 127.

Fé é amar a Deus, só por ele,
quanto se pode amar,
por ser ele singular,
não por interesse dele:
e se mais quereis saber,
crer na Madre Igreja santa,
e cantar o que ela cantar
e querer o que ela quer.[53]

Faith is loving God, only Him, as much as it is possible to love, not for his regard, for He is unique; and should you wish to know more, you must believe in our Holy Mother the Church, singing what she sings, and desiring what she desires.

---

[53] *Auto da Fé*, in *Compilaçam e Todalas Obras de Gil Vicente*, i, 75.

CHAPTER SEVEN

Tyndale

Henry Wansbrough

In the latter part of this chapter I intend to examine a sample of William Tyndale's translation of the New Testament to show why it is such an exciting translation, and has – through the medium of the King James Version – proved so enduring. First, however, I wish to discuss why the very fact of the translation was such a great and timely achievement. Because of the backlash against Lollardy, England was lagging behind in the matter of biblical translation; there was practically none. This has often been connected with a supposed underdeveloped state of literature in English. In any case, Tyndale's achievement was that the translation which has endured into the twenty-first century, and which remains the unavoidable basis for any new translation, sprang fully-fledged from him. He was in a unique position, at the joining of the ways, one coming from the Lollard tradition, that grumbling undercurrent of fourteenth-century England, and the other from the burgeoning classical tradition. Each of these is represented by one of Tyndale's two great heroes, Wyclif and Erasmus.

It has long been fashionable to set Tyndale's achievement against the background of the primitive state of literature in England. English, they say, was no literary language. Even the facilities for printing were backward. There is certainly some truth in this contention, but I would suggest that it has been exaggerated, and for reasons of propaganda at that. The roughness of the English language and the prevailing illiteracy were both used as arguments against translating the Bible into English. Opponents of the persistent Lollard yearning to have an English Bible used these arguments to stifle that yearning.

Certainly the cultural loss to the English language consequent on the Norman Conquest had delayed its development for several centuries. Only the French-speaking aristocracy could afford books, and French remained their language until in the mid-fourteenth century the Hundred Years War began to give French the *allure* of being the language of the enemy. Henry V (1387–1422) is the first king of England of whom we possess a letter written in English, though the famous scene of the English lesson in the last act of Shakespeare's *Henry V* may well exaggerate his ignorance of French.

This does not mean that no English prose existed, but simply that it was not yet considered a literary language.[1] English as a prose medium was still characterized as 'rude' and 'barbarous'.[2] I would suggest that this was as much a literary convention as the truth. Sir Philip Sidney famously in 1561 laments the lack of English poetry: 'It shall be but a little more lost time to enquire why England (the mother of excellent minds) should be grown so hard a stepmother to poets. Poesy thus embraced in all other places should only find in our time a hard welcome in England.'[3] Sir Thomas Elyot similarly, in the Preface to *The Boke named the Governour* (London, 1531) complains of the difficulty made by the poverty of the language. He in fact invented in that book such terms as 'modesty', 'mediocrity', 'industrious', 'frugality', 'beneficence', but the complaint has all the marks of a literary convention.

It is possible to quote contemporary figures about illiteracy, but it is important to remember that these testimonies are suspect because their authors have an axe to grind. Thus Thomas More in his *Apology* (1523) argues that there is no point in Englishing the Bible, when he makes the estimate that 'people far more than four parts of all the whole divided into ten could never read english yet, and many now too old to go to school'.[4] A quarter of a century later Bishop Stephen Gardiner of Winchester's estimate is still more pessimistic, when he writes in May 1547 that 'not one in a hundredth part of the realm' could read.[5] These are not serious estimates, let alone reliable statistics, and evidence to the contrary may be garnered from the numerous heresy trials where possession and use of heretical books forms a regular part of the accusation, even among the artisan classes. There were plenty of good plain works, manuals of instruction on medicine, hawking, cooking, behaviour. There were letters, such as the Paston and Stonor letters, which are often playful and merry. There was the English Chronicle, which Tyndale claims to have read as a child,[6] and which may

---

[1] A useful survey is given in H.S. Bennett, *Chaucer and the Fifteenth Century*, Oxford History of English Literature, 2 (Oxford, 1947), ch. 7.

[2] R.F. Jones, *The Triumph of the English Language* (London, 1953), ch. 1. Cf. I.A. Gordon, *The Movement of English Prose* (London, 1966), pp. 95–101.

[3] Sir Philip Sidney, *The Defence of Poesy: An Apology for Poetry*, ed. Geoffrey Shepherd (London, 1965), p. 131.

[4] *The Apologye of Syr Thomas More, Knyght* (1523), quoted by H.S. Bennett, *English Books and Readers 1475–1557* (Cambridge, 1969), p. 28.

[5] Letter to Edward Vaughan, 3 May 1547, in *The Letters of Stephen Gardiner*, ed. J.A. Muller (Cambridge, 1933), p. 274.

[6] Tyndale, *The Obedience of a Christian Man* (Antwerp, 1528). Facsimile of the 1528 edition (Aldershot, 1970), fol. xv^v.

well have had no small influence on his purposeful, episodic style. There were devotional works, such as Walter Hilton's *The Scale of Perfection* (London, 1494), or Nicholas Love's *Mirror of the Life of Christ*.[7] This was based on John de Caulibus' Latin work *Meditationes vitae Christi*, but Love's own contribution to the work was considerable. It is full of warm and memorable passages which make its popularity in English still easy to appreciate. The field was clearly open and ready for some major works in English.

Of course the academic language was still Latin. Scholars all over Europe corresponded with each other in Latin. More's *Utopia* was written in Latin, and Cuthbert Tunstall, Bishop of London, thought it necessary to ask More specifically to write in English when he was writing against Tyndale. As late as 1605, of the 60 000 volumes listed in the *First Printed Catalogue of the Bodleian Library*,[8] only sixty are in English. Similarly, of the 1830 books listed as sold by the Oxford bookseller John Dorne in 1520, the overwhelming majority is in Latin, with only the occasional intrusion of such works as 'Robin Hod' or 'balets' (ballads). This is perhaps not so surprising for a university city. Even a popular manual of etiquette for children in the dining-room is written in Latin, *Stans puer ad mensam*, of which Dorne sold several copies.

A real factor of backwardness in England was in the matter of printing, which was far less advanced than on the Continent. Caxton learned printing as late as 1471/72 in Cologne, and it was not until 1477 that he published at Westminster the first book to be printed in England. For contrast we may compare the printing of biblical translations on the Continent. A German Bible had already been printed in 1466, and before Caxton's first printed book there were already Bibles printed in Italian (1471), French (1474) and Dutch (1477), to be closely followed by printed versions in Catalan (1478) and Czech (1488). The sophistication of Greek printing, which had long been common on the Continent in Italy and Switzerland, and certainly in the magnificent Complutensian Polyglot Bible, now virtually ready for publication in Spain, was light-years beyond English standards. The market remained small, and before he embarked on a book Caxton was always careful to ensure that he would be able to

---

[7] Nicolas Love, *The Mirrour of the Blessed Lyf of Christ*, written some time around 1410. Its popularity is shown by the number of times it was printed: by Caxton in 1484 and 1490, by Pynson and de Worde in 1494, by Pynson again in 1506, and four more times by Pynson before 1530. It survives in fifty-six complete (or once complete) versions, which is equalled only by Walter Hilton's *Scale of Perfection*.

[8] *Catalogus librorum bibliothecae publicae quam vir ornatissimus Thomas Bodleius eques auratus in Academia Oxoniensi nuper instituit. The first printed catalogue of the Bodleian Library. 1605. A facsimile* (Oxford, Bodleian Library, 1986).

cover his costs, securing patrons to cover the costs for twenty-three of his seventy-seven printed books. After Caxton's death in 1491 there remained only two printers of any note, Richard Pynson and Wynkyn de Worde, who were responsible for 70 per cent of the English output.[9]

However, the major factor militating against biblical translation in England was clearly the backlash against Lollardy. The provision of the Scriptures in the vernacular had been one of the principal aims of Wyclif and his followers. In 1408, as part of the reaction against Wyclif, the Constitutions of Oxford, at the instance of Archbishop Arundel of Canterbury, had forbidden any translation of the Bible into English 'whether in the time of John Wyclif or since', unless it was approved by the diocesan. Special permission was occasionally given to specific persons to possess a translation of the Bible, and some translations did survive well into the sixteenth century, though they were never diffused by the new invention of printing. How widespread these were it is impossible to tell, but in 1529 Sir Thomas More differentiated between on the one hand the translation of the 'great arch-heretic Wycliffe' who 'purposely corrupted the holy text', and on the other 'Bibles fair and old written in English which have been known and seen by the bishop of the diocese'. It was to fill the resultant gap of a genuine version of vernacular Scriptures, and to provide for meditation and spiritual reading on Gospel themes, that Nicholas Love's *Mirror of the Life of Christ* was intended, for it was written in the years immediately after the prohibition of translation of the Bible. In the *Memorandum* at the beginning, Love states that Archbishop Arundel 'commanded by his metropolitan authority that it be published universally for the edification of the faithful and the confutation of heretics or Lollards'.

After the abortive march on London of Sir John Oldcastle in 1414 there was no more public manifestation of Lollardy, but this merely meant that it went underground. 'Lollardy became a pertinacious rather than a heroic faith, occupying quiet groups of tradesmen and artisans, but here and there attracting a few priests, merchants and professional men.'[10] Nevertheless, Lollardy was continually felt to remain a danger, and the witch-hunt against it continued. The term seems to have been used in general for any heterodox opinions.[11] In 1458 the statutes of

---

9 Bennett, *English Books and Readers*, p. 188.

10 A.G. Dickens, *The English Reformation* (London, 1989), p. 49.

11 'The term *lollard* had, as was evident from examples in the last chapter, come by the mid-fifteenth century to be a generic term for "heretic".' Anne Hudson, *The Premature Reformation: Wycliffite Texts and Lollard History* (Oxford, 1988), p. 446.

King's and Queens' Colleges, Cambridge, were modified to require an oath against the heresies of Wyclif and Pecock, and in 1476 the University of Oxford assured the King that a search for Wyclif's and Pecock's books had been made and that a few had been burnt.[12] As late as 1523 Tunstall wrote of the current unorthodox tendencies, 'It is no question of pernicious novelty; it is only that new arms are being added to the great crowd of Wycliffite heresies.'[13] Indeed, Richard Hilles held that a young man burnt in 1541 for Lutheran heresies had in fact merely held the opinions of 'our Wycliffe'.[14] Lollardy seems to have merged almost seamlessly into Lutheranism, and in the early years of the sixteenth century investigations for heresy continued to turn up the same themes: John Godwyn is reported in 1504 to have held that images are only 'stokkis and stones', that pilgrimages are pointless and so is confession to a priest. John Whitehorn of Letcombe Bassett near Newbury was arraigned in 1508, when he had a hidden English Bible, and said that the eucharist was 'pure brede and nowght else'.[15]

For our theme it is significant that Lollardy seems to have been concentrated in a number of local centres. There were occasional outbreaks in London,[16] but we hear of it most often in East Anglia, the Chilterns round High Wycombe, Marlow, Henley, Reading. There was another concentration in West Oxfordshire round Burford, Standlake and Asthall, and considerable activity in Bristol. None of this is far from Tyndale's views,[17] nor from his geographical area. The religious authorities were sensitive to such tendencies, and ready to pounce. Just how jumpy they were may be seen in the precautions taken by the bishops against the arrival of heretical books in the country. In December 1524 the booksellers of London were called together by Tunstall and warned against importing or selling Lutheran books. Again

---

[12] J.L. Catto, 'Theology after Wycliffism', in *History of the University of Oxford*, ii (Oxford, 1992), p. 278.

[13] In a letter to Erasmus, *CWE* x, 26.

[14] Letter, Richard Hilles to Henry Bullinger, in *Original Letters Relative to the English Reformation*, edited for the Parker Society by the Revd Hastings Robinson (Cambridge, 1846), i, p. 221.

[15] Hudson, *The Premature Reformation*, p. 468.

[16] In 1511 Archbishop Warham condemned Agnes Trebill of Kent as a heretic. She said that the bread and wine were unchanged after the consecration, and disapproved of confession, pilgrimages and worship of saints. Charles Sturge, *Cuthbert Tunstal: Churchman, Scholar, Statesman, Administrator* (London, 1938), p. 128.

[17] Heretical elements included objection to the eucharist ('not the veray body of Criste but a commemoration of Cristis passion, and Cristis body in a figure'), to images ('hit wer as good offer a candell to an owll in the wode as to an image of our Lady') and to pilgrimage ('folks go on pilgrimage more for the green way than for any devotion'). See Hudson, *The Premature Reformation*, pp. 468–9.

in February 1525 they were called together by Wolsey and solemnly harangued. To look ahead, one of the most amusing and ludicrous incidents of the reaction to Tyndale's translation was in 1529, when Tunstall, finding the policy of burning the books as they arrived in England to be insufficently effective, arranged for his agent Augustine Packyngton, whom he had met at Antwerp, to buy up Tyndale's whole stock. This effectively cleared Tyndale of debt, 'so the bishop had the books, Packyngton the thanks and Tyndale had the money'.[18]

Doctrinal suspicion was, then, one more factor militating against translation of the Bible into English. There were also factors which made such a move appropriate and indeed inevitable. The phenomenon of the revival of classical learning is too well known to require documentation. However, since it was at Oxford that Tyndale received his formation, a sketch of that revival at Oxford will not be out of place.

The beginning of Greek in Oxford seems to have been at the hands of Emmanuel of Constantinople, who was already teaching Greek there in 1462. John Farley and William Grocyn signed their names in the university letter-book in Greek letters in 1464 and 1476 respectively; if one may judge from modern schoolboy behaviour, this argues less rather than more knowledge of Greek. In the 1490s both Grocyn and William Lily found it necessary to go to Florence to gain an adequate knowledge of Greek, and John Colet's famous lectures on Romans in 1496–99 were still based on the Latin text. Cambridge seems to have been more advanced than Oxford. Some would date the graffiti in the monastic cells of Magdalene College before 1500, but even there the breakthrough was taking place during the whole course of the first two decades of the century. Erasmus was in Cambridge from 1511 to 1514, thoroughly bored and complaining about the quality of the beer. In 1518 the University's first Reader in Greek was appointed, while Thomas More was encouraging Oxford to emulate its sister university. Erasmus wrote to the President of the newly founded Corpus Christi College that he numbered the College *inter praecipua decora Britanniae* on account of its *bibliotheca trilinguis*.[19] But this was no serious evaluation of the extent of Greek learning. Its flattery is shown up in its true colours by the chance observation that in 1537 the only Hebrew book in the library catalogue was that classic Hebrew grammar, Reuchlin's *De rudimentis hebraicis*.

---

18 Edward Hall, *Hall's Chronicle ... Collated with the Editions of 1548 and 1550* (London, 1809), p. 763.

19 Letter 990 in *CWE* vi.

More to the point is the invaluable booklist of John Dorne for 1520, which inevitably gives a picture of what people in Oxford were reading in that year. It was a fairly comprehensive bookshop, selling ballads in quantity (perhaps the equivalent of modern airport-bookstall trash), eight copies of the notorious Albertus *De secretis mulierum* (which Tyndale castigates as clerical pornographic reading), a couple of lives of St Catherine and of St Margaret, as well as the scholastic works which must have been the standard textbooks of the time (including a big text of the *Sentences* for three shillings and fourpence). A lot of Latin classical texts were being read. Many copies of Tully, especially *De officiis*, were sold, but also a good number of other authors, such as Ovid, Vergil, Lucan, Sallust, Terence. There is, however, quite a clutch of Greek texts: Aesop, Aristophanes' *Plutus*, Lucian, Dionysius Areopagita (uncertain whether in Greek or Latin), and a big Greek dictionary for the price of six shillings and fourpence. There is even an *Alphabetum Ebraicum*, though at a price of two pence this cannot have been a very extensive work. There are two valuable indications of the buzz-interests of the day. First, the clutch of indications already of Lutheran controversy: several copies of Luther's *De potestate papae* were sold for three pence each. One investigative purchaser got to the heart of the controversy by buying (for a shilling) this work, plus the *Resolutio*, plus the *Responsio Lutheri*. The very next year, in 1521, one of Bishop Longland of Lincoln's first actions was to attempt to protect the minds of the susceptible young students of Oxford by ordering 'these corrupt works as Luther and others' to be sought out in the Oxford bookshops.[20]

The second important indication of what was afoot at Oxford just after Tyndale went down is the large number of books by Erasmus that were sold. David Daniell calculates that one in every seven customers bought a book by Erasmus.[21] Besides his theoretical works, the *Adagia*, the *Colloquia* and the *Enchiridion*, interest centres on the extraordinary hunger for his grammatico-rhetorical works; these will have been important in training any rhetorician or translator. Chief among them are two. *De utraque verborum ac rerum copia* has some valuable writing on the use of synonyms, advising the user to observe the difference of nuance between them (Lib. I, fol. vii), giving lists of synonyms, for example, near-synonyms for the negative, *non, haud, neque, haudquaquam, neutiquam, minime, minus, parum* (Lib. I, fol.

20 Lincoln Archives Office, Register 26, fol. 101.

21 David Daniell, *William Tyndale: A Biography* (Yale, CT, 1994), p. 346, n. 31. Any writer on Tyndale must be vastly indebted to this admirable book, and to Professor Daniell's editions of Tyndale.

xxvi).[22] Of this book, *De copia*, John Dorne sold sixteen copies in the year. Of another grammatical work by Erasmus, *De constructione verborum* (actually by William Lily, first High Master of St Paul's School, and revised by Erasmus) he sold a staggering thirty copies in the year. These must have been textbooks in the hands of every student, showing the importance of such literary exercises, an invaluable propaedeutic for any translator. Practice in saying the same thing in several different ways is an essential training for a translator.

It was into this atmosphere that young William Tyndale – admittedly, just a decade earlier, though we may assume that not everything had changed in the course of the decade – arrived from the borders of Wales in the early years of the century, taking his BA in 1512 and his MA in 1515. What the methods of linguistic training were in those years we can divine somewhat from the book sales catalogued above. We know more about theological studies. In the Preface to *The Obedience of a Christian Man* (1528) Tyndale has some hard remarks to make about scholastic disputations, which were presumably the staple fare in Oxford. One complaint is that Scripture may be studied only after several years of previous study: 'Ye drive them [students] from God's word and will let no man come thereto until he have been two years master of arts.'[23] What he thought of that study may be gathered from another comment: 'Of what text thou provest hell, will another prove purgatory, another limbo patrum and another the assumption of our lady; and another shall prove of the same text that an Ape hath a tail.'[24] His basic complaint is that this is putting the cart before the horse, or as he put it, measuring the meteyard by the cloth.[25] The Scripture should provide the yardstick for understanding of the Fathers, not vice versa, as was so often the case. A mere glance at the staple material for theological study, the Glosses, will show that this complaint was not without justification. Only too often scholastic theologians worked backwards to the scriptural text through the glosses.[26] On the contrary, argues Tyndale, once readers

---

[22] The popularity of this work struck me when I looked for it in the Bodleian. The standard modern copy is missing, but there are editions published in 1513, 1514, 1517, 1519 (two editions), 1521 (two editions), 1526, 1528, 1532, 1535, and so on. Similarly *De constructione verborum* features editions of 1513, 1514, 1515 (two), 1516, 1521 (two), 1522 (three editions) in Bodley's catalogue. These are chance holdings; there are many more editions.

[23] Tyndale, *The Obedience of a Christian Man*, fol. xviii[r].

[24] Ibid., fol. xix[r].

[25] Ibid., fol. xvi[r].

[26] My colleague Anthony Marett-Crosby has pointed out to me two examples, Gen. 2: 21 and 2 Cor. 5: 13. In the former case the Glossa Ordinaria interprets Adam's 'deep sleep' as elevation to the *angelica curia*; consequently, both Albert and Aquinas interpret Adam's experience as rapture to God's presence. In the latter case Aquinas interprets the

have learnt how to read Scripture itself, 'if they go abroad and walk by the fields and meadows of all manner doctors and philosophers, they could catch no harm: they should discern the poison from the honey and bring home nothing but that which is wholesome'.[27]

Foxe's *Book of Martyrs* mentions laconically and without further detail that after Oxford Tyndale went to Cambridge. Speculation about his activities there and his possible contact with heretical groups there are fruitless; we have no information other than this simple, perhaps inaccurate, mention by Foxe. To judge, however, from his impatience with the traditional theology and from his own pugnacious and argumentative temperament, he will not have avoided the first buds of Lutheran influence there. By contrast with this guesswork, Tyndale's activities at his next post provide an invaluable picture of his temperament and state of mind. It is the immediate preface to his work as translator of the Bible.

After his time at university Tyndale secured a place as tutor to the children of a Gloucestershire squire, Sir John Walsh, a man of substance who was twice High Sheriff of the county. Foxe tells a couple of stories about Tyndale during this period which show the development of his passionate concern to provide the text of the Bible to every man. The first is the story of a confrontation between Tyndale and a learned country cleric who held that Canon Law was more important that Scripture. This is a confrontation between traditional attitudes and the impetus of Lollardy, which had been smouldering in the countryside for a century and a half.

> Master Tyndale happened to be in the company of a certain divine, recounted for a learned man, and in communing and disputing with him he drave him to that issue, that the said great doctor burst out into these blasphemous words, and said, 'We were better to be without God's laws than the pope's'. Master Tyndale, hearing this, full of godly zeal and not bearing that blasphemous saying, replied again and said, 'I defy the pope and all his laws', and further added that, if God spared him life, ere many years he would cause the boy that driveth the plough to know more of scripture than he did.[28]

---

verse in the light of an unrelated saying of Augustine attached to the verse by the Glossa Ordinaria. The Vulgate verse includes 'sive mente excedimus', meaning 'if we have been unreasonable'. The gloss relates to it Augustine's definition of ecstasy, 'excessus mentis', and Aquinas then concludes that Paul had two experiences of ecstasy, described respectively in 2 Cor. 5 and 2 Cor. 12.

[27] Tyndale, *The Obedience of a Christian Man*, fol. xviii[r].

[28] John Foxe, *Acts and Monuments of Matters Happening in the Church* (London, 1563), commonly known as 'Foxe's Book of Martyrs'.

Important here is Tyndale's mention of the ploughboy. This must surely be a reminiscence of Erasmus' preface to his 1516 first printed edition of the Greek New Testament.[29] There Erasmus wrote about the farm worker singing the Scripture: 'I could wish that all women should read the Gospel and St Paul's Epistles. I wish the farm worker might sing parts of them at the plough and the weaver might hum them at the shuttle, and the traveller might beguile the weariness of the way by reciting them.' Tyndale expresses the same idea, but with his own customary vigour and clarity.

This brings us to the second profound influence on Tyndale at this time. Foxe recounts that his employer, Sir John, kept a good table, so that 'there resorted to him many times sundry abbots, deans, archdeacons with divers other doctors and beneficed men'. Master Tyndale 'spared not to show unto them simply and plainly his judgement in matters, and lay plainly before them the open and manifest places of the Scriptures, to confute their errors and confirm his sayings', to such good effect that 'at length they waxed weary, and bare a secret grudge in their hearts against him'. The secret of Tyndale's devastating effectiveness was surely Erasmus. During this period Tyndale translated Erasmus' *Enchiridion militis Christiani* and presented it to his master and lady[30] – with significant effect on the Walshes' social life! 'After they had read well and perused the same, the doctorly prelates were no more so often called to the house, neither had they the cheer and countenance when they came as before they had.' Erasmus, already the intellectual guru of Europe, provided the backbone for the varied yearnings of Lollardy. Tyndale's programme is strikingly similar. It must be remembered that Tyndale was already in one of the heartlands of Lollardy, giving regular open-air sermons in Bristol, less than a dozen miles from his position in Little Sodbury, on what is now College Green. The secret of Tyndale is that he was the combination of the rural dissatisfaction of Lollardy and the academic dissatisfaction of Erasmus and the Renaissance. A couple of examples must suffice of sentiments expressed in the *Enchiridion* which can be paralleled in a dozen depositions from the investigations into Lollardy:

---

[29] The reaction to this in some circles was not dissimilar to that of Tyndale's learned divine. The Professor of Philosophy at Louvain could see no point in returning to the Greek text, on the grounds that the Latin Vulgate could not possibly be wrong since it had been approved by the Councils of the Church.

[30] The first published English translation of this appears in 1533. There seems no reason to suppose that this was Tyndale's translation, the manuscript of which may still be languishing in Gloucestershire.

Against pilgrimage: 'Would you like to win the favour of Peter and Paul? Imitate the faith of the one and the charity of the other and you will accomplish more than if you were to dash off to Rome ten times.'[31]

Against veneration of the saints: 'You worship the bones of Paul preserved in a relic casket but do not worship the mind of Paul hidden in his writings.'[32]

Against superstition: 'I am ashamed to mention with what superstition many of them [priests and theologians] observe silly little ceremonies instituted by mere men.'[33]

The next we hear of Tyndale is the decisive move to break the jinx on translations of the Bible into the vernacular. He offered himself in 1520 as a translator to that noted humanist and friend of Erasmus, Cuthbert Tunstall, Bishop of London. Tunstall, however, refused his request, on the grounds that he had no room for him in his household, a feeble excuse. The subsequent history makes it quite clear that Tunstall was a dedicated opponent of Bible translation (see above). Tyndale's own fiery temperament may well have played a part in his rejection, and even the reputation he had won himself in Gloucestershire. It is striking that as his sample submission to Tunstall Tyndale chose so luxuriant and artificial a rhetorical author as Isocrates. In any case, it was this refusal which pushed Tyndale into exile and into the arms of the Lutheran theologians. Tyndale had clearly already given thought to the requirements of biblical translation. It would be intriguing to know how long he had held so strongly, as he writes in *The Obedience of a Christian Man* (1528):

> The Greek tongue agreeth a thousand times more with the English than with the Latin. The manner of speaking is both one, so that in a thousand places thou needest not but to translate it into the English word for word, when thou must seek a compass in the Latin, and yet shall have much work to translate it well favouredly, so that it have the same grace and sweetness, sense and pure understanding with it in the Latin, and as it hath in the Hebrew. A thousand parts better may it be translated into the English than into the Latin.

The outline of Tyndale's actual career as translator of the Bible can be quickly rehearsed. It is an exciting story of sixteenth-century intrigue and skulduggery on which I do not propose to delay. The outline may

---

[31] Erasmus, *Enchiridion militis Christianae*, in *CWE* lxvi (Toronto, 1988), p. 71.

[32] Ibid., p. 72.

[33] Ibid., p. 74.

be read in Foxe's *Book of Martyrs*, and a fuller, more rounded account in Professor Daniell's biography of Tyndale. I propose to give no more than a sketch, before going on to make a few suggestions about the qualities of the translation itself.

Having been cold-shouldered by Tunstall, Tyndale went abroad to Flanders in April 1524, to pursue his objectives in the more tolerant air of the Continent. He first set about translating the New Testament, and by the summer of 1525 he had got as far as printing the middle of Matthew Chapter 22 at Cologne, when the authorities set out to arrest him. However, he fled to Worms, where he finished and published the New Testament. This he revised in 1534, not long before he was kidnapped and incarcerated. It should be well known that he was, at the instigation of the English authorities, garrotted in 1536, and his body burnt at the same stake. The only other fragment of biography I shall offer is a quotation from a letter written to the prison governor shortly before his execution. It shows his undaunted spirit and his continuing passion for language and translation. It is still the same Tyndale sitting in prison as sat in the ale-house to confront the learned cleric.

> I suffer greatly from cold in the head and am afflicted with perpetual catarrh. I ask to have a lamp in the evening; it is indeed wearisome sitting alone in the dark. Most of all I beg and beseech Your Clemency to urge the Commissary that he will kindly permit me to have the Hebrew Bible, Hebrew grammar and Hebrew dictionary, that I may pass the time in that study.

Finally I wish to offer some remarks about this first printed translation of the New Testament, Matthew 1–22. I believe that the focus on this short section of text is quite sufficient to illustrate the qualities of Tyndale's achievement. Little is to be gained by repeating the more general assessments, for example of C.S. Lewis,[34] or of David Daniell in his wide-ranging survey in the preface to his edition of Tyndale's New Testament.[35] It would be possible to list the household words coined by Tyndale (C.S. Lewis lists 'passover', 'long-suffering', 'scapegoat', and also – wrongly – 'peacemakers'). It would be possible to enumerate the expressions drawn from Tyndale's translation which have become proverbial in the English language ('the powers that be', 'the fat of the land', 'not unto us, O Lord, not unto us'). It is necessary to point out that, for the portions of the Bible translated by Tyndale, between 70 per cent and 80 per cent of the King James Version is verbatim Tyndale's

---

34 *Oxford History of English Literature*, iii (Oxford, 1954), pp. 205–7.
35 David Daniell, *Tyndale's New Testament* (New Haven, CT, 1989).

version. I am well aware that I leave out of discussion many fascinating topics which deserve attention in a chapter on Tyndale in the book *The Bible in the Renaissance*. Two topics I will mention summarily before considering the original piece of translation. They are both concerned with More's objections to Tyndale's translation.

Firstly, when Tyndale's translation reached England, Thomas More, the leading literary figure of his time in England, and enjoying an international reputation, was commissioned by Tunstall to attack it. He attempted to pillory it as 'Luther's Testament'. This is a fair comment only as regards the theological notes, which were highly dependent on Luther. With regard to the translation, it is clear to me that Tyndale acted as any sensible translator of a much-translated text will do; he consulted and made use of existing versions, while retaining his own independence. In some places he agreed with Luther, in others he did not.[36] To give but one example, Tyndale corrects Matthew 3: 3, to 'the voyce *off a cryer* in wyldernes', where Luther has *ein ruffende stymme*, 'a voice crying', as though the participle βοῶντος agreed with the φωνή.

Secondly, More's objections centre round three translation options, Tyndale's preference for 'senior' or 'elder' instead of 'priest', for 'congregation' instead of 'church', and for 'love' instead of 'charity'. There is, of course, a hidden agenda, the legacy of Lollardy, for at least the first two of these. Tyndale's versions are, however, all thoroughly defensible translations. It is simply a matter of emphasis on one particular set of theological overtones rather than another, and More's objections are heavy with the overtones of ecclesiastical tradition, which is precisely what Tyndale meant to avoid.

'Priest' is, of course, a corruption of πρεσβύτερος, but in Christian parlance 'priest' includes the concept of a sacrificing priest. A sacrificing priest is far from the New Testament usage of the word, where the word retains the organizational and communitarian sense of 'elder', or (as Tyndale translated it) 'senior', the original, classical Greek usage of the word. The πρεσβύτεροι are simply members of the council of elders. In this item of translation Tyndale is certainly true to the original meaning of the New Testament.

Similarly, 'congregation' as a translation of ἐκκλησία deliberately avoids the ecclesiastical overtones of 'church' and returns to the Old Testament overtones of a group called together, called out of a mass. No doubt the Lollard objection to everything ecclesiastical was Tyndale's reason for refusing the word and preferring 'congregation'. It is perhaps

---

[36] F.F. Bruce gives the interesting opinion that Tyndale was a better Greek scholar than Luther, who did, after all, have Melanchthon to help him. F.F. Bruce, *The English Bible* (London, 1961), p. 36.

a little heavy and Latinate for the Hebrew *qhl-YHWH*, but on the whole fits at least the Pauline contexts better than 'church'. 'Church' does not suggest a local grouping and does suggest an entity far more developed than the Pauline local Christian assembly. When the King James Version reverts to 'church', this is principally a statement of which theological overtones it wishes to emphasize.

The case of 'love' seems to me rather different. The preference for 'love' over 'charity' is part of Tyndale's preference for English words over latinate ones. It also enabled him to distinguish between two Greek words used in the New Testament, ἀγάπη and χάρις. The latter is etymologically cognate with 'charity' and also with 'grace', accordingly Tyndale translates it sometimes 'grace' and sometimes (correctly) 'thanks'. It seems to me that 'love' renders far better the meaning and feel of the Hebrew *hsdh*, which stands behind the Greek ἀγάπη. I would suggest that in this case Tyndale's preference is partly a preference for the fresh and direct English word, partly a rejection of the whole medieval structure of the institutional Church associated with 'charity'.

In these three linguistic matters, then, although Tunstall might legitimately claim that Tyndale's New Testament was 'naughtelie translated',[37] it was also accurate.

I wish finally to draw attention to three qualities of Tyndale's version of Matthew 1–22. Before doing that I must stress what a staggering achievement it is to have translated the whole of the New Testament without precedent. This is an achievement which no English-speaker has subsequently been able to do. Not only does any responsible translator consult the work of predecessors, but the very rhythm and modes of expression have been shaped by Tyndale through the King James Version. Every subsequent version of the Bible in the English language, no matter how fresh and original it claims to be, must be, and indeed is, indebted to Tyndale. This makes his version unique, at any rate in English. He himself had no such model in English, though he certainly used Luther's German and - as we shall see - must have received at least echoes from the Wyclifian Middle English translation. Neither of these could solve his translation problems for him.

The first quality I wish to stress is the rhythmical quality of the language. For this the Beatitudes may serve as an example:

> Blessed are the povre in sprete: for theirs is the kyngdome off heven.
> Blessed are they that morne: for they shalbe comforted.
> Blessed are the meke: for they shall inheret the erth.
> Blessed are they which honger and thurst for rightewesnes: for they
>   shalbe filled.

---

[37] As Humphrey Monmouth reported to Wolsey (British Library, Harl. 425, fol. 11).

> Blessed are the mercifull: for they shall obteyne mercy.
> Blessed are the pure in herte: for they shall se God.
> Blessed are the maynteyners of peace: for they shalbe called the
>   chyldren of God.
> Blessed are they which suffre persecucion for rightewesnes sake: for
>   theirs ys the kyngdome off heven.
> Blessed are ye when men shall revyle you, and persecute you and
>   shall falsly say all manner of yvell saynges agaynst you ffor my
>   sake. Reioyce and be glad, for greate is youre rewarde in heven.

It is tempting here to enter into an exposition of the balance and rhythm of the original Greek (the first eight beatitudes composed in two fours corresponding to each other in verbs and word-count, and the whole bracketed by the banner, 'for theirs is the kingdom of heaven'), but that is not my subject. Tyndale's version is so familiar that we take it for granted, which only reinforces the point. Tyndale's second 1534 version makes only two changes, one from 'maintainers of peace' to 'peacemakers', which is more accurate for εἰρηνοποιοί as well as more rhythmical, and the other removing the future from 'shall revile you' (an odd grammatical mistake, made also in 'shall say', which is perpetuated in the King James Version).[38] The KJV makes only two further changes, inserting '*do* hunger and thirst *after* righteousness' (which seems to me rhythmically inferior and linguistically unnecessary), and preferring '*are* persecuted' to Tyndale's 'suffer persecution', a pedantic change which slightly diminishes the force.

The achievement of this may be seen by comparison with Wyclif's version, which lacks both rhythm and balance (I have ventured to italicize elements where Tyndale's version seems to me a significant improvement – and Tyndale's 'suffer persecution' suggests that he was familiar with the Wycliffite version):

> Blessed ben poor *men* in spirit, for the kingdom of heaven is herne.
> Blessed ben mild *men*, for they schulen welde the earth,
> Blessed ben they that mournen, for they schulen be comforted.
> Blessed ben they that hungren and thristen righteousness, for they
>   schulen be *fulfilled*.
> Blessed ben merciful *men*, for they schulen get mercy.
> Blessed ben *they that be of* clean heart, for they schulen see God.
> Blessed ben peaceable *men*, for they schulen be cleppid Goddis
>   children.
> Blessed ben they that suffren persecution for rightfulness, for the
>   kingdom of heaven is herne.

A second quality on which I would like to dwell is the vigour and directness of language, a quality which one would expect from someone

---

38 The verbs are aorist subjunctive, not future, as is clear from εἴπωσιν.

whose directness of speech had early got him into trouble.[39] Striking in this respect is the reply of Jesus to the Rich Young Man who wanted to enter the kingdom of heaven (Matt. 19: 18): Τὸ Οὐ φονεύσεις, Οὐ μοιχεύσεις, Οὐ κλέψεις. In the 1534 revision Tyndale eventually reaches the splendid 'Break no wedlock, kill not, steal not'. He changes the order and simplifies. It is hardly surprising that the KJV backs off to 'Thou shalt do no murder, thou shalt not commit adultery, thou shalt not steal', returning almost exactly to Tyndale's earlier rendering. This directness occurs again and again, recreating especially the vigour of the sayings of Jesus. 'Ask and it shall be given unto you. Seek and ye shall find. Knock and it shall be opened unto you' sharpens the Wyclifian 'Ask ye ... Seek ye ... Knock ye'. Immediately afterwards the KJV weakens Tyndale's vigorous 'whosoever asketh receiveth' into 'everyone that asketh receiveth', in the interests of pedestrian accuracy (πᾶς).[40]

A third delightful quality of the translation is its humour. Here I must depart from my chosen text of Matthew 1–22, in order to indulge in my two favourite pieces of Tyndale's light-heartedness. One is the serpent to Eve, where the serpent begins the seduction of Eve with the splendid but quite unjustified 'Tush, ye shall not die'. In the KJV this fades to the dully respectable, 'Ye shall not surely die' (Gen. 3: 4). Another delightful touch is the relaxed *al fresco* feeling at the Feeding of the Five Thousand in Mark 6: 40, when the crowd sits down 'here a rowe and there a rowe', a free rendering of πρασιαί πρασιαί spurned by the KJV's sober 'they sat down in ranks'. Finally, Tyndale is certainly enjoying himself in the story of the Canaanite Woman (Matt. 15: 21–8), who comes to Jesus and says, 'My doughter is *pytiously* vexed with a devyll' [κακῶς δαιμονίζεται – KJV: 'grievously vexed']; '*And he gave her never a worde to answer*' [KJV: 'But he answered her not a word']. Tyndale also catches

---

[39] Homely images come readily to Tyndale. I treasure especially two in the Preface to *The Obedience of a Christian Man*: (i) the accusation that George Ioye 'playeth boo pepe and in some of his books putteth in his name and style and in some keepeth it out'; (ii) the humour of the age is reflected also in 'as the fox when he has pissed in the grayes [badger's] hole challengeth it for his own'. These have the same earthy countryman's wisdom as the scintillating animal proverbs of the Rylands MS 394, for example: 'the catte wolle fysshe ete, but she wol not her fete wete', or 'while the welp playes, the old dog grennys' (W.A. Pantin, 'Medieval Latin and English Proverbs from the Rylands Latin MS 394', *Bulletin of the John Rylands Library*, 14 (1930), pp. 81–114).

[40] There are, of course, occasions where Tyndale seems to have made a simple mistake, which is corrected by the KJV. One can hardly defend on grounds of vigour 'If the salt be once unsavery, *what* can be salted *therwith?*', for ἐν τίνι ἁλισθήσεται at Matt. 5: 13, and the KJV corrects to '*wherewith* shall *it* be salted?' The 1526 version contained a few curious errors which were corrected in 1534, for example, 'fifty fold' for 'sixtyfold' in the parable of the Sower (Matt. 13: 8), and the price of the ointment at Bethany being given as 'two houndred pens' instead of 300 (Mark 14: 5).

perfectly the wit and playfulness of the exchange by: 'It is not good, to take the childrens breed, and to cast it to *whelpes*' [κυναρίοις, so KJV, dully: 'dogs']. On the other hand the impatience of Jesus is brilliantly rendered by 'Why are youre mindes *cumbred* because ye have brought no breed' [Matt. 16: 8: not quite fair for τί διαλογίζεσθε ἐν ἑαυτοῖς and toned down by the KJV to 'Why reason ye among your selves?'].

For accuracy Tyndale's first translation of the Bible from Greek into English has been surpassed, for its spirit and verve it reigns supreme.

CHAPTER EIGHT

English Fears of Social Disintegration and Modes of Control, 1533–1611

Vincent Strudwick

During the second half of the fifteenth century, the Renaissance spirit, together with the availability of 'lost' resources, gave rise to a renewed interest in the Holy Scriptures. This interest and scholarship flowered gently throughout western Europe, and then in the early sixteenth century, with the development of the printing press and a concern to renew the Church on the basis of biblical scholarship, there was a visionary impetus for a rapid increase in new translations into the vernacular, and the spread of the knowledge of the text of the Scriptures beyond the confines of what later was to be called 'the clerisy'.

The complex threads of conflict and change that came to be known as 'the Reformation' ensured that this did not happen as quickly as once might have been envisaged, but in England, following the break with Rome, the slow progress of the availability of the Bible in English is surprising. While some have thought that this was due to influential theological conservatives impeding progress, it is my contention that it was the *social* conservatism of some reformers – notably Archbishops Cranmer and Whitgift – and fears that unfettered reading of the Bible in the nation at large might lead to political disruption and change that caused the introduction of modes of control over the reading of the Bible throughout the sixteenth century and into the seventeenth.

My story begins in Italy. In the Church of Santa Maria Novella in Florence there is an unexpected and wonderful monument to an Orthodox patriarch named Joseph. Underneath is this inscription which, in accordance with Orthodox custom, is written in the first person, but out of respect for the location is in Latin:

> ECCLESIAE ANTISTES FVERAM QVI MAGVS EOAE:
> HIC IACEO MAGNVS RELIGIONE IOSEPH:
> HOC VNVM OPTABAM MIRO INFLAMMATVS AMORE:
> VNVS ET EVROPAE CVLTVS VT VNA FIDES:
> ITALIAM PETII FOEDVS PERCVSSIMVS VNVM:
> IVNCTAQVE ROMANAE EST ME DVCE GRAIA FIDES:

NEC MORA DECVNVI NVNC ME FLORENTIA SERVAT:
QVA TVNC CONCILIVM FLORVIT VRBE SACRVM:
FELIX QVI TANTO DONARER MVNERE VIVENS:
QVI MORERER VOTI COMPOS ET IPSE MEI[1]

The story behind the monument is that on 8 February 1438 the
Byzantine emperor John VIII and the patriarch Joseph II, head of the
Church in Constantinople, arrived in Florence where the papal court
was currently based, together with twenty Byzantine bishops. In
attendance were 700 priests, monks and lay people making up a
splendid delegation whose purpose was to reunite the Christian Church
in the fiery love that motivated Joseph. They also had a political motive,
in that the East needed support from the West to resist a possible
Turkish occupation, for they believed that the Western powers would
regard with horror any further encroachment into Europe by Islam. The
splendour of the occasion, as well as reflections on its theological
significance, were captured by the painter Benozzo Gozzoli in his
wonderful mural in the Medici chapel in Florence. Here the emperor, the
patriarch and the young Lorenzo de' Medici are depicted in a
magnificent procession entitled 'The Procession of the Magi', in which
people from East and West intermingle behind the chief characters as
they make their way to worship the Christ Child together; a single
church on pilgrimage. The poignancy of the situation is not only in the
immediate failure of the union, which was quickly disowned when the
delegations returned to base; but also because the lasting monument to
that meeting between East and West was the quickening of the flow of
books, pictures and artefacts of different kinds from eastern countries
into western cities, which helped to assuage that 'thirst for sources'
which was characteristic of Renaissance humanists. This 'return to
sources' became a cause of further division in Christendom, as
Renaissance learning intertwined with other forces to produce conflict
and change.

The Council of Florence was a catalyst in a continuing process which
brought the pagan authors, the Greek fathers and Greek texts of
Scripture into Europe; and these in turn brought not unity but further
disintegration to the Church for whose unity Joseph had so passionately

---

[1] 'I who was an official of the Church and a wise man from the East, here I lie, Joseph,
great in religion. This one thing I longed for with a fiery love – that Europe should have a
single Church as it has a single faith. I came on quest to Italy and there we struck a treaty
of union. While I was at the helm Greek and Roman faiths were joined together.
Straightway I laid me down to sleep and now Florence has me in her keeping, the city
where that sacred council blossomed. Happy am I who in my life was graced with so great
a gift, and who died having reached my goal and my heart's desire.'

longed. Before Constantinople fell to the Turks in 1453, the flow of treasures, including books and manuscripts, to the west grew into a flood. They gave rise to new visions of how the Church should and might be, and there were plenty of visionaries, including those who wished to place the Scriptures at the disposal of ordinary people. Erasmus of Rotterdam, an admirer of Lorenzo Valla (he wrote to a critic that he would be glad to stand as Valla's champion),[2] expressed his vision for the psalms, that 'the farmer sing some of them at the plough, that the weaver hum some part of them to the rhythm of his shuttle and that the traveller lighten the weariness of his journey'.[3] If Joseph's vision was that Europe should have a single Church as it had a single faith, that of Erasmus was that all in Europe in every social class should have access to the stories on which the Church's faith is based.

The early part of the sixteenth century was a honeymoon period for those who were passionately fired with the idea of a vernacular version of the Scriptures. There were those, of course, who feared that vernacular Scriptures might be the excuse for religious polemic, as had happened with Wyclif's Bible in England; there were also some who doubted whether the Scriptures in the vernacular could be regarded as the real word of God. But these were relatively few in number, and the visionaries held the day. The invention of printing gave promise of the vision being fulfilled in ways that an earlier generation could not have envisaged; large numbers of pocket-sized Bibles which could be owned by individuals were now a possibility, and this was to raise an important issue that was to cause some early enthusiasts of the vernacular translations to hesitate.

In 1522 Luther published his New Testament, and since this followed his excommunication and the beginnings of ecclesial divisions within the Empire, the vernacular Bible once again became associated in some people's minds with heresy and schism. Tyndale's work followed, and his translation of 1526 is prefaced by a version of the foreword that Luther had offered with his New Testament. This ensured that both at the time and later, the translation of the Scriptures into the vernacular ceased to be a purely visionary process and became involved in the battlefront of a war. As David Daniell puts it in his biography of Tyndale, 'Bursting its containment of learned Latin enclaves and clerical outposts, it was carrying the war into the market-place and would arm the common man with an ageless weapon of religious revolution.'[4]

---

2 Erasmus to Cornelius Gerard (Aurotinus), no. 29 in *Opus epistolarum Des. Erasmi Roterodami*, ed. P.S. Allen (Oxford, 1906; repr. 1992), pp. 119–20; see also letter 26, pp. 112–15.

3 Erasmus, Preface to his New Testament (1516).

4 David Daniell, *William Tyndale: A Biography* (New Haven, CT, 1994).

Many people have interpreted the subsequent history of the English Bible during the sixteenth century in this way – that it was one of the battlefronts in which theological conservatives and reformers engaged in conflict. But there was another issue involved.

After King Henry VIII broke with Rome in 1534, there was some expectation among reformers that an official English Bible might emerge. Indeed in that very year the Convocation of Canterbury petitioned the King 'that the whole Bible might be translated into English'. From the king there followed a deafening silence. The piece of translation that was occupying the king at that time was the translation into English of Marsiglio of Padua's *Defensor Pacis*, which could be read as a helpful tract in giving a medieval theological basis for the Royal Supremacy, one of the fundamental pillars on which England's separation from Rome was based. It was not a best-seller but it shows where the king's interest lay. Through a time of change, with part of the historic authority structure removed, it was important for social order that the basis of authority in the monarchy should be absolutely clear. After all, it was in the interests of the long-term political and social cohesion of the country that Henry had justified taking the momentous step of breaking with the Pope's authority. He wished for a male heir, a smooth succession and no repetition of the horrors of the Wars of the Roses, which were still fresh in the minds of his elderly subjects. So the king wished to concentrate on giving theological backing to the Supremacy.

However, while there was no official encouragement for an English Bible forthcoming, Miles Coverdale attempted to offer a theologically 'clean' version of the Scriptures and tried to get the king's tacit assent for this venture. Coverdale had been an Augustinian friar in Cambridge where, under the influence of his prior, the notorious Robert Barnes, he embraced the cause of reform. His preaching was too radical for safety in slowly changing England, with a theologically conservative king and many bishops light half-believers in the cause of reform. In the preface to his 1535 translation, dedicated to the king, Coverdale writes that he had ventured it 'to the intent that if anything therein be translated amiss (for in many things we fail even when we think to be sure) it may strode in your Grace's hand to correct it, to amend it, to improve it, yea and clean to reject it if your godly wisdom shall think it necessary'.[5] Again, there is no evidence of a reply, although Coverdale's translation of the Psalter was included by Cranmer in the first Prayer Book of 1549, and it became the

---

[5] *Writings and Translations of Miles Coverdale, Bishop of Exeter*, ed. G. Pearson (Cambridge, 1844).

familiar text of all subsequent editions until the Alternative Service Book of 1980. Coverdale became Bishop of Exeter in the reign of Edward VI, was exiled by Queen Mary and restored by Elizabeth I. His version of the Psalms was rhythmic, and suitable for recitation or singing.

What I would call visionary energy for an 'official' vernacular Bible was still around, and there was a move in 1536 for an English version of the Bible to be put in churches alongside the Vulgate. This was in the form of a draft injunction which was never formally published. In 1537 a revised English Bible known as Matthew's Bible appeared. The text consisted of Tyndale's Pentateuch, a version of Joshua to 2 Chronicles translated from the Hebrew, and more from Coverdale and Tyndale's New Testament of 1535. It carried the royal authorization, but for a more satisfactory version Thomas Cromwell, the king's Vicar General for Church Affairs, persuaded his royal master that there should be a Bible in English in each church of the land, and that each local church should be required to purchase one. This version, called the Great Bible, was printed in Paris in 1539. On the title-page it claims to have been made from the Hebrew and Greek 'by the diligent study of divers excellent learned men'. However, it was Coverdale who was the chief editor, revising his earlier material. The Great Bible was reissued in a new edition of 1540 with a preface by the Archbishop himself, Thomas Cranmer. All notes and controversial matter were deliberately excluded.

The message of the preface was one of social unity. In the design of the frontispiece we see the two estates, clerical and lay, harmoniously and gratefully receiving the Word of God from the hands of a benevolent monarch. The 'spin' on the vernacular text was the king's preferred message of discipline and obedience, which differs from the vision of Erasmus and others who believed in the unfettered dissemination of vernacular Scriptures. For this vision is about the political and social coherence of the nation – and this was the king's vision.

In his preface Cranmer faces the reality of the situation. Those who would deny the common people the Scriptures are 'peevish, perverse and obdurate'; lay and vulgar people who live in the world *need* Scripture more than the holy. They need more of ghostly succour and comfort, for Scripture is the guide to *life*. But interestingly, Cranmer goes on to weave into the vision of the vernacular Scriptures the king's vision of social order. He says – and he cites John Chrysostom – that Scripture by itself is not enough. Scripture is the basis for discipleship but it will not be understood by common people without interpretation. So the lay reader is advised, 'Go to thy curate and preacher.'[6]

There is no doubt that Cranmer saw the Bible as a tool for the church rather than for the individual, and he warns against unfettered discussion of it in the taverns. Cranmer's fear of biblical pub talk was not fear that Lutheran or other heretical opinions might emerge, but rather it was fear of unsettling and rebellious social and political opinions which would in some way emerge in an alehouse discussion, and be the basis for social disruption and for breaking the unity of the Commonwealth.

So in answer to the question, 'Shall everyone have total access to the Scriptures and be able to interpret them, or shall the church control their use?' the Archbishop says: 'Let us keep our bounds and let us neither go too far on the one side lest we return into Egypt, neither too far over the other lest we be carried away to Babylon.' We may interpret Egypt as Rome and Babylon as Geneva; it was a popular convention at the time.

It is in this context that Gillian Brennan's article 'Patriotism, Language and Power' is important.[7] She argues that the split in the English Church over vernacular translations from the middle of the 1530s until the turn of the century was not between conservatives who feared Lutheranism and radicals who wanted a true church, but between those who wanted to ensure the control of access to knowledge through the use of classical languages or vernacular literature interpreted by the Church, and those progressives who thought that the unlimited dissemination of vernacular Scriptures was the best way to achieve a godly commonwealth. She cites one of Cranmer's letters, showing that Cranmer saw the Bible as the basis for a stable society: 'Herein may princes learn how to govern their subjects; subjects obedience, love and dread to their princes; husbands how they should behove to wives, how to educate their children and their servants; and contrary, that wives, children and servants may know their duty to their husbands, parents and masters.' But it is clear that by 1540 Cranmer felt that the Bible would not do this on its own without being mediated through the Church, and this is what he set out to do. Cranmer and his reforming group questioned how far down the social scale you could go and expect intelligent understanding and response. Instruction was also required.

---

[6] 'Cranmer's Preface to the Great Bible 1540', in *Documents of the English Reformation*, ed. Gerald Bray (Cambridge, 1994). The Injunctions of 1538 ordered that a Bible should be provided in each church in the land by the following Easter. The Great Bible was not available from the printer until April 1539. Copies were soon sold, and another edition was needed. Cranmer's Preface was written for this 1540 edition.

[7] Gillian Brennan, 'Patriotism, Language and Power: English Translations of the Bible 1520–1580', *History Workshop Journal*, 27 (1989), pp. 18–36.

An Act of 1543 restricted Bible reading on the grounds that it created disorder among the uneducated. Noblemen could read the Bible to their families at home; merchants, noblewomen and gentlewomen could read the Bible to themselves; but it was forbidden to lower-class women and merchants, artificers, apprentices, journeymen, serving men of the degree of yeoman or under, husbandmen and labourers.

The king expressed himself as sorry to know and hear how unreverently that most precious word of God was disputed, rhymed, sung and jangled in every alehouse and tavern. Fears were of 'dumbing down the Bible' and of subsequent social unrest.

The Archbishop's immediate code of control was to ensure that only large Bibles were printed, and that these were chained in church, and were to be read and expounded by Masters of Arts of Oxford and of Cambridge. The reading itself was important. Robert Atwell in his introduction to his selection of daily spiritual readings for the Christian Year writes:

> Patristic and medieval commentators on Scripture display [great] interest in the sounds of words and in the literary devices of rhythm, rhyme, alliteration and assonance ... They related to its performative value, and what it actually felt like as it was articulated in the mouth, spoken with the tongue, and heard with the ear. They would repeat the words of the sacred text with their lips again and again, so that the body and not just the mind entered into the process. They sought to cultivate their capacity to listen to the Word of God at ever deeper levels of inward attention.[8]

Atwell goes on to say that they borrowed from the vocabulary of digestion to describe the process of ingesting Scripture, and wonderfully expressive words were used, such as *ruminatio* and *manducare*, the verb to chew the cud; and the slow digestive process of cows is well suited to describe the process of engaging with Scripture. It is this that is reflected in the collect that Archbishop Cranmer composed for the second Sunday in Advent when he prepared the first Prayer Book in 1549. It is one of his very few 'original' collects, and this may reflect the importance that he attached to it:

> Blessed lord, which hast caused all holy Scriptures to bee written for our learnyng; graunte us that we maye in suche wise heare them, read, marke, learne, and inwardly digeste them; that by pacience, and coumfort of thy holy woorde, we may embrace, and euer holde fast the blessed hope of euerlasting life, which thou hast geuen us in our sauiour Jesus Christe.

The Archbishop's ultimate code of control for Bible reading was the

---

[8] Robert Atwell, *Celebrating the Seasons* (Canterbury, 1999), Introduction, p. v.

Book of Common Prayer itself. The first version appeared in 1549, another in 1552, and a third at the beginning of the reign of Queen Elizabeth, in 1559. Part of the pattern of ordered worship which it set out included selected Bible readings which would be heard in the context of the Church's worship.

At Morning and Evening Prayer, and in the Holy Communion service, the Bible was heard by the laity with a 'spin' which Cranmer emphasized and underlined through his clever formulation and positioning of collects which helped to sum up the message of the readings chosen. In this way it was hoped that the Bible would percolate through the nation, not as a tool for individualism but as part of an interpretation of life which had the royal authority at its root and the unity, peace and concord of the nation as its aim. This was a priority concern for Tudor monarchs, and after Queen Mary had briefly returned allegiance to Rome, Elizabeth reintroduced the Book of Common Prayer with its Bible readings set out in the lectionary of 1559.

But in 1560 the Geneva Bible appeared, following an initiative by William Whittingham, who had married into Calvin's family. Miles Coverdale and John Knox were among his associates, who both revised previous translations and provided new translations, for this edition, in parts of the Old Testament. The quarto editions came with maps and concordances, and chapters were divided into verses for easy reference in group study. 'Geneva' had ecclesial as well as geographical overtones. In the New Testament words like 'elder' and 'congregation' replaced 'priest' and 'church', and indeed the preface begins with the story of Zerubbabel and the rebuilding of the Temple, offering him as a model for the queen, 'whom God has made as our Zerubbabel'. Perhaps the queen was not flattered by the comparison, nor by the closing reference to the transience of earthly kingdoms: 'All other kingdoms and monarchies as the Grecians and Romans have fallen and taken end.'

In any case the New Testament was presented to conform to Calvinist understanding and practice, and the marginal notes were full of interpretations which focused on reformed practice. Worse still from the point of view of *social* conservatives, who included many who had reformed sympathies, the Geneva Bible was printed in a format suitable for domestic use. In other words, there were lots of small 'pocket' copies which people could thumb through either in the tavern or at home, a form which made it a possible source of social unrest.[9] For the first great

---

[9] My own copy of the Geneva Bible, published by Christopher Barker in 1580, includes a section entitled 'Certain questions and answers touching the doctrine of predestination, the use of God's Word and Sacraments'. There are also 'Two Right Profitable Concordances' and an injunction to the owner to 'read two chapters each day'.

defender of the Church of England, it was of no great importance and he was able to sit on the fence. Bishop John Jewel's *Apology of the Church of England* was published in Latin in 1562 for an international audience, and translated into English in 1564 by Anne, Lady Bacon, wife of Sir Nicholas Bacon, Lord Keeper of the Great Seal, and mother of the illustrious Francis Bacon.

Jewel was definitely a reformer and had been deprived of his Fellowship at Corpus Christi College, Oxford, for his opinions. One of those who voted for his expulsion, John Moran, is quoted as saying: 'I should love thee, Jewel, if thou wert not a Zwinglian. Thou art a heretic in thy faith, but certainly an angel in thy life. Truly, thou art an honest man; but thou art a Lutheran.'[10] Jewel, a friend of Peter Martyr Vermigli, was also a visionary as far as the Bible was concerned, and put the following about it in his Apologia. In contrasting the Church of England with Rome, it tops Jewel's list that 'We turn Scripture into all tongues; they scant suffer them to be had abroad in any tongue. We allure the people to read and to hear God's word; they flee to come to any trial. ... We reverence, as it becometh us, the writings of the Apostles and Prophets.'[11] But he avoids the questions already raised by the Geneva Bible.

Archbishop Parker, however, was ambivalent about the Geneva Bible, although he did lend his support to the printing of new editions. But in 1575 Parker died, and was succeeded as Archbishop of Canterbury by Edmund Grindal, a disciple of Martin Bucer, whose religious convictions were extremely radical. Within two years of Parker's death, Christopher Barker printed four new folio editions of the Geneva Bible, and two pocket editions. In addition, he offered impressions of Tomson's translation of Beza's New Testament, dedicated to Mr Secretary Walsingham. Between 1560 and 1603 nineteen editions of the Geneva Bible were printed.

In 1578, an edition appeared 'with every appearance of official sanction', and this was bound with a version of the Prayer Book, which had been tampered with. Certain words had been changed, including the substitution of the word 'minister' for 'priest'; the popish names of Mattins and Evensong were changed to Morning and Evening Prayer, and the orders for private baptism, confirmation and the churching of

---

[10] Preface to John Jewel, *An Apologie or Answere in Defence of the Church of England* (London, 1564). This preface takes the form of a life of Bishop Jewel by an anonymous 'friend'.

[11] See the modern edition, *The Apology of the Church of England by John Jewel, Bishop of Sarum. Translated by Anne, Lady Bacon, and published 1564*, ed. R.W. Jelf (London, 1859), p. 113.

women were all omitted. This combination went through sixteen editions and helped to provoke the row which ended with the suspension of Archbishop Grindal.

The Geneva Bibles were the main resource for 'prophesyings'. Prophesyings were biblical conferences where the Bible was studied and 'a man shall speak or enquire of God as shall move his heart'. They had been introduced into England during the reign of Edward VI, both as a means of doing biblical study and for improving the educational and preaching abilities of the clergy. Attenders at the prophesying would sit, Bibles in lap, and discuss texts and meanings. They were not just for clergy, but all of them were there: 'men, women, boys and girls, labourers, workmen and simpletons'. The issue of prophesying was the chief focus of the Queen's complaint about Grindal. She ordered Grindal to suppress them, because of the possible threat to social and political stability that she supposed they contained. Grindal refused: 'I am forced with all humility and yet plainly to confess that I cannot with safe conscience and without the offence of the majesty of God, give my assent to the suppressing of the said exercises.' This challenge to the Queen's authority was accompanied by a request that she should refer all ecclesiastical matters of doctrine and discipline to her bishops. To accompany this challenge came the reminder: 'Remember, Madam, that you are a mortal creature.' This missive drove Elizabeth to a pitch of fury; however, she was advised that she could not get rid of him, and therefore she suspended him from his juridical duties as archbishop. He continued to hold office for another five years, thus causing a 'suspended' archbishop to be added to the indiscipline of the Church that Elizabeth was so keen should be broad but ordered.

Following the appointment of Archbishop Whitgift in 1583 there was an attempt to restore order in the Church but it is clear that group Bible study continued. The Jesuit William Weston, travelling incognito round the country in the decade between 1588 and 1598, records in his autobiography, published in 1611, an account of such a group: 'Each of them had his own Bible and assiduously turned pages and looked up the text cited by the preachers, discussing the passages among themselves to see whether they had quoted them to the point and accurately.'[12] Now this may not have been as irreverent as an alehouse disputation; it was deemed nevertheless to be potentially even more dangerous.

However, within the continuing Roman Catholic Church, the successors to those early visionaries of the early sixteenth century were continuing to press for vernacular Scriptures which would not be tainted

12 *William Weston: The Autobiography of an Elizabethan* (London, 1955).

by heresy and error, as many of the vernacular translations were deemed to be. English Catholic exiles at Rheims undertook to produce their own translations based on the Latin Vulgate. They were particularly targeting the Puritans in England as their real enemies, but they were not preparing their translations for the kind of popular use that was later described by our visiting Jesuit. In the Preface to the Rheims Bible (1582), the editors write:

> The Protestants, such as St Paul calleth *ambulantes in astutia*; walkers in deceitfulness [2 Cor. 4: 2] have so abused the people, and many other in the world, not unwise that by their false translations they have, instead of God's Law and Testament and for Christ's written will and word, given them their own wicked writing and fantasies most shamefully in all their versions, Latin, English and other tongues, corrupting both the letter and the sense by false translation, adding, detracting, altering, transposing, pointing, and all other guileful means; especially where it serves for the advantage of their private opinions.[13]

The issue of social control also preoccupies the writer of the Rheims preface. There is a description of how the laity in the primitive church read Scripture: 'The virgins did meditate upon the places and examples of chastity, modesty and demureness; the married, on conjugal faith and continency; the parents how to bring up their children in faith and fear of God; the prince, how to rule; the subject, how to obey; the priest, how to teach; the people, how to learn.' This reflects the kind of thinking expressed in 'ruminatio' and also Cranmer's instinct as he was writing his preface to the Great Bible forty years earlier. The English Catholics at Rheims were clear that in former times it was not possible to put translated Bibles 'in the hands of every husbandman, artificer, apprentice, boys, girls, mistress, maid, man'; or that they should be

> sung, played, alleged, of every tinker, taverner, rhymer, minstrel; that they were for table talk, for ale benches, for boats and barges, and for every profane person and company. No, in those better times men were neither so ill, nor so curious of themselves, so to abuse the blessed book of Christ; neither was there any such easy means before printing was invented, to disperse the copies into the hands of every man, as now there is.[14]

In fact at this date only the New Testament was produced and the Catholics had to wait until 1609, when the Old Testament was completed and the Bible was reissued in what became known as the 'Douay' version. In the preface to that completed Bible, it is stated:

---

[13] 'Preface to the Rheims New Testament 1582', in *Documents of the English Reformation*, ed. G. Bray, pp. 375–6.

[14] Ibid., p. 378.

'Seeing therefore that dangers and hurts happen in many, the careful chief pastors in God's Church have always moderated the reading of Holy Scriptures according to persons, times and other circumstances; prohibiting some and permitting some, to have and read them in their mother tongue.'[15]

When in 1583 Grindal died, Elizabeth nominated as his successor John Whitgift. A former professor of divinity and Master of Pembroke Hall and of Trinity College in Cambridge, Whitgift was theologically Calvinist but, in matters of church order, a convinced Church of England person. He wished for a strong and unified national church, impervious alike to papal and extreme Puritan influence. He was the perfect archbishop for Richard Hooker, who was to become the great exponent of the Church of England and of its particular and especial place. Hooker was a protégé of Jewel and became a Fellow of Corpus Christi College, Oxford, in 1577. Among his students were George Cranmer, a great-nephew of the archbishop, and Edwin Sandys, whose father became Archbishop of York.

According to Izaak Walton, it was after Hooker had forfeited his Fellowship by marrying Joan Churchman 'who brought him neither portion nor beauty',[16] that he was visited by his former students while he was rector of Drayton Beauchamp. They found him beset by domestic duties, unhappy and unable to pursue his scholarship. Sandys wrote to his father, the Archbishop of York, who nominated Hooker for the post of Master of the Temple. The Archbishop of Canterbury's own candidate had not been acceptable and Hooker was appointed. It was here that he made his reputation; it was later that he began his great work, *A Treatise on the Laws of Ecclesiastical Polity*.

Book V of *The Laws* was published in 1597 and dedicated to John Whitgift, the Archbishop of Canterbury, who was having particular trouble with the Puritan wing of the church, which was perceived as trying 'to erect a popular authority of elders and take away episcopal jurisdiction'. Hooker, like Whitgift, perceived the Church of England to be concerned with *to konos* – the public and common good as opposed to 'my particular good'. As he goes on to explain, Hooker perceived the basis for private judgement made for 'my particular good' as deriving from a partial and partisan interpretation of Scripture. Hooker acknowledges that there are problems in reading and interpreting the Scriptures, and that there are apparent contradictions in Scripture. In a list of such interpretations, Hooker writes:

---

15 Ibid., p. 403.
16 Izaak Walton, *The Life of Mr Richard Hooker* (1665), republished in R. Hooker, *Works*, ed. John Keble, based on the text of 1836 (Oxford, 1841), p. 17.

In setting down that miracle at the sight of which Peter fell down astonied before the feet of Jesus, and cried, 'Depart, Lord, I am a sinner', the Evangelist St Luke saith the store of fish which they took was such that the net they took it in 'brake' and the ships which they loaded therewith sunk; St John recording the like miracle saith, that albeit the fishes in number were so many, yet the net with so great a weight was 'not broken'.[17]

In suggesting that two miracles are here being described, rather than different versions of the same one, Hooker relies on the authority of the Church as the proper interpreter of Scripture. 'The principal cause of *writing* the Gospel was that it might be preached upon or interpreted by public ministers authorized thereunto.' It would seem that Hooker is still following the precept of his friend's great-uncle in expecting that the Scriptures should be read publicly in church. 'The reading therefore of the Word of God, as the use has ever been, in open audience, is the plainest evidence we have of the Church's Assent and Acknowledgement that it is his Word.'[18] Hooker criticizes Puritan preachers for using the Scriptures as jumping-off points for their sermons, and choosing without care and discrimination. For him the ordered and open reading of Scriptures in the public services authorized by the Church in the Book of Common Prayer meant that there was not a pick-and-mix system, but that the whole of God's Word was unfolded publicly in an orderly way and in a prayerful context. That is the way that Scripture should be dealt with, and the way it is dealt with in this Church of England. For such kind of reading there needs to be a translation which lies somewhere between 'the rigour of literal translators and the liberty of the paraphrasts'.[19]

Hooker's views not only sum up the position of Whitgift in his struggles to bring order to the Church in the decades between 1580 and the turn of the century, but also set the tone for the way in which the Church of England was to use and expound Scripture in the following century. It seems to me that the struggle throughout the century was not mainly about differences in faith between those of large opinions, as for example between Church of England and Lutheran or Church of England and Calvinist; many of the Church of England divines espoused views which were held in such categories. Rather the concern was for private opinions formed either alone or in groups outside the Church's influence, which might give rise to personal idiosyncratic behaviour or a public disorder.

---

17 Richard Hooker, *Of the Laws of Ecclesiastical Polity*, in R. Hooker, *Works*, ed. J. Keble.
18 Ibid.
19 Ibid.

Of course it is important that we do not idealize the manner in which the Word was preached with authority in the ordinary parish church. A Puritan source noted in the 1570s:

> In all their order of service [that is, the Church of England] there is no edification according to the rule of the Apostle, but confusion. They tosse the psalms in most places like tennise balles. The people, some standing, some walking, some talking, some reading, some praying by themselves, attend not to the minister. ... When the Old Testament is read, or the lessons, they make no reverence; but when the Gospel cometh then they al stand up. ... When Jesus is named, then of goeth the cappe, and down goeth the knees, with suche scraping on the ground, that they cannot hear a good while after, so that the Word is hindered, but when other names of God are mentioned they make no courtesie at all.[20]

The Word was also sometimes ignored: 'Verily a man may come into some churches and see the Bible so inclosed in dust, evenes the pulpit is in like manner with both dust and cobwebs, that with his finger he may write on the Bible this epitaph, *ecce nunc in pulvero dormio*'.

When, on Elizabeth's death in 1603, James VI of Scotland became James I of England, he travelled immediately to London under the new style of King of Great Britain. He was met by Puritans who presented the Millenary Petition. Prevaricating, he suggested a conference, to be held at Hampton Court. And it was here that he responded to the urging of Dr John Rainolds, President of Corpus Christi College, Oxford, that a new translation of the Bible should be undertaken, and this appeared as the 'Authorized Version' of 1611. Although it was seven years in preparation, nine-tenths of the Authorized Version's New Testament is Tyndale's. The same is true of the first half of the Old Testament, which was as much as Tyndale had been able to translate before he was executed outside Brussels in 1536.

By the beginning of the new reign, the codes of control imposed by the Elizabethan establishment had worked only to a limited degree. The Book of Common Prayer was firmly in place and had become extremely popular with 'middle England'. It had received minor alterations before being reissued by royal authority in 1604. There was a solid core who continued to receive the social message of the vernacular Bible in the way that the Establishment desired. But people of all sorts, including young men educated at university, had discovered biblical alternatives to the hierarchical society and episcopal church that the Establishment was seeking to preserve; and the vernacular Bible in its different versions – but

---

[20] Quoted in Judith Maltby, *Prayer Book and People in Elizabethan and Early Stuart England* (Cambridge, 1998).

chiefly the Geneva Bible – had already sowed seeds of private judgement in a society where political and social tensions were accumulating.

During the sixteenth century, as the vernacular Bible was struggling to make its influence felt, there had also been various attempts to revise Canon Law, notably in 1553 and 1571. Indeed, the process had started soon after Henry VIII's break with Rome, but there was a majority reluctance to proceed with it until it was clear what sort of church the Church of England was to become, and therefore what canons were needed to guide it. There was a strong desire to keep a familiar structure in place until what was needed to support the new royal structures was clear. So there was piecemeal legislation until the canons of 1604. While much of the content of the new canons grew from the old pre-Reformation Canon Law and there was confirmation of revisions that had occurred in legislation deemed necessary to meet particular circumstances, the new canons contained three of importance to the Bible. They covered the same ground as a proclamation issued in 1573, and were aimed to ensure that priests of the Established Church should not take part in the kind of Bible readings and prophesyings that led to 'private' interpretations of the Scriptures which might have a diverse and potentially dangerous social and political outcome. Canon 71 states that ministers are not to preach nor administer communion in private houses, Canon 72 states that they are not to appoint public or private fasts or prophesies or to exorcise but by authority, and Canon 73 forbids clergy of the Established Church to 'hold private conventicles'.[21]

This attempt to tighten up and make relevant the disciplinary procedures of the Church of England shows that the forms of social control introduced during Elizabeth's reign had not proved sufficient to win over everybody in a totally comprehensive church with a traditional view of hierarchical authority and social order. Permanent non-conformity had arrived, and with it an ever-present challenge to the Establishment.

The Authorized Version was essentially a work of revision, rather than an original work, and, as I have indicated, relied heavily on Tyndale. But the fifty-four divines, who ranged from the Puritan John Rainolds of Corpus Christi to the scholarly high churchman Lancelot Andrewes, paid careful attention to textual accuracy, correcting archaisms and ensuring a translation that would be readily understandable. They avoided theological controversy.

It is significant, but easily overlooked, that the title-page reminds the reader of earlier anxieties surrounding the vernacular Bible. It is

---

21 *Constitutions and Canons Ecclesiastical 1604* (Oxford, 1923).

'Appointed to be read in Churches', which is not only a way of saying that this is an approved official version, but a reminder that Bible reading is meant for church; this is the proper place for it to be read, rather than the home, the tavern or the conventicle. It was also assumed that it would be read aloud in churches, and the translators paid especial attention to words and cadences that would encourage *ruminatio* and *manducatio*. It was this very language that had an effect on the English people which it is difficult to find elsewhere. France, Italy and Holland had vernacular translations much earlier, and there were fourteen different versions of a vernacular German Bible between 1466 and Luther's Bible, but even there it can be argued that the influence on the language was not as great as in England.

Liah Greenfield writes that 'the reading of the Bible planted and nurtured among the common people in England a novel sense of human – individual – dignity, which was instantly to become one of their dearest possessions'.[22] It was Tyndale's translation, revised in the Authorized Version, that developed this special sense that the text was 'theirs', anglicizing God and making the Gospel culturally English, and contemporary. In a similar way to the manner in which artists were painting Nativity scenes in the cultural setting and dress of sixteenth-century life, so this text made the Gospel available to the English with such contemporary force that it widened the gap between England and Europe, reinforcing theological differences with a powerful cultural expression of English religion that was to encourage Euro-scepticism, even into the twentieth century.

But within England, in spite of the attempts to control and regulate Scripture throughout the sixteenth century and into the new reign, there was an inevitable shift in the English religion from what was basically a religion of ceremony to a religion based on conscience. Once individual conscience has been awakened and given authority by the ready availability of a text which can become memorable, there is always the potential for change. As Christopher Hill has said: 'Ceremonies are fixed by custom and authority; the society in which they are all-important ticks over in a changeless routine. The appeal to individual conscience opens up possibilities of disagreement.'[23]

In groups, these disagreements were discussed and possible new outcomes debated. Memorability was accentuated in word and song

---

[22] Quoted in Gerald Hammond, 'Tyndale's Bible and the Emergence of the English Nation State', in *'Reformation': Papers from the Oxford International Conference*, i (Oxford, 1996), p. 11.

[23] Christopher Hill, *The English Bible and the Seventeenth-Century Revolution* (London, 1992).

which often focused group purpose and identity. Songs based on the vernacular texts and frequently borrowing from their rhythms enlivened group Bible study, and sharpened its political edge as the seventeenth century proceeded. George Wither, described as 'a fanatical rhymer and an intemperate Puritan', published his *Hymns and Songs of the Church* in 1623. An example of his theme and style is to be found in his celebration of Jael, the wife of Heber the Kenite:

> She in her left hand took a nail
> And raised up in the right
> A workman's hammer wherewithal
> She Sisera did smite;
> His head she took
> When she had struck
> His pierced temple through;
> He fell withal
> And in the fall
> He at her feet did bow.[24]

Set to music by Orlando Gibbons, such songs brought biblical stories to life and stirred people up for action.

While the disruption to the social order, and the eventual civil war, that came to England in the seventeenth century cannot entirely be blamed on the influence of the vernacular Bible, it was a powerful ingredient, for the English had become a people of the Book, and this transition brought fragmentation to the monolithic concept of society that Tudor monarchs had tried to create and Stuart monarchs attempted to preserve.

Looking back to the beginnings of the story, it is an ironic and sad twist of fate that the Patriarch Joseph on his visit to Florence in 1438, fired with a dream of a single church and a single faith in Europe, should have contributed to further divisions and disagreements, both theological and cultural.

---

[24] George Wither, *Hymns and Songs of the Church* (1623).

CHAPTER NINE

The Bible and Protestant Inculturation in the *Homilies* of the Church of England

Luc Borot

To propagate the faith of the newly separated Church of England, the leaders of the episcopates of Henry VIII, Edward VI and Elizabeth I found it expedient to provide preachers with a ready-made set of homilies.[1] The two volumes of *Homilies* were to become one of the pillars of the established Church of England, along with the legislation on supremacy and uniformity, the *Book of Common Prayer*, Hooker's *Laws of Ecclesiastical Polity* and the Authorized Version of the Bible. The *Homilies* implicitly propound an original system of doctrinal authority, based on the Fathers and on Scripture. Though such sermons were supposed to be read to wide audiences, sophisticated references to the patristic tradition were offered for the meditation of the congregations. Scripture, whose presence was meant to emphasize the Protestant nature of the new Church, is used in a variety of ways, often changing the rhetorical status of biblical references in the *Homilies*. Scripture can be quoted, paraphrased, interpreted, or – more surprisingly in the case of prose meant to be vocally delivered – merely referred to in the marginalia of the book. To approach this very complex nexus of problems, I shall first set the *Homilies* in their historical context, then analyse the homilies that take the Bible as their subject matter, then examine the argumentative uses of Scripture, and finally

---

[1] I quote the facsimile edition, *Certaine Sermons or Homilies appointed to be read in Churches, in the time of the late Queen Elizabeth of famous memory*, eds Mary Ellen Rickey and Thomas B. Stroup, *STC* 13675 (London, 1623; Gainesville, FL, 1966). This is the edition, ordered by James I, that I shall refer to throughout this chapter. In quotations, the volume number will precede the page reference, as each volume has a separate pagination in the book. The first edition of the first volume was published in 1547, the first edition of the Elizabethan volume was issued in 1563, with an enlarged version in 1571. The marginalia pointing to biblical references are shown in square brackets in the quotations. *STC* references are to A.W. Pollard and G.R. Redgrave, *A Short-Title Catalogue of Books printed in England, Scotland and Ireland ... 1475–1640*, 3 vols (London, 1986, 1976, 1991).

look at some extra-biblical *exempla*. Behind these rhetorical questions, a double sociological and cultural question looms: in the deepest recesses of rural England in the Elizabethan era, were there many parishioners with the culture required to catch the subtleties of the patristic and biblical erudition of these landmarks of English prose? And as far as those endowed with the proper culture were concerned, could their consciences be properly edified, when the said masterpieces were droned from the pulpit by some semi-literate 'dumb dog', certainly baffled by the matter he was asked to read?

The history of the *Homilies*, close as it is to the history of the 'protestantization' of England, is a very political one.[2] The ideological orientations of the sermons were as closely scrutinized by the governors as their theological foundations. Cranmer had begun to write the first homilies about 1539, but their publication was postponed by the objections of some Catholic bishops of Henry VIII. The publication of the first volume was a capital political event, sealing the authorities' motivation in propagating the new faith. Among the churchmen who wrote the homilies, some, like Bishop Bonner, were less than convinced of the justification for the religious change that was happening, yet, when Bonner was leading the restoration of Catholicism in England under Mary, he retained the same political device, and he reissued some of the homilies, adding orthodox Catholic ones. At the accession of Elizabeth, she and her bishops, through the 1559 *Injunctions*, once more enforced the use of the 1547 text,[3] and before the publication of the second volume in 1563, the first had been reprinted four times. The last homily of the second volume, added for a new edition in 1571, was written for strictly political motives: after the Northumberland rebellion, it had seemed necessary to compose a more powerful discourse on obedience than the already available 'Exhortation to

---

2 The information about the history of the work comes from Ian Lancashire's introduction to his remarkable electronic critical edition of the *Homilies* in his series *Renaissance Electronic Texts*, on the Internet server of the University of Toronto, at the URL http://www.library.utoronto.ca/utel/ret/homilies/elizhom.html (Toronto, 1994); introductory material can be reached at the URL http://www.library.utoronto.ca/utel/ret/homilies/elizhomi.html.

3 *Iniunctions Geven by the Quenes Maiestie. Anno Domini M.D.LIX. The fyrst yeare of the raigne of our Soueraigne Lady Quene Elizabeth*, STC 10100 (London, 1559); *Tudor Royal Proclamations*, eds Paul L. Hughes and James F. Larkin, 2 vols (New Haven, CT, and London, 1969), ii, Proclamation 460, pp. 117–32; in the same collection, see also no. 461, 'appointing Homilies to be read in Churches', STC 13648, pp. 132–3; both are dated 'before 19 July 1559'.

Obedience' of the Edwardian volume. The 'Homily against Disobedience and wilful Rebellion' was to become the longest item of the whole volume.

It is not original to describe the Reformation in England as a political process resulting from a descending scheme of authority, but it is still difficult for some scholars to admit that massive popular adhesion to the new belief was far from widespread in the beginning. Yet the work of religious historians in the past twenty years has shown, in different ways, that Protestantism was not adopted with spontaneous enthusiasm by the English masses, and that the enforced 'stripping of the altars' was not everywhere popular.[4] It has been shown that Mary's reign saw a rise in the number of ordinations, whereas the number of ordinands under Edward VI had dwindled to almost nothing.[5] The English that Elizabeth began ruling at her accession in 1558 were still a Catholic people, which only a political design could forcibly convert into a 'Protestant nation'. It was to take a very long and agitated reign to achieve this: at the queen's death in 1603, the generations that had been brought up in Catholic England were almost extinct, and the dangers of recusancy had prompted many a formal conversion, a process that was only effectively perfected in the second generation, when parents who were 'Church Papists' had let their children be educated in the established Church. The development of sound, orthodox preaching, the 'reformation' of the clergy and the gradual spread of biblical knowledge were important factors in this inculturation of the new faith, but one should not underestimate the effect of the disappearance of the men and women who embodied the memory of the old religion in the families and local communities. The African thinker Amadou Hampate-Bâ compares the death of an old person in an oral culture with the burning of a library; Renaissance English society was such a culture.[6] The *Homilies* were, like

---

[4] Patrick Collinson, 'Elizabethan and Jacobean Puritanism as Forms of Popular Religious Culture', in Christopher Durston and Jacqueline Eales (eds), *The Culture of English Puritanism, 1560–1700* (London, 1996), pp. 1–31; Eamon Duffy, *The Stripping of the Altars: Traditional Religion in England c. 1400–c. 1580* (New Haven, CT, and London, 1992); Christopher Haigh, *English Reformations: Religion, Politics and Society under the Tudors* (Oxford, 1993); Ronald Hutton, *The Rise and Fall of Merry England* (Oxford, 1994); Kenneth Hylson Smith, *The Churches in England from Elizabeth I to Elizabeth II*, 2 vols (London, 1996), i: 1558–1688.

[5] Haigh, *English Reformations*, pp. 182, 215–16.

[6] Ibid., prologue: 'The Religious World of Roger Martyn', pp. 1–11, describes the mental world of the pre-Reformation English parishioner as it was remembered in Elizabeth's reign; Roger Martyn's text is printed in David Cressy and Lori Anne Ferrell (eds), *Religion and Society in Early Modern England, a Sourcebook* (London, 1996), 'The State of Melford Church as I, Roger Martyn, did know it', pp. 11–13. Martyn lived

many other printed artefacts of the time, instruments for the oral transmission of a new religious conception, imposed on the illiterate by the highly literate, a religious vision that was to be presented as a better support for social order, as well as a better path to salvation.

The two successive volumes combined theological information and moral education, both social and individual. The civil and religious authorities who sponsored the composition of the books seem to have intended to raise the people's moral standards at least as much as to sanctify them through the Protestant religion. The composition of the first volume reveals this double purpose: 'A fruitful Exhortation to the Reading of Holy Scripture', 'Of the Misery of all Mankind', 'Of the Salvation of all Mankind', 'Of the true and lively Faith', 'Of good Works', 'Of Christian Love and Charity', 'Against Swearing and Perjury', 'Of the Declining from God', 'An Exhortation against the Fear of Death', 'An Exhortation to Obedience', 'Against Whoredom and Adultery', 'Against Strife and Contention'. Of these twelve homilies, eight directly deal with theological issues of some difficulty, the other four with matters of morality and social behaviour, though some can be related to explicit commands of God, like those against swearing and adultery, whereas the others betray the authorities' preoccupation with civil disobedience in the kingdom and social peace in the local communities.

The second volume contains twenty-one homilies in the edition of 1571: 'Of the Right Use of the Church', 'Against Peril of Idolatry', 'For repairing and keeping clean the Church', 'Of Good Works: And first, of Fasting', 'Against Gluttony and Drunkenness', 'Against Excess of Apparel', 'An Homily of Prayer', 'Of the Place and Time of Prayer', 'Of Common Prayer and Sacraments', 'An Information of them which take Offence at certain Places of Holy Scripture', 'Of Alms Deeds', 'Of the Nativity', 'Of the Passion: for Good Friday', 'Of the Resurrection: for Easter Day', 'Of the worthy Receiving of the Sacrament', 'An Homily concerning the coming down of the Holy Ghost: for Whitsunday', 'An Homily for Rogation Week', 'Of the State of Matrimony', 'Against Idleness', 'Of Repentance and True Reconciliation unto God', 'An Homily against Disobedience and Wilful Rebellion'.[7] Apart from one

---

c. 1527–1615, and his memoir bears witness to the hopes that some 'Church papists' still entertained at the end of Elizabeth's reign, to see the old religion sanctioned again. Cressy and Ferrell quote William Parker, *The History of Long Melford* (London, 1873), pp. 70–73. Martyn must have been one of the oldest men alive in England at his death.

7 The titles of the homilies in these two lists are here given as in the list of contents at the beginning of the volume. As will be seen from the references in subsequent footnotes, the title at the head of each individual homily at times differs in details from these.

obviously political subject already mentioned, four homilies reveal the concerns of the Elizabethan clergy with the private morality and social manners of their flocks. Seven sermons are more directly concerned with doctrine and spirituality. Five homilies were meant to be used on specific liturgical occasions. The rest, though naturally religious, define matters of ecclesiastical practice and parish ordinance.

The tradition of the pre-Reformation Church is not systematically rejected. For instance, the persistence of some pre-Reformation ceremonies (matrimony, ordination, anointing of the sick, funerals, churching of women) was justified in the homily on common prayer and sacraments by their symbolic and pedagogical usefulness in the Church, with a particular insistence on the assertion that they could in no wise be considered as sacraments. Similarly, the second volume includes a series of sermons to be used during Rogation week, including a particular text to be used by the preacher on the occasion of the perambulation of the parish boundaries, to remind the participants of the fundamental principles of a society based on property. The Rogation rites happened to be one of the Puritans' main grudges against the alleged papistry of the Church of England, one of the marks of the insufficiency of the Reformation in the kingdom. The association of the compulsory homilies with the ceremonies of the 'Babylonian whore' helped to focus their opposition to the episcopal institutions.

In the two successive versions of the homilies, specific directions enforced the use of these official texts in the parishes wherever and whenever no authorized preacher was available. On Elizabeth's succession, one of the first measures taken by her administration in the field of religion was the regulation of preaching.[8] The Queen also issued injunctions to the clergy directing how worship should be conducted and how parishes should be furnished and organized, imposing the homilies published under her brother's reign as delivering the only doctrine fit to be preached.[9] The pretence to authority of the exiled radical Calvinists, as of those of the clergy who had accepted to return to Catholic practices under Mary, could thus be countered, and royal supremacy practically restored and asserted. The preface to the 1562 reprint of the Edwardian *Homilies* justifies the necessity to have the sermons imposed on the Church in these terms:

> to auoyd the manifold enormities which heretofore by false doctrine
> haue crept into the Church of God: and how that all they which are

---

[8] *Proclamation* [*forbidding unlicensed preaching*], 27 December 1558, STC 7889, *Tudor Royal Proclamations*, no. 451, pp. 102–3.

[9] *Iniunctions*, § 4, sig. A2^v–3^r, *Tudor Royal Proclamations*, p. 119; § 27, sig. C1^r, *Tudor Royal Proclamations*, p. 124.

appointed Ministers, haue not the gift of preaching sufficiently to
instruct the people, which is committed vnto them, whereof great
inconueniences might rise, and ignorance still be maintayned, if
some honest remedy be not speedily found and prouided.[10]

They were to be used by all ministers in the whole kingdom in a very
clearly defined liturgical framework:

> All which *Homilies*, her Maiesty commandeth, and straitly chargeth
> all Parsons, Vicars, Curates, and all other hauing spirituall cure,
> euery Sunday and Holyday in the yeere, at the ministring of the holy
> Communion, or if there be no Communion ministred that day, yet
> after the Gospel and Creede, in such order and place as is appointed
> in the *Booke of Common Prayers*, to reade and declare to their
> Parishioners plainely and distinctly one of the sayd *Homilies*, in
> such order as they stande in the Booke, except there be a Sermon,
> according as it is enioyned in the Booke of her Highnesse
> Iniunctions, and then for that cause onely, and for none other, the
> reading of the sayd *Homilie* to bee deferred vnto the next Sunday,
> or Holyday following. And when the foresayd *Booke of Homilies* is
> read ouer, her Maiesties pleasure is, that the same be repeated and
> read againe, in such like sort as was before prescribed.[11]

Once a month, a sermon was expected to be preached by the incumbent
or by an appointed preacher. The foreword to the second volume
exhorts the ministers to select the most appropriate homily and to divide
it between the morning and evening services, to accommodate the
listening capacities of their congregations, as it were, but it never
questions the necessity of making use of the set texts. The second
foreword also allows the ministers to change the Old Testament reading
for a New Testament passage if it seems more appropriate to the
edification of the flock, but the liturgical reference remains the
constitutionally compulsory *Book of Common Prayer*.[12]

Another legal document quoted in the two forewords is the
Injunctions issued by Elizabeth in 1559. These injunctions define the
duties of the ministers and parish officers in providing the clergy and the
community with the means to read and study the Bible directly. A large
Bible must be provided, with a Latin and Greek New Testament for the
minister to study by himself for his edification; the commentaries of
Erasmus on the New Testament must be available in the church,
alongside the Bible.[13] Some items must be purchased by the minister for

---

10 *Homilies*, I. sig. a2^r.

11 *Homilies*, I. sig. a2^v–3^r.

12 'An Admonition to all Ministers Ecclesiasticall', *Homilies*, II, unpaginated.

13 *Iniunctions*, § 6, sig. A3^{r-v}, *Tudor Royal Proclamations*, p. 119; § 16, sig. B1^v–2^r,
Tudor Royal Proclamations, p. 121.

his own use, others by the parish for the minister or for the community. The *Injunctions* involve the body of the Church, clergy and laity alike, in the national effort to inculturate the Bible and Protestantism in England. It should therefore be no wonder that the reading, studying and understanding of the Bible should be the topic of two homilies, one in each volume.

The first homily of the first volume, 'A Fruitful Exhortation to the Reading and Knowledge of Holy Scripture', was intended to strike the keynote of the religious changes undertaken by the Crown and by the clergy who were actively supporting the new form of religion. It addresses the individual believer, suggesting a new orientation for his or her spiritual life, which now ought to concentrate on the word of God, rather than on Mary and the saints, and strive towards an intimate knowledge of God's will, not the accumulation of good works through – often repetitive – devotion. The private scrutiny of the Bible was expected to replace such vocal prayers as the rosary in the personal devotion of the English Christian. The other sermon, in the second volume, which is not an 'exhortation' but an 'information', aims at clearing the Scriptures from aspersions cast by opponents, such as the alleged 'uncleanness' of the patriarchs of the Old Testament. After about a quarter of a century of 'reformation', some objections seem to have kept emerging from some people, and from some of the clergy who still looked back to the old religion; and there were fears that immoral arguments might be derived by antinomians from the same places of Holy Writ. The implied audience of 1563 was less ignorant of Protestantism and Scripture than the implied audience of 1547, and both sceptics and recusants – hidden or public – had to be convinced, edified and converted. The same evolution seems true of the authors themselves, since in neither volume did they use a single translation as their source, but rather seem to have translated or paraphrased the original texts. For instance, the histories are still called after their names in the Septuagint or Vulgate, a practice which endured in the 1563 and 1571 texts. Likewise, the Psalms were still numbered as in the Vulgate.

The first volume of *Homilies* aptly begins with an 'exhortation' to become acquainted with what, according to the reformed religion, was the foundation of all Christian belief. *Scriptura sola, fide sola*: the theology of the book conforms with these two crucial axioms of the Reformation. Scripture is the food and support of faith, the light of the soul. The sermon defines what the Bible is, why it should have a primordial importance in the Christian's life, and how it should be read and digested.

The Bible is less described than defined. The list of books and the division between New and Old Testaments are never touched upon. On the other hand, the encomium of the Holy Writ dominates the rhetorical strategy in the first section:

> For in holy Scripture is fully contayned what we ought to doe, and what to eschew; what to beleeue, what to loue, and what to looke for at Gods hand at length. In these Books we shall finde the father from whom, the sonne by whom, and the holy Ghost, in whom all things haue their being and keeping vp, and these three persons to be but one God, and one substance. In these books we may learne to know our selues, how vile and miserable we be, and also to know God, how good he is of himselfe, and how hee maketh vs and all creatures partakers of his goodnesse.[14]

The teaching of Scripture reveals orthodox Trinitarian theology, it makes the believer aware of his condition and of God's bounty. To embrace true Christianity and reject the old superstitions, the believer is exhorted to look for 'the Well of Life in the bookes of the New and Old Testament, and not to runne to the stinking puddles of mens traditions (deuised by mens imagination) for our iustification and saluation'.[15] Such theological additions as the doctrine of Purgatory, transubstantiation or auricular confession are the matters to be understood by the phrase 'the stinking puddles' of human invention. Human tradition is here denied authority, but the Fathers are more than once called upon to support the preacher's argument with the mere sound of their names: Augustine, St John Chrysostom and Fulgentius add credit to the praise of the Word.[16]

When trying to explain why the Bible should be the core of the faithful's religious lives, the names of the Reformers are never called upon; neither is the intellectual movement of the previous decades ever mentioned in either book of *Homilies*. The version of Reformation history that the listeners received was a story of purification, not a dramatic breach from a tradition to which most English Christians were deeply attached. The author of the first homily seems more inclined to present the sweetness of reformed devotion than to launch an attack on the polluted streams of superstition. God's own argument should be sufficient to justify the demand to base one's spiritual life on His word, but the very scope of the Bible is a valid argument with which to open the sermon:

---

14 *Homilies*, 'A Fruitfull Exhortation to the Reading and Knowledge of Holy Scripture', I. 2.

15 Ibid.

16 Ibid.

> To a Christian man there can bee nothing either more necessarie or
> profitable, then the knowledge of holy Scripture, forasmuch as in it
> is conteyned Gods true word, setting foorth his glory, and also mans
> duety. And there is no trueth nor doctrine necessarie for our
> iustification and euerlasting saluation, but that is (or may bee)
> drawne out of that fountaine and Well of trueth.[17]

Twenty-one marginalia refer the reader to biblical passages, four of them
to the Old Testament; but the books of the Bible are not mentioned in
the actual text, which the congregation were expected only to hear. Was
the preacher allowed to quote from them to his audience? The logic of
the foreword of 1563 seems to allow for it, but there is no clear evidence
for it, and none in the 1547 edition. Yet the Gospels are paraphrased
whenever Christ's own words are alluded to. When the preacher says
that the Bible is the best part, the one which Mary chose, is the illiterate
listener supposed to know that he is referring to Martha's sister, not to
the mother of Jesus? When he uses Paul's image of the two-edged sword,
could anyone – in 1547 or even in 1563 – but another cleric draw a
parallel with the Apostle to the Gentiles, unless the preacher added the
information for the sake of catechizing? The rhetoric of the author
mostly consists in weaving evangelical allusions into a specific idiom,
whose brilliance is only accessible to the happy very few who could
listen for them in English, whereas most of these few would certainly
have a better acquaintance with the Latin than with the English text:

> [I]t is a more excellent iewell or treasure, then any gold or precious
> stone, it is more sweet then hony, or hony combe, it is called the best
> part, which Mary did choose [Luke 10], for it hath in it euerlasting
> comfort. The wordes of holy Scripture be called words of euer
> lasting life [John 6]: for they bee Gods instrument, ordayned for the
> same purpose. They haue power to turne through Gods promise,
> and they be effectuall through Gods assistance, and (being receiued
> in a faithfull heart) they haue euer an heauenly spirituall working in
> them: they are liuely, quicke, and mighty in operation, and sharper
> then any two edged sword, and entreth thorow, euen vnto the
> diuiding asunder of the soule and the spirit, of the ioynts and the
> marrow [Heb. 4]. Christ calleth him a wise builder, that buildeth
> vpon his word [Matt. 7], vpon his sure and substantiall foundation.
> By this word of God, wee shall bee iudged: for the word that I
> speake (sayth Christ) is it, that shall iudge in the last day [John 12].
> Hee that keepeth the word of Christ, is promised the loue and
> fauour of God [John 14], and that hee shall bee the dwelling place
> or temple of the blessed Trinity.[18]

The author or editor could also have added 1 Corinthians 3: 16 and 6:

---

[17] Ibid., I. 1.
[18] Ibid., I. 2–3.

19, and 2 Corinthians 6: 16 in the margins for the last metaphor, based on Paul's image of the 'temple of God' or 'temple of the Holy Ghost'. Weaving, as it were, the Apostle's shifted metaphor of the sword into the expression of Christ's promises, the author sets himself on a level with Paul, the first commentator of Christ's words in the Scriptures themselves. By omitting to name Paul as the author of the most powerful metaphors, the author silently establishes the preacher's rhetorical stance as one of the most authoritative human voices in the Bible. Paul is a mirror for preachers, as Christ must be a mirror for every Christian, a model which can properly be imitated only by those who appropriate his word by reading.[19]

'These Bookes therefore ought to bee much in our hands, in our eyes, in our eares, in our mouths, but most of all in our hearts', the preacher says.[20] The rhetorical progression from the sense of touch to the seat of feelings conveys the programme of the Reformation for the individual who wishes to deepen his love of God: own a Bible, read the Bible, listen to the Word of God and to the ministers thereof, and appropriate its message with love. The first part of this homily explains why the Bible must be read and meditated on, but the second describes the method for such reading and answers some objections to the reading of the Bible by all believers.

Two main objections are raised rhetorically by the author: (i) the Bible is too difficult; (ii) the individual's capacities are too weak to enable him to read it with profit. Each objection is met with proper reasons, to persuade the listeners that they should not listen to such arguments from difficulty or weakness. Shifted metaphors and similes are applied to strike the imagination, Augustine's authority is much invoked, and his own similes are repeated to confirm the preacher's point. As a landscape, the Bible has low and high points, some parts that can be easily reached, others for which stronger capacities are required, but how shall the weak become strong if they do not exert their powers?[21] Neither difficulty nor ignorance can be entertained as reasons for abstaining from reading the Word. Similes from the people's professional lives also bring the matter closer to their daily experience.[22]

To counter the objection that weakness of parts may lead the ignorant into error, the preacher praises humility:

---

[19] Though Paul's authorship of the Epistle to the Hebrews is no longer regarded as a valid hypothesis, the epistle was generally believed in the sixteenth century to have been written by him.

[20] *Homilies*, 'A Fruitfull Exhortation ...', I. 2.

[21] Ibid., I. 5–6.

[22] Ibid., I. 4–5.

> Read it humbly with a meeke and lowly heart, to the intent you may
> glorifie God, and not your selfe, with the knowledge of it: and read
> it not without dayly praying to God, that he would direct your
> reading to good effect: and take vpon you to expound it no further,
> then you can plainely vnderstand it. ... For humility will only search
> to know the truth, it will search, and will bring together one place
> with another, and where it cannot finde out the meaning, it will
> pray, it will aske of other that know, and will not presumptuously
> and rashly define any thing, which it knoweth not. Therefore the
> humble man may search any trueth boldly in the Scripture, without
> any danger of errour. And if he be ignorant, he ought the more to
> read and to search holy Scripture, to bring him out of ignorance.[23]

The humble reader, comparing, collating places, will try and test both
the texts and his capacities, and be exalted by his findings. As
presumption and pride can indeed conduce to error, so the humble and
ignorant are those *par excellence* who must peruse the Word with profit.
Prayer and reading are not exclusive of each other, but collaborate to
improve the Christian's intimacy with his God: the devout soul
presented in this passage is praying for wisdom, like Solomon, so to
speak, with similar benefit.

Against the argument from the obscurity of the texts, an already
classic Protestant argument is offered: for the individual, as for the
Church, the Spirit will, in time, bless the readers with a light that will
make mysteries seem obvious:

> Although many things in the Scripture be spoken in obscure
> mysteries, yet there is nothing spoken vnder darke mysteries in one
> place, but the selfe same thing in other places, is spoken more
> familiarly and plainly, to the capacity both of learned and
> vnlearned. And those things in the Scripture that be plaine to
> vnderstand, and necessary for saluation, euery mans duty is to
> learne them, to print them in memory, and effectually to exercise
> them. And as for the darke mysteries, to bee contented to bee
> ignorant in them, vntill such time as it shall please God to open
> those things vnto him. In the meane season, if he lacke either
> aptnesse or opportunity, God will not impute it to his folly: but yet
> it behoueth not, that such as bee apt, should set aside reading,
> because some other be vnapt to read: neuerthelesse, for the
> hardnesse of such places, the reading of the whole ought not to be
> set apart.[24]

These arguments strengthen the previous ones. Humility is necessary,
too, to be 'contented' with temporary ignorance, if confidence teaches
the believer that he will in time be enlightened. Humility, patience,

---

[23] Ibid., I. 5.
[24] Ibid., I. 6.

confidence are virtues that the moral homilies frequently praise and commend in man's life in society, but they are also necessary for the proper development of reformed religiosity. In this homily, the devotional and cultural project of the volume's designers was producing its first model of reformed Christian devotion.

However, the author, or authors, were neglecting an important social and cultural dimension of the religious change they were promoting: reading the Word of God required a basic skill for which as yet there was no systematic and voluntarist development in England (contrary to what was happening in Scotland). Literacy ought to have been sponsored throughout the realm, but it was not. Under Edward VI, grammar schools were created, and school foundations were encouraged, but they only concerned an elite of the young people; and though at the time of the reprinting of the first volume, Elizabeth's *Injunctions* would exhort richer clergymen to present gifted boys with exhibitions to help them become ministers in their turn, and would instruct schoolmasters to teach their pupils formulae from the Scriptures, there was no basic encouragement of systematic popular education in the most basic skills of literacy.[25] This may explain this incidental remark in our homily: 'I say not nay, but a man may prosper with onely hearing, but hee may much more prosper, with both hearing and reading.'[26] Two orders of believers were henceforth delineated: those who could only trust their ministers' preaching, and those who could search the Bible for themselves. In the cultural construction of the 'Puritan' mentality, this distinction was to be of no little value. Some theological and cultural provision was also to prove necessary to avoid the alienation from Christianity of those who might find in the Word an occasion for scandal.

The early Elizabethan bishops were aware of disagreements with the liberty to read the Bible that the Reformation was granting to every Christian. The 'Information for such as take Offence at some Parts of Holy Scripture', in the second volume, was there to identify the enemies of the Word and to explain why the Bible contained such scandalous stories as, for instance, the episode of Lot's daughters.

---

[25] *Iniunctions*, § 12, sig. B1ʳ, *Tudor Royal Proclamations*, p. 121; § 40–42, sig. C3ʳ, *Tudor Royal Proclamations*, pp. 126–7. On literacy and schooling, see David Cressy, 'Levels of Literacy in England, 1530–1730', *Historical Journal*, **20**.1 (1977), pp. 1–23, and Margaret Spufford, 'First Steps in Literacy: The Reading and Writing Experiences of the Humblest Seventeenth-Century Spiritual Autobiographers', *Social History*, **4**.3 (1979), pp. 407–35. I have synthesized the cultural implications of illiteracy in Luc Borot, 'Culture des élites et culture(s) populaire(s) du règne d'Elisabeth à la Restauration: ponts et points de passage dans les productions visuelles et écrites', *XVII–XVIII. Bulletin de la Société d'études anglo-américaines des XVIIᵉ et XVIIIᵉ siècles*, 46 (June 1998), pp. 7–34.

[26] *Homilies*, 'A Fruitfull Exhortation ...', I. 5.

After a summary of the reasons for reading the Bible already expressed in the first homily, the preacher draws a list of objections to the widespread knowledge of the book. To some 'delicate wits' and courtiers, the language of the Bible is too coarse; to others, some characters commit actions against the laws of God and man, and against 'public honesty'. Another set of critics objects to the example of the diversity of rites under the ancient law. Worse, some consider that the people's knowledge of the principles of charity taught by Christ is a hindrance to the advancement of their worldly business, for, the writer says, 'carnall reason, being alway an enemie to God, and not perceiuing the things of Gods spirit, doth abhorre such precepts, which yet rightly vnderstood, infringeth no iudiciall policies, nor Christian mens gouernements'.[27] The first 'exhortation' insists that the Bible is good for all Christians, whatever rank they occupy in society; this 'information' stresses from the beginning that some men in authority or in high places are enemies of God's Word and slaves to the flesh.

The modern reader may be surprised that the preacher should start his polemic by a point of form in the law of the levirate: the widow whose husband had died without issue by her would spit in her brother-in-law's face and take off his shoe if he refused to marry her. That practice seems to have struck some critics as ridiculous, but the issues of incest or polygamy possibly involved are not raised. The form of the rite is justified: it means opprobrium on the man and his descent.[28] The metaphor of the horns, standing for power, in Psalms 75 and 132, also has to be cleared of the accusation of impropriety:[29]

> Now I pray you, what vncomely manner of speech is this, so vsed in common phrase among the Hebrewes? It is a shame that Christian men should bee so light headed, to toy as ruffians doe with such manner speaches, vttered in good graue signification by the holy Ghost. More reasonable it were for vaine men to learne to reuerence the fourme of Gods wordes, then to sport at them to their damnation.[30]

The language of the Bible belonged to a certain historical people's culture, as far as its imagery is concerned, though it remains relevant for the Christians of the present. The Holy Ghost is eternal and his message is universal, though he first addressed mankind in the language of the Hebrews, the chosen people. This looks like a historicization of the

---

[27] *Homilies*, 'An Information of them which take Offence at certain Places of Holy Scripture', II. 146.

[28] Ibid.

[29] Ibid.

[30] Ibid., II. 147.

sacred text, but one should be wary of such anachronistic interpretations, as we shall see.

A historical and sociological explanation is provided for the number of wives and concubines of the patriarchs in Genesis. The marriage practices that obtained in the world of Genesis are described and explained, and the commentary explains how far this could be made legal for those exceptional figures:

> The plurality of wiues, was by a speciall prerogatiue suffered to the fathers of the olde Testament, not for satisfying their carnall and fleshly lustes, but to haue many children, because euery one of them hoped, and begged oft times of God in their prayers, that that blessed seede, which God promised should come into the world to breake the serpents head, might come and be borne of his stocke and kinred.[31]

The exception is theologically justified through an anachronistic device: the first generations after Adam are depicted as a people eager to bring about mankind's redemption in the nearest possible future. While this reveals some knowledge of Judaism, since every Jewish newborn boy is potentially the Messiah, it cannot be supported within the book of Genesis, since the promise of a redeemer is never expressed in it, unless a typological reading is applied to the whole Bible (a traditional mode of interpretation that the Reformation was to develop in its own way). This is one of the reasons why the Elizabethan bishops' sense of 'historical' criticism should not be exaggerated.

When referring to Noah's drunkenness and nakedness, Lot's incest, or David and Solomon's polygamy, the exemplarity of the biblical figures is reversed, and the sense of God's law is invoked as the Christian's moral common sense:

> Which things wee see plainely to bee forbidden vs by the law of God, and are now repugnant to all publike honestie. ... But wee ought rather to beleeue and to iudge that Noe in his drunkennesse offended God highly. Lot lying with his daughters, committed horrible incest. Wee ought then to learne by them this profitable lesson, that if so godly men as they were, which otherwise felt inwardly Gods holy Spirit inflaming in their hearts, with the feare and loue of God, could not by their owne strength keepe themselues from committing horrible sin, but did so grieuously fall, that without Gods great mercy they had perished euerlastingly: How much more ought wee then, miserable wretches, which haue no feeling of God within vs at all, continually to feare, not onely that we may fall as they did, but also be ouercome and drowned in sinne, which they were not?[32]

---

[31] Ibid.
[32] Ibid., II. 148.

It is not easy, then, to draw a line between the patriarchs' legitimate, and Solomon's sinful polygamy. Was Moses' law a factor of differentiation between them? The Bible appears much more complex a document in this homily than in the previous one, since it now seems open to contradictory modes of interpretation: how is the reader to know when polygamy is right or wrong? The first homily has given a clue: those who do not understand some passages must ask those who are likely to know, who were likely to be the clergy. Yet this quotation adds another clue: if we know the law of God, we are aware that these practices are forbidden to us, and we cannot go astray in our interpretation of these cases.

The second part of the 'Information' deals with evangelical morality. 'Politique wise men' scorn the precepts of the Sermon on the Mount and the rules of charity defined in the Gospels and Epistles of the New Testament. These men deem the Gospels 'to destroy all order in gouernance',

> for that Christes precepts should seeme to destroy all order in gouernance, as they doe alleadge for example, such as these bee. If any man strike thee on the right cheeke, turne the other vnto him also. If any man will contend to take thy coate from thee, let him haue cloke and all. Let not thy left hand know what thy right hand doeth. If thine eye, thine hand, or thy foote offend thee, pull out thine eye, cut off thine hand, thy foote, and cast it from thee. If thine enemie (saith Saint Paul) be an hungred, giue him meate, if hee bee thirstie, giue him drinke: so doing thou shalt heape hote burning coales vpon his head.[33]

The preacher weaves together several fundamental evangelical quotations to heap shame on the critics' heads. Christ wants his followers to be self-denying people, averse to revenge, and this has nothing to do with political disobedience. The Christian who follows the precepts of the Gospels will be renewed in the spirit and must change his mode of thinking when he tries to understand the Word:

> [R]eason must giue place to Gods holy spirite, you must submit your worldly wisedome and iudgement, vnto his diuine wisedome and iudgement. Consider that the Scripture, in what strange fourme soeuer it bee pronounced, is the word of the liuing God.[34]

The rules of Bible-reading are here repeated in different terms, but the principle of humility which the first homily of 1547 had defined remains valid. The antitheses between the spirit and the flesh, God and the world, are extended to an opposition between the spirit and reason.

[33] Ibid., II. 149.
[34] Ibid.

Two difficulties must now be considered, at the end of the presentation of the *Homilies'* defence of private biblical devotion. Which intellectual or spiritual currents are hidden behind the 'offences' denounced by the author of the 'Information'? And even after such a potent encomium of the Scriptures, what are the potential dangers of free Bible-reading that seem to remain in the minds of the *Homilies'* promoters?

The dangers of private interpretation were often put forward by Catholics on the grounds of man's weakness of understanding, and of the difficulties of some parts of the text. The assertion that it was offensive could also be a hypocritical way of advocating the prohibition of Bible-reading, without necessarily revealing one's attachment to the old religion. The points at issue selected by the author of this homily on this account are singularly extra-religious, as if the general line of the homily's argument against them was the 'carnality' of the opponents it intended to expose. The worldly-wise politicians are countered with more religious arguments, advocating Christianity's most primordial principles in Christ's own words, as if the enemy were more insidiously dangerous than the papists. Who are these carnal politicians? Is the author pointing towards a Machiavellian influence in English political circles? Is he referring to a surge of Roman or Athenian influence that might sever political reflection from Christian principles? He may be referring to a nexus of such continental intellectual influences in the wake of humanism, with which members of the gentry and nobility could sympathize. Practical politicians could be tempted to emancipate themselves from the rules of charity for efficiency's sake, opposing the laws of nature to God's principles of self-denial, turning their backs on the Bible for the sake of a near-stoic, pagan system of moral values independent of transcendent revelation. When such a movement was only in the process of emerging, this open attack against ruthless would-be governors reveals a very astute perception of some ideological and intellectual movements in the elites of English society.[35]

The conclusion of the homily answers, in passing, the objection concerning the diversity of rites under the old covenant. It does so by a reference to the device of typology:

> And though in sundry places of the Scriptures, bee set out diuers
> Rites and Ceremonies, oblations and sacrifices: let vs not thinke

---

[35] See Emile Gasquet, *Le Courant machiavélien dans la pensée et la littérature anglaises du XVIᵉ siècle* (Paris, 1974); Felix Raab, *The English Face of Machiavelli* (London, 1964); or Luc Borot, 'Conseiller, courtisan, citoyen: trois figures de la participation politique du sujet dans l'Angleterre moderne', in Luc Borot (ed.), *Civisme et citoyenneté: une longue histoire* (Montpellier, 1999), pp. 93–141.

strange of them, but referre them to the times and people for whom they serued, although yet to learned men they be not vnprofitable to be considered, but to be expounded as figures and shadowes of things and persons, afterward openly reuealed in the new Testament.[36]

Typology presents the faithful with a pattern of progress in the revelation of God's truth to men, since the New Testament opens the meaning of some obscurities of the Old. The process of meditation and revelation outlined in the first homily is supposed to continue this revelation for the Church and for each of its members.

The very idea of this homily seems, however, to betray an anxiety on the part of the Protestant elites of the country, and in particular on the part of the clergy: the homily is based on questions, doubts, objections and attacks probably reported from various quarters of English society. Puritan prophesyings could begin to encourage 'wild' preaching by uneducated people. Sectarian movements were also likely to break the unity of the Church. Worse than this, the memory of the Anabaptist rising of Münster in the 1530s remained a European trauma forever associated with the excesses of unbridled religious reformation. If the promoters of each book of *Homilies* were so sincere and enthusiastic about the private reading of the Bible, they would never have imposed their sermons on the whole Church.

When the authors of the *Homilies* are not preaching on the Bible, they keep quoting it in different ways. There are several ways to approach or use the biblical texts, most of which are illustrated in the two volumes of *Homilies*, but only two will be considered here: how they are used and applied, or even manipulated, and how they are commented on and interpreted.

One of the rhetorical difficulties of the English Reformation resulted from the descending structure of authority that imposed it on the parishes. It could lead to paradoxical stances that the 'godly party' would be very keen to use to the Church's detriment. On the other hand, many English Christians must have been wondering why they were being liberated in such an authoritarian way from a yoke whose weight they had never felt, and the homilies seem to have been written from a comparatively traditionalist point of view to avoid offending such parishioners. The rhetorical stance adopted was that of an authoritative voice, warranting with its own authority the substitution of the Bible's for the Pope's authority. The Church hierarchy as author of the *Homilies*

---

[36] *Homilies*, 'An Information ...', II. 152.

chose, as we have understood by now, to sit in the Apostles' chair and, having imposed on the parishioners, through their rhetoric and their theological expositions, the Bible as the final source of truth, they now had to resort to Scripture whenever a doctrinal change had to be vindicated in a homily, or when a traditional rule needed a reformulation.

The most basic way to conjure up biblical authority was by mentioning names of biblical books, characters or authors. Christ himself is of course the most frequent object of this name-dropping that allowed the author, after a textual allusion, to moralize the passage to his purpose. Unfortunately, in the identification of rhetorical manipulation in our analysis of this example, we can only rely on the printed copy of the text. Oratorical devices would have enabled the parish preacher to distinguish between the voices involved in the reference. In the homily against whoredom and uncleanness, in the first volume, the text first states: 'Now hath Christ our Master commanded vs that wee should forsake all vncleannesse and filthinesse both in body and spirit: this therefore must wee doe, if wee looke to please.'[37] The text alleged is Matthew 15: 11: 'Not that thing which entreth into the mouth defileth the man, but that which commeth out of the mouth defileth the man.' As no quotation marks are used in the book, a reader (and perhaps also a listener, if the careless parish preacher had not checked his texts beforehand) might have understood that the following conclusion also belonged to the Gospels, whereas it was penned by the author of the homily: 'For those things which proceed out of the mouth, come forth from the heart, and they defile the man. For out of the heart proceede euill thoughts, murders, breaking of wedlocke, whoredome, theftes, false witnesse, blasphemies: these are the things which defile a man.'[38] This sort of rhetorical confusion about voices and *personae* generates an identification of the preacher's *persona* with Christ's voice, which both authenticates and authorizes the moral lesson as Christ's.

Another device, involving summary and paraphrase, could generate *exempla* from well-known biblical stories, or create new ones. In the same homily against whoredom, the story of Herod and John the Baptist, though never literally quoted, is reported and moralized at the same time.[39] In the parishes where the stained-glass windows had not been destroyed, there may have been some representation of the scenes, or, if the paintings were still on display, they may have included a picture or sequence from that common topos, and the parishioners may have

---

[37] *Homilies*, 'A Sermon Against Whoredome and Uncleannesse', I. 79.
[38] Ibid.
[39] Ibid., I. 80.

kept the memory of such figures; but in the later Elizabethan period, in areas where iconoclasm had been efficient, such spoken allegories would have constituted the only means for the illiterate majority to store up biblical stories for meditation or edification.

To strengthen the arguments against traditional beliefs and practices, the authors often wove together references and quotations or paraphrases to produce an impression of indubitable authority through accumulation. To assert the heterodoxy of the invocation of the saints' mediation in the Catholic conception of the communion of saints, the authority of the converging statements of Christ, Paul and John about the sufficiency of the Saviour's intercession is enhanced by the accumulation and frequency of references, under the invocation of the Holy Spirit as the implied author of the Scriptures:

> For there doeth the holy Ghost plainely teach vs, that Christ is our onely Mediatour and Intercessour with God, and that we must not seeke and runne to an other. If any man sinneth, sayth Saint Iohn, we haue an aduocate with the Father, Iesus Christ the righteous, and hee is the propitiation for our sinnes [1 John 2: 1–2]. Saint Paul also sayth, there is one God, and one Mediatour betweene God and man, euen the man Iesus Christ [1 Tim. 2: 5]. Wherevnto agreeth the testimonie of our Sauiour himselfe, witnessing that no man commeth to the Father, but only by him, who is the way, the trueth, the life [John 14: 6], yea and the onely doore whereby we must enter into the kingdome of heauen, because God is pleased in no other but in him [John 10: 9]. For which cause also he cryeth, and calleth vnto vs that we should come vnto him, saying: Come vnto me, all ye that labour and be heauy laden, and I shall refresh you [Matt. 11: 28]. Would Christ haue vs so necessarily come vnto him? and shall we most vnthankefully leaue him, and runne vnto other?[40]

Obviously, quoting was a means to bring evidence to support the new theology, but, unless the new means to establish the authority of an argument was applied by the ecclesiastical hierarchy that sponsored the *Homilies*, there may have been fears lest the hesitant doubt. Another effect of the device of literary accumulation, as of other easy devices applied in the *Homilies*, was to provide partisans of the cause with a ready-made method to state their beliefs. Nor should one neglect the possibility that official apologetics were also intended to encourage popular imitators, since one of the aims of the promoters of the book was the deep inculturation of reformed Christianity. Yet emulation also worked in unexpected ways, as it was to provide the critics of the 'unfinished' Reformation with argumentative methods.

The 'Information' on the apparently offensive passages of the Bible

---

[40] *Homilies*, 'An Homilie or Sermon concerning Prayer', II. 115.

has given us an instance of exegesis and meta-exegesis at work in the *Homilies*. Yet moral and theological matters were not the sole message of the official sermons: ideological positions were also heavily proved by scriptural exegesis, and obedience happened to be one of the obsessions of the authors. In the first volume, the second part of the homily on obedience copiously comments on David's respect for Saul, and his behaviour towards his predecessor's murderer.[41] The commentary covers more than half of that particular section meant for one reading during a single service. The rhetorical technique appears to proceed once more through accumulation of evidence, but this time, each paraphrase or quotation is commented on. Several moments in the conflict between reproved Saul and 'holy David'[42] are presented, building up towards a climax with the execution of the messenger who announced the king's murder.[43] In a sequence referring to 1 Samuel 18–20, 1 Samuel 24: 4–22 and 1 Samuel 26: 5–24, the righteous hero is presented as the most perfect example of a subject respecting a ruler who was his persecutor. In spite of his grudges against Saul, in spite of his knowledge of Saul's reprobation by God, he refrained from killing Saul each time the king was within his reach, and he explicitly prevented his soldiers or servants from killing him, because Saul was the Lord's anointed.[44] It is God's role to punish evil rulers, and no mortal may wilfully murder them: 'for as truly as the Lord liueth (except the Lord smite him, or except his day come, or that he goe downe to warre, and perish in battaile) the Lord be mercifull vnto me, that I lay not my hand vpon the Lords anoynted.'[45] The commentary on 2 Samuel 1 and the punishment of the murderers is introduced by a reference to Psalm 89 (verse 20: 'I have found David my servant; with my holy oil have I anointed him'),[46] which enables the author to present David implicitly as both a prophet and a hero, whose words and actions must be considered as inspired by God, whether he appears in the Bible as a historical character or as a prophet of the Holy Spirit in his Psalms.

And by these two examples, Saint Dauid (being named in Scripture

---

41 *Homilies*, 'An Exhortation concerning Good Order, and Obedience to Rulers and Magistrates', I. 69–77. This is one of the few three-part homilies; the second part is pp. 72–5.

42 In the 1547 volume, David is very frequently called 'Saint David', 'Holy David', or 'the prophet David', forms that hark back to representations with which later attitudes towards biblical characters in reformed Churches will deliberately break.

43 *Homilies*, 'Exhortation concerning … Obedience …', I. 74.

44 Ibid., I. 73–4.

45 Ibid., I. 73.

46 Ibid., I. 74. The whole of Ps. 89 could be quoted to support the message of the homily, and this interpretation of David's attitude to Saul.

a man after Gods owne heart) [Ps. 8[9]] giueth a generall rule and lesson to all subiectes in the world, not to withstand their liege lord and king, not to take a sword by their priuate authority against their king, Gods annointed, who onely beareth the sword by Gods authority for the maintenance of the good, and for the punishment of the euill, who onely by Gods Law hath the vse of the sword at his command, and also hath all power, iurisdiction, regiment, correction and punishment, as supreme gouernour of all his Realmes & Dominions, and that euen by the authority of God, and by Gods ordinances.[47]

The listeners were certainly expected to gather for themselves that the lesson on obedience taught by the *exemplum* of David was the Spirit's own message on kings and rulers. By dint of accumulation and commentary, the homilists were able to build up arguments that could seem to stifle opposition, as long as the hearers were not theologians or experienced Bible readers. The monopoly of public exegesis involved some risks, however: if the parishioners began to read their Bibles and interpreted the texts for themselves, who could absolutely guarantee that the homilies would not be generally contradicted by the people?

Religious history is by no means an easy branch of historical research, but a history of religious indifference would be even more difficult to write than a history of atheism or unbelief. It would be extremely hard to collect evidence about the reactions of indifference or hostility that some parishioners may have experienced and kept secret: the public expression of unbelief was indeed dangerous. The changes in orthodoxy and authority that occurred between 1533 and 1558 may have generated scepticism among both the learned and the lowly. The repetition of identical sermons throughout the year, and year after year, in the parishes whose parson was too lazy or too uneducated to preach, may have caused the same effect. The homilies themselves did not always raise the listeners' souls with spiritual topics. Indeed, those dealing with social morality did not systematically use the Bible in their argument, and the exalted tone of some very practical texts hardly makes up for their lack of spiritual elevation. The morality of the *Homilies* could have been voiced and vindicated in much the same terms before the breach from Rome and under Mary's reign. In these texts, tradition and the Fathers go a long way with the preachers.

The extreme case of a homily arguing in general terms and on

---

[47] *Homilies*, 'Exhortation concerning ... Obedience ...', I. 74. The marginal note has 'Psalm 88', according to the Catholic Psalter, whose numbering is used throughout the volume. The numbers have been adjusted for this chapter.

tradition is the one on matrimony, which uses only five biblical arguments in all.[48] When taking Abraham as an instance of patriarchal matrimony, the author does not directly use the texts of Genesis, but constructs a story that he can moralize; and he reads the stories through the pedestrian prism of commonplace patriarchal morality, advocating severity on the part of the husband, and allowing moderation for affection's sake.[49]

Another frequent source was the patristic tradition, already mentioned. It is mostly used to ground theological notions on foundations prior to the scholastic corruption of divinity. It is used with great rhetorical efficiency in the homily on the sacraments and on the use of the vernacular in the liturgy. In particular, the Fathers provide patterns from the original liturgy of the Churches in the early centuries of Christianity to vindicate the prohibition of some parts of the mass: in the space of two pages, eight fathers are invoked to describe the fundamental origins of the liturgy.[50]

More surprisingly in the context of sacred eloquence, the authors regularly evoke ancient – and therefore pagan – examples or authorities. The rhetorical device is not unlike the comparison of the sins of the patriarchs with those of the present Christians, but its semantics work in a slightly different way. A classic device consists in comparing the virtuous behaviour of pagans with the vices of the Christians, who can thus be shown not to have profited from the lessons of the Gospel. In the 'Homily against Excess of Apparel', the authors find it expedient to contrast Christian women's inordinate taste for luxury with the austere tastes of female figures from pagan Antiquity. Tertullian, as patristic authority, is quoted alongside ancient thinkers or writers like Democrates, Sophocles, Aristotle or Socrates, with stories about Dionysius and Pyrrhus.[51]

More representative still of the encounter of biblical knowledge with para-biblical traditions is the beginning of the homily against disobedience. The authors quote the Bible with great insistence and frequency throughout the six parts of the homily, but the beginning has to present the listeners with a striking *exemplum*, which can be no other than the traditional myth of the beginning of evil: the fall of Lucifer. To

---

[48] *Homilies*, 'An Homilie of the State of Matrimonie', II. 239–48.

[49] Ibid., II. 244.

[50] *Homilies*, 'An Homilie wherein is declared that Common Prayer and Sacraments ought to be ministred in a tongue that is understood of the hearers', II. 138–9.

[51] *Homilies*, 'An Homilie against Excess of Apparel', II. 106–8. Other pagan *exempla* can be found in the 'Exhortation concerning ... Obedience ...', I. 72–3, or in the homily against strife and contention, I. 94–6.

start before the Fall of man, they resort to the legend of what had made the serpent evil, a point never considered in Genesis. The classical story, drawn from pseudepigraphal writings of the Old Testament like the lives of Adam and Eve, and from references to their tradition in later books of the Old Testament, and in the New Testament, has pride of place.[52] Lucifer, then Adam, are types of every disobedient Christian Englishman, most of all of the Northumberland rebels, as the rest of the homily demonstrates.

> For as long as in this first kingdome the subiects continued in due obedience to God their king, so long did God embrace all his subiects with his loue, fauour, and grace, which to enioy, is perfect felicity, whereby it is euident, that obedience is the principall vertue of all vertues. ... But as all felicitie and blessednesse should haue continued with the continuance of obedience [Matt. 25: 41], so with the breach of obedience, and breaking in of rebellion, al vices and miseries did withall breake in, and ouerwhelme the world. The first authour of which rebellion [John 8: 44], the root of all vices, and mother of all mischiefes, was [2 Peter 2: 4] Lucifer, first Gods ... most bounden subiect [Jude 6], who by rebelling against the Maiestie of God, of the brightest and most glorious Angel, is become the blackest and most foulest fiend and deuill [Rev. 12: 7]: and from the height of heauen, is fallen into the pit and bottome of hell [Gen. 3: 1]. Here you may see the first authour and founder of rebellion, and the reward thereof [Wis. 2: 24], here you may see the graund captaine and father of rebels, who perswading the following of his rebellion against God their Creatour and Lord, vnto our first Parents Adam and Eve [Gen. 3: 8, 17: 23–4], brought them in high displeasure with God, wrought their exile and banishment out of Paradise ... into this wretched earth and vale of misery: procured vnto them, sorrowes of their mindes, mischiefes, sickenesse, diseases, death of their bodies, and which is farre more horrible then all worldly and bodily mischiefes, he had wrought thereby their eternall and euerlasting death and damnation [Rom. 5: 12, 19], had not God by the obedience of his Sonne Iesus Christ repaired that, which man by disobedience and rebellion had destroyed, and so of his mercy had pardoned and forgiuen him: of which all and singular the premisses, the holy Scriptures doe beare record in sundry places.[53]

This very long quotation perfectly demonstrates the *modus operandi* of the homilists' exegetical rhetoric. Though most people had not read the Bible for themselves in 1571, everyone in Christendom, even before the Reformation's injunction to read the Bible, knew the story of Adam and Eve, and the myth of the fall of Lucifer and his angels. To convey the ideological message that set obedience above all other virtues, it was

---

[52] *Homilies*, 'An Homilie against Disobedience and Wilful Rebellion', II. 275–6.
[53] Ibid.

more efficient to begin with the origin of man's estate, which is also the cause of salvation by Christ. Augustine called the Fall of man 'felix culpa', but he also advocated the power of sovereigns as one of the consequences of the Fall, and as a very special instrument of mankind's penance for it. Rulers, evil or good, were God's agents in the administration of temporal punishments for the original sin. By insisting on the bliss of a harmonious kingdom, in which obedient subjects were wisely ruled by a saintly princess, the homilists were perhaps trying to take the sting out of political augustinianism, but the homily abounds with reminders of the temporal and spiritual doom awaiting transgressors of divine and royal order. For Renaissance Christians, the myth of Satan would have seemed perfectly orthodox and biblically founded; but by scholarly standards, its absence from Genesis in the sequence reporting the story of the original sin sets it outside the pale of biblical exegesis, though it is not irrelevant to the political theology of the period, and indeed the references to Genesis in the text do not point to elements that could identify Satan as the serpent.

When reading this excerpt from the first two pages of the last homily, a modern reader is reminded – by hindsight – of the first lines of Milton's *Paradise Lost*: 'Of mans first disobedience, and the fruit / Of that forbidden tree ...'. It is not totally improbable that such an official episcopalian and royalist text could have inspired the author of *Eikonoklastes* when he composed the incipit of his poetic masterpiece. The influence of the *Homilies* can be discovered even among the people who actively struggled against their usage in the Church. The last sentence of the above quotation reminds the listeners of the duty taught to them by the first homily they had heard in the current cycle: that they should read their Bibles to be good subjects and good Christians. This ultimate homily was there to teach them that no one could call himself a good Christian who was not a good subject. Indeed, the Roman Catholics had started the Northumberland rebellion, but the 'godly' were already threatening the stability of Church and State.

What is also revealed in this very long addition to the 1571 volume, is that Elizabeth ought then to be regarded as an antitype of God the Father against whom Satan and Adam rebelled, and of Christ who conquered death through obedience to the Father. At their own level, the obedient parishioners could also regard themselves as antitypes of Christ, since they abode by the law, as he had taught his disciples to render unto Caesar what was his, and had not rebelled against Pilate's sentence. The theology of our quotation from this homily is fully Christian, though its initial argument has more to do with religious myths than with the very complex composition of the 'Elohist' and

'Yahvist' manuscripts of Genesis, as modern biblical scholarship has taught us to read it. Throughout this homily, which can be regarded as a climax of the inculturation of Protestantism and absolute monarchy in England, the authors have applied all the possible rhetorical and apologetic devices that could blend ideological arguments with biblical authority. The ideological and theological foundations of what James I and VI would call 'the true law of free monarchies' were ready to support a new political exercise: the construction of the modern State.

The *Homilies* are a window open onto the religious culture of the English Renaissance, but they also embody the tensions and contradictions of the English Reformations. The uses of the Bible in these two volumes bear witness to the difficulties that the bishops who were the promoters of the book experienced with the protestantization of the established religion. Even in the second volume, which was constructed along strictly Protestant lines, the religious imagination of the sermons is still very closely related to the mind of medieval Christianity. The rhetoric of the homilies dealing with central theological issues demonstrates the validity of the doctrinal changes, and the Scriptures are then copiously applied to the matter in hand. The authors were probably aware that they were not only teaching new doctrines, but also teaching them in a new way; they were teaching two elements of the Reformation at once, in the message itself, and through the medium conveying the message. The spirituality which is proposed for the believers' practice is not new in that it centres on Christ, since *devotio moderna* was already Christ-centred, but it is new in that it intends to remove a whole crowd of intercessors from the mental world of the English Christian, and not least the Blessed Virgin. At the beginning of Henry VIII's reign, Marian shrines in England were visited by thousands of pilgrims, devotion to Mary was universal; and yet the same generation was asked to forsake Marian devotion without replacing it with anything else. The collective unconscious must have found it difficult to fill the gap, and the propaganda depicting Elizabeth as the Virgin Queen, the pageants during which she was carried in a sedula on noblemen's shoulders like Spanish madonnas, may have been semi-conscious attempts to work on the religious need for a holy mother-figure to worship. Esther or Judith were types that the queen seems to have preferred, but the staging of her appearances could not but remind the viewers of the processions of old. Biblical devotion, involving reading, meditation, interpretation and application of all this to one's life, was mostly open to the literate, and had a potent influence on the 'Puritan' current of spirituality. On the other hand, the moral doctrine of the *Homilies* was not new in any way, and neither were the conclusions of their political theology. The most polemical issue was the independence of the Church of England from the Holy See, and the doctrine of the last homily, though aimed in part at the tyrannicide theories of some Jesuits which were particularly intended for the English Catholics (though the latter were not all systematically hostile to the person of the queen), would have been difficult to distinguish from the doctrine preached by most Catholic bishops to their flocks on the Continent in normal circumstances. As an essential vehicle of the inculturation of Protestantism in England, it is therefore possible to say that the *Homilies* made the Bible and most of Christian culture available to most English Christians, even to the illiterate, but that the Puritans were not totally unjustified in blaming them for hindering the proper practice of biblical devotion among the people and the ministry alike. Their continued mention in the *Book of Common Prayer* at the beginning of the twenty-first century, in the Thirty-nine Articles, symbolically bears witness to the enduring position of this collection of sermons in the identity of the Church of England.[54]

---

[54] *The Book of Common Prayer* (Prayer Book [Further Provisions] Measure, 1969), Article XXXV.

CHAPTER TEN

The Welsh Bible and Renaissance Learning

Ceri Davies

For nearly a year, from the autumn of 1587 until the late summer of 1588, Dr William Morgan, a clergyman from the village of Llanrhaeadr-ym-Mochnant in north-east Wales, was staying in London. During those months the realm held its breath at the prospect of a Spanish invasion, and the religious implications of that threat had their bearing – at least indirectly – on William Morgan's presence in London at that time. For he was in the metropolis to supervise the printing of his translation of the Bible, including the Apocrypha, into Welsh. The printing was the responsibility of George Bishop and Ralph Newbury, deputies of the royal printer Christopher Barker, and William Morgan made his way daily to the press, in St Paul's Churchyard, from the deanery in Westminster. There he stayed as the guest of Dean Gabriel Goodman, himself a native of north Wales. In a postscript to the Latin address with which he prefaces the translation, William Morgan thanks Goodman for his hospitality and many other kindnesses: *vir re et nomine valde bonus*, 'truly a good man, in deed as well as in name'. He also thanks the Archbishop of Canterbury, John Whitgift, for offering to accommodate him, but adds (with a nice glimpse of sixteenth-century London) that staying at Lambeth would have necessitated crossing the Thames every day, an undertaking which clearly did not appeal to one brought up in the mountain fastnesses of Snowdonia.

The Welsh translation of 1588, 'Bishop Morgan's Bible' as it is often called (for William Morgan was to become Bishop of Llandaff in 1595, subsequently of St Asaph in 1601), became the single most important force in the Wales of the centuries that followed. Not only did it shape the religious life of Wales, but it also left its indelible imprint on the country's language and culture. Dr Isaac Thomas, the leading authority on the Welsh translations of the Bible, puts it thus:

> Without this Welsh Bible, that scriptural Christianity which became such a tremendous force in the religious and social life of Wales would not have been activated and would not have been sustained. Without this Welsh Bible the Welsh language would gradually but surely have disappeared from the churches, the parishes and the

land. The Wales of the last four centuries would have been a very different Wales without William Morgan's Bible.[1]

In the later sixteenth century, however, it was by no means obvious to everyone that translating the Scriptures into Welsh was either necessary or desirable. My threefold aim in this chapter is briefly to outline some of the steps which led to making the Bible available at that time in Welsh; to illustrate something of the linguistic and literary aspects of the versions which were produced; and especially to demonstrate the humanistic concerns which combined with Protestant convictions to motivate the translators.[2]

Wales, at the beginning of the sixteenth century, was in a culturally ambivalent position. On the one hand, things appeared remarkably flourishing. The thousand-year-old literary tradition of the country still thrived, as poets who practised the ancient skills of their strict-metre craft enjoyed the support of landed patrons. The turmoils created by Owain Glyndŵr's rising, early in the fifteenth century, had subsided, and a modicum of political stability was given a further boost by the victory of that part-Welshman Henry Tudor at the Battle of Bosworth in 1485. Henry's descent from Owain Tudur of Anglesey led poets and politicians alike to see in him the tangible fulfilment of the prophecy made to Cadwaladr, at the end of Geoffrey of Monmouth's *Historia Regum Britanniae*, that the day would come when the British – by which the Welsh understood themselves – would again rule the whole island. Many of the Welsh gentry class found themselves afforded opportunities, at court and in administration, in a way that would have been undreamt of a century earlier. On the other hand, the so-called Acts of Union, passed in 1536 and 1543 under Henry Tudor's son Henry VIII, completed the political integration of Wales into the English realm. Welsh people, at any rate the articulate among them, did not complain. The process led, however, to the outlawing of Welsh as a language of administration in Wales. The Acts also meant that the English

---

[1] Isaac Thomas, *William Morgan a'i Feibl/William Morgan and his Bible* (Cardiff, 1988), p. 87.

[2] I am much indebted to the extensive research conducted over the last twenty-five years into the Welsh Bible and its background. Of fundamental importance are two magisterial volumes by Isaac Thomas, *Y Testament Newydd Cymraeg, 1551–1620* (Cardiff, 1976) and *Yr Hen Destament Cymraeg, 1551–1620* (Aberystwyth, 1988). On the historical context, the work of a lifetime is elegantly distilled in Glanmor Williams, *Recovery, Reorientation and Reformation: Wales c. 1415–1642* (Oxford, 1987) and *Wales and the Reformation* (Cardiff, 1997). On literary aspects of the translations and their cultural influence, and on the literary background, see especially *Y Gair ar Waith: Ysgrifau ar yr Etifeddiaeth Feiblaidd yng Nghymru*, ed. R. Geraint Gruffydd (Cardiff, 1988) and *A Guide to Welsh Literature c. 1530–1700*, ed. R. Geraint Gruffydd (Cardiff, 1997).

Reformation was applied to Wales, and the decrees of the 1530s and 1540s, concerning the use of the English Bible and the Book of Common Prayer in every church in the realm, included Wales in their remit. For the bulk of the native population, nearly all monoglot speakers of Welsh, this meant being compelled to worship in a language that was no less alien to them than the Latin of the Vulgate and the old Catholic liturgy. Whatever the merits or demerits of the imposition, there was clearly a chink here in the Protestant armour, and in the claim that the liturgy, and especially the reading of the Scriptures, should be conducted in a language which was intelligible to the hearer. Recusancy, and Roman Catholic sympathizing, continued on no small scale in parts of Wales throughout the later part of the sixteenth century.[3] John Whitgift's encouragement and support for William Morgan was no doubt in part born of the awareness that, in Wales, the Protestant credibility of the church of which he was archbishop was compromised. Should Whitgift be tempted to forget it, the strictures of the Puritan John Penry were a constant reminder to him of the state of things in Wales.[4]

I have indicated that the bulk of the native population of Wales in the early sixteenth century was monoglot Welsh-speaking. There were, however, those (the Cambridge-educated John Penry among them) for whom the closer ties with England provided a vast widening of educational and cultural horizons. George Owen, an engaging Pembrokeshire antiquary of the Elizabethan period, put it like this:

> Since the time of Henry VII and Henry VIII that we were emancipated, as it were, and made free to trade and traffic throughout England, the gentlemen and people in Wales have greatly increased in learning and civility; for now great numbers of youths are continually brought up and maintained at the Universities of Oxford and Cambridge and in other good schools in England, where some prove to be learned men and good members of the Commonwealth of England and Wales.[5]

The result was that far more Welshmen than ever before came in contact with classical learning and the study of the ancient languages. It also meant that they became increasingly open to the influence of Renaissance humanism, as they encountered it in the two universities and the Inns of Court. For many, the benefits of the new learning led to a not unconscious distancing of themselves from the Welsh language and its literature. It was Wales's good fortune, however, that in the sixteenth century there emerged a group of remarkably able young Welshmen

---

[3] D. Aneurin Thomas, *The Welsh Elizabethan Catholic Martyrs* (Cardiff, 1971).

[4] Glanmor Williams, *Wales and the Reformation*, pp. 305–8.

[5] *The Description of Pembrokeshire*, Part III, ed. H. Owen (London, 1906), p. 56. (The orthography of the quotation is modernized.)

whose scholarly and cultural perceptions were sharpened by the new learning, and who did not lose their interest in and their concern for their Welsh heritage. Many of them (though by no means all) also became Protestants, and their conviction that the benefits of neither the Renaissance nor the Protestant Reformation should be denied to Wales led them to aspire to see the Bible translated into Welsh. There was, of course, a religious agenda. There was also a humanistic one – to restore the Welsh language, the original 'British' tongue, to its rightful position among the recognized languages of learning. As I suggested earlier, the concept of the Welsh as the true 'Britons' was founded in large measure on a biased interpretation of Geoffrey of Monmouth's myth of Brutus and his successors. Geoffrey was also used for Protestant purposes. His story of the conversion of King Lucius to what was taken to be a quasi-Protestant form of Christianity carried much weight not only with Welshmen but also with English antiquaries, notably Archbishop Matthew Parker. Geoffrey's *Historia* came under severe attack from Polydore Vergil and others, but Welshmen were very reluctant to have their faith in it shaken.[6]

William Salesbury (*c.* 1520–?99)

The great pioneer in the task of Welsh biblical translation in the sixteenth century was a layman, William Salesbury.[7] He was born about 1520 in the parish of Llansannan, Denbighshire, and brought up in Llanrwst in the Conway Valley, areas where the native Welsh literary tradition was particularly thriving. Salesbury was of gentle stock, and his family was sufficiently affluent to send him to school in England (probably in Leicestershire), then to Oxford, and possibly also to one of the Inns of Court. A friend of his, the poet Gruffudd Hiraethog, paid tribute to his learning in an Oxford still largely dominated by the medieval Trivium and Quadrivium:

> Fo ŵyr dy gorff, wrda, i gyd
> Foddion y Saith Gelfyddyd:
> Ystryw holl soffestri hen
> Yw'r dichell o Rydychen.[8]

---

6 Saunders Lewis, *Meistri'r Canrifoedd* (Cardiff, 1973), pp. 116–39; Glanmor Williams, *Reformation Views of Church History* (London, 1970), esp. pp. 63–5.

7 On Salesbury, see especially Isaac Thomas, *William Salesbury a'i Destament/William Salesbury and his Testament* (Cardiff, 1967); W.A. Mathias, in *Y Traddodiad Rhyddiaith*, ed. G. Bowen (Llandysul, 1970), pp. 27–78, and in *Llên Cymru*, **16** (1989), pp. 40–68; R. Brinley Jones, *William Salesbury* (Cardiff, 1994).

8 *Gwaith Gruffudd Hiraethog*, ed. D.J. Bowen (Cardiff, 1990), 23, lines 51–4 (p. 84).

Your body knows, good man, all the ways of the seven arts; the cleverness of all old sophistry is the skill from Oxford.

In the same poem, Gruffudd Hiraethog also tells of his friend's mastery of languages. In addition to English, he had five languages at his command: Latin, Hebrew, Greek, Welsh and French.[9] Another contemporary, the lexicographer Thomas Wiliems, added German and other languages to the list of those which Salesbury knew.[10] It is, of course, important to notice the emphasis on knowledge of Hebrew and Greek, in addition to Latin. For all his familiarity with the sophistries of the seven liberal arts, Salesbury is presented as that new kind of scholar, *vir trium linguarum gnarus*, learned in the three languages of the Scriptures (Hebrew and Greek as well as the Latin of the Vulgate), the three sacred languages of the inscription on the Saviour's Cross.

William Salesbury was a remarkably rounded scholar. A great admirer of Erasmus, he refers to the Dutchman as 'the most learned, most eloquent and most recognized teacher in all Christendom' (*yr athro dyscedickaf, huotlaf, ac awdurusaf yn Cred oll*).[11] Likewise, in a prefatory letter addressed in English to Richard Colyngbourne at the beginning of one of his books, he speaks of Erasmus as 'the head learned man of all our tyme'.[12] To some measure the multi-faceted nature of Erasmus' learning was reflected, albeit on a smaller scale, in the range and variety of Salesbury's scholarly pursuits. Between 1547 and 1552 he translated a Latin work (Linacre's version of Proclus' *De sphaera*) into English, published his friend Gruffudd Hiraethog's collection of Welsh proverbs, compiled a Welsh–English dictionary to help his fellow-countrymen to become familiar with English, wrote a guide to the pronunciation of Welsh and produced a study of rhetoric. His main concern, however, was with seeing the Scriptures translated into Welsh, and he viewed the matter in a humanistic light. In the preface to the collection of proverbs *Oll Synnwyr pen Kembero ygyd* (1547) he addresses his fellow-Welshmen with the words, 'If you do not wish to abandon utterly the faith of Christ, ... insist on having Holy Scripture in your language' (*A ny vynwch ymado yn dalgrwn dec a fydd Christ, ... mynwch yr yscrythur lan yn ych iaith*). But in the same place Salesbury says, 'If you do not wish to be worse than animals, which have not been born like man for understanding, insist on having learning in your

---

[9] Ibid., lines 39–44.

[10] National Library of Wales, Havod MS 26, p. 204. (T. Parry, *Bulletin of the Board of Celtic Studies*, 9 [1937–39], p. 109.)

[11] *Oll Synnwyr Pen Kembero Ygyd* (1547), Preface, in *Rhagymadroddion, 1547–1659*, ed. Garfield H. Hughes (Cardiff, 1951), p. 14.

[12] *A Briefe and a playne introduction* (1550), sig. Aiii[r].

language' (*A ny vynwch vynet yn waeth nag aniueilieit, y rain ny anet y ddyall mal dyn, mynuch ddysc yn ych iaith*).[13] The Scriptures in Welsh, learning in Welsh: the two go together for him.

By 1551 Salesbury had, on his own initiative, completed and published *Kynniver Llith a Ban*, a Welsh translation of the liturgical Gospels and Epistles prescribed by the Book of Common Prayer of 1549 for use in the communion service on Sundays and holy days. It is a volume of 176 pages, the first large work to be printed in Welsh.[14] Isaac Thomas has shown that the translations, for all the occasional signs of haste, are far more than renderings into Welsh of the English prayer book lessons, taken from the Great Bible. Salesbury evidently had before him Erasmus' Greek New Testament in one of its editions, and probably Tyndale's English and Luther's German versions. In a lengthy Latin preface, addressed to the four Welsh bishops together with the Bishop of Hereford (in whose diocese there were many Welsh-speaking parishes in the sixteenth century), Salesbury's Protestant concern emerges that the Word of God was being imprisoned by walls of foreign tongues, as if in chains (*menia pregrinarum* [sic] *linguarum, ... quibus in uinculis – proh dolor – dei uerbum coercetur*). He also asks the bishops to examine his translation and lend it their authority. Further, he explains that he has viewed it as his responsibility strictly to translate, not to paraphrase (*notent, me arctam uertentis regulam obseruasse non paraphrastis libertate functum fuisse*); and, to achieve that end, he went back to the Greek, preferring, as he puts it in a nice expression of the *ad fontes* principle, 'the fountainhead to the river' (*preponens fontem riuo*).[15]

In less than two years after the publication of *Kynniver Llith a Ban* Salesbury was obliged to lie low, for Mary Tudor's reign. In 1558, however, on Elizabeth's accession, he was again free publicly to continue with his mission. It is virtually certain that Salesbury was the driving force behind a petition to the Privy Council which led to an Act of Parliament in 1563, requiring the five bishops to arrange for the translation into Welsh of the Bible and the Book of Common Prayer, the

---

13 *Rhagymadroddion*, ed. Hughes, p. 11.

14 Modern diplomatic edition by J. Fisher, *Kynniver Llith a Ban* (Cardiff, 1931).

15 Fisher's edition includes the Latin preface (pp. [li–lii]) and an English translation of it (pp. 174–6). A Welsh translation is available in C. Davies, *Rhagymadroddion a Chyflwyniadau Lladin, 1551–1632* (Cardiff, 1980), pp. 18–21. Salesbury interestingly says that, for passages from the Gospel of Matthew, he was attracted to the Hebrew text (*multum addictus fui contextui Hebraico*). Isaac Thomas (*Y Gair ar Waith*, ed. Gruffydd, p. 49; *A Guide to Welsh Literature*, ed. Gruffydd, pp. 161–3) explains that he probably had before him Shem Tob b. Sharprut's Hebrew translation (1385) of Matthew, based on the Vulgate, which was revised and published by Sebastian Münster (1537). By 1567 Salesbury knew what the 'Hebrew Matthew' was and rejected it.

work to be completed by St David's Day 1567. The successful passing of that Act was largely thanks to the active support of two influential figures: in the House of Commons, Humphrey Llwyd, MP for Denbigh in the 1563 Parliament, and himself a hugely significant figure on the humanist scene; and in the House of Lords, the learned Bishop Richard Davies, a Marian exile in Frankfurt between 1555 and 1558, by 1563 Bishop of St David's and one of the five prelates charged under the Act with responsibility for arranging the translation.[16] In fact, Davies seems to have been the only one of the five to take his duty seriously. He invited William Salesbury to his episcopal palace at Abergwili outside Carmarthen, and there, in what was a small Renaissance court of learning in west Wales, they together set the work in train. It was intended that it be a collaborative undertaking, but Davies's diocesan duties, coupled with his responsibilities as a contributor to the English Bishops' Bible, meant that the bulk of the work was carried out by William Salesbury. It had been wildly unrealistic to expect that the whole Bible, together with the Book of Common Prayer, would be ready by 1567. Even so the Prayer Book together with the Psalter did appear in May of that year, followed by the New Testament in October. Both books were printed in London, by Henry Denham.

The 1567 New Testament is, without any doubt, a work of outstanding scholarship. In the period of less than twenty years since Salesbury worked on *Kynniver Llith a Ban*, Robert Estienne's 1550 and 1551 editions of the Greek text of the New Testament, Beza's Greek text and Latin version (1565), and the Geneva Bible (1560; New Testament, 1557) had all appeared, and Dr Isaac Thomas's meticulous studies have shown that Salesbury was familiar with all of these.[17] We also have a glimpse of Salesbury's principles as translator in the title-page, which reads:

> Testament | Newydd ein Arglwydd | Jesv Christ. | Gwedy ei dynnu, yd y gadei yr ancyfia= | ith, 'air yn ei gylydd or Groec a'r Llatin, gan | newidio ffurf llythyreu y *gairiae-dodi*. Eb law hyny | y mae pop gair a dybiwyt y vot yn andeallus, | ai o ran llediaith y 'wlat, ai o ancynefin= | der y devnydd, wedy ei noti ai eg= | lurhau ar 'ledemyl y tu da= | len gydrychiol.

The New Testament of our Lord Jesus Christ drawn, as far as the

---

16 On Humphrey Llwyd see R. Geraint Gruffydd, 'Humphrey Llwyd of Denbigh: Some Documents and a Catalogue', *Denbighshire Historical Society Transactions*, 17 (1968), pp. 54–107; *idem*, 'Humphrey Llwyd: Dyneiddiwr', *Efrydiau Athronyddol*, 33 (1970), pp. 57–74. On Richard Davies, see Glanmor Williams, *Bywyd ac Amserau'r Esgob Richard Davies* (Cardiff, 1953); *idem*, 'Bishop Richard Davies (?1501–1581)', in G. Williams, *Welsh Reformation Essays* (Cardiff, 1967), pp. 155–90.

17 Thomas, *Y Testament Newydd Cymraeg*, pp. 126–261.

different idiom allowed, word for word from the Greek and Latin, changing the form of the letters of the inserted words. Beside this each word deemed to be unintelligible, either because of the local dialect, or because of the unfamiliarity of the matter, has been noted and explained in the margin of the same page.

The concern that every particular in the original be translated follows the emphasis of the Geneva translators. The concern also that any insertion, made for clarity's sake, be indicated in the text, is in accordance with the principle adopted by Beza and the Geneva Bible: black-letter, or gothic, type is used for the text, but the inserted words are printed in roman type. Furthermore, in the margin Salesbury has added (as he implies) a variety of alternative words, where he thought matters of dialect or 'unfamiliarity of the matter' might pose problems. This actually imports one of the major difficulties with Salesbury's New Testament, at least for reading in public. Salesbury was so concerned with scholarship, and so interested in philological as well as theological matters, that the work can appear very difficult to read. R. Geraint Gruffydd puts the matter succinctly:

> [Salesbury] was, in one sense, too much of a humanist with too deep a respect for two of the basic principles of humanism, *antiquity* on the one hand, *variety* or *copiousness* on the other. If he could give a word or grammatical form a Middle Welsh guise or, preferably, a Latin one, so much the better. And if he could give six alternative spellings, especially if a word appeared more than once on the same page, better still.[18]

For Salesbury the connection between Latin origins and orthographical practice was of paramount importance. He knew that countless words in Welsh were derived from Latin, and had discussed the matter in his Welsh–English dictionary of 1547. Many of the Latin words had entered Brythonic, the old Celtic mother-tongue, at the time of the Roman occupation, and as the Welsh language evolved they had gone through the same morphological changes as native Brythonic words. But Salesbury, time and time again, insists on printing such Welsh words in a Latinate manner. Here, taken at random, are two verses from the Gospel of Matthew, chapter 21. First, verse 20, recording the reaction of Jesus's disciples to the cursing of the fig tree:

> A' phan ei gwelawdd y discipulon, y ryveddasant, gan ddywedyt, Pan'd ebrwydd y gwywodd y fficusbren?

> And when the disciples saw it, they marvelled, saying, How soon is the fig tree withered away?

---

[18] R. Geraint Gruffydd, *The Translating of the Bible into the Welsh Tongue* (Cardiff, 1988), p. 14.

The Welsh for 'disciple' is *disgybl*, plural *disgyblion*, derived (like the English word) from Latin *discipulus*. So Salesbury prints the word in a Latinate manner. Likewise, the Welsh word for 'fig tree' is *ffigysbren*, from Latin *ficus*, and Salesbury insists on displaying the derivation by the way he spells the word. Three verses later (verse 23a) one reads:

> A' gwedy y ddyvot ef ir Templ, yr Archoffeiriait, a' Henafieit y popul a ddaethan attaw.

> And when he was come into the temple, the chief priests and the elders of the people came unto him.

The Welsh for 'temple' is *teml*, and for 'people' it is *pobl*; both words derive from Latin (*templum, populus*), and the forms which Salesbury prints are as close to the Latin root as possible.

Salesbury's Latinate orthography is just one example of the kind of thing which made his translation hard going for a not too learned priest to read in public. Another of his quirks was not to print initial mutations of consonants. For example, in Matthew 21: 23 above, the rules governing mutation require that initial *t* in *Templ* be changed to *d*, and initial *p* in *popul* to *b*: *i'r Deml, y bobl*. Of course Salesbury expected that the words would be pronounced as contemporary speech required, but his scholarly concerns saw no need to relate spelling to pronunciation. The consequence was that an outstanding work, remarkably accurate in its rendering of the Greek text and brilliant in the way it embraced the whole range of Welsh vocabulary and creatively extended it, was vitiated by excessive learning. As a later Welsh humanist, Maurice Kyffin of Oswestry, put it in 1595: 'the printed version was so full of solecisms and foreign words that the ear of a true Welshman could not bear to listen to it' (*yr oedd cyfled llediaith a chymaint anghyfiaith yn yr ymadrodd brintiedig, na alle clust gwir Gymro ddioddef clywed mo 'naw'n iawn*).[19] Complaints were made to the publisher. It is also possible that it was cool public reaction to the New Testament which dampened Salesbury's enthusiasm for seeing through the translation of the Old Testament. It is known that for some years he and Richard Davies worked on it, possibly until 1575, but they parted company before any further publication was ready for the press. According to one colourful authority, Sir John Wynn of Gwydir, 'variance' happened between them 'for the general sense and etymology of one word, which the Bishop would have to be one way and William Salesbury another'.[20] Whether John Wynn's account is correct or

[19] Maurice Kyffin, *Deffynniad Ffydd Eglwys Loegr* (1595), 'Annerch at yr howddgar ddarlleydd Cristnogawl', in *Rhagymadroddion*, ed. Hughes, p. 92.
[20] Sir John Wynn, *The History of the Gwydir Family and Memoirs*, ed. J. Gwynfor Jones (Llandysul, 1990), p. 62.

not, it is certainly the case that William Salesbury, in his younger days perhaps the most versatile of all the Renaissance scholars connected with Wales, moved into obscurity, leaving to another the task of completing the Welsh Bible.

It appears that, for a period, the work on the Old Testament was in abeyance. One imagines that there was much speculation concerning who would fulfil the requirements of the 1563 Act and complete the job. There is evidence that about 1576 Bishop Richard Davies invited one of his relations, the Anglesey-born Dr Siôn Dafydd Rhys, to undertake at least part of the work. Siôn Dafydd Rhys was a notable scholar, educated in Oxford and Siena. While in Italy he had published, among other things, his *De italica pronunciatione ... libellus* (1569), a guide in Latin to the pronunciation of Italian.[21] The plan, such as it was, that Rhys should devote himself to the biblical work seems not to have materialized. In any case, his religious loyalties were suspect, and he subsequently returned to the Roman Catholic faith which had attracted him in Italy.[22]

William Morgan (1545–1604)

It is to William Morgan, with whom we started, that we must look to find the scholar who was to bring the work on the Welsh Bible to fulfilment. He was born at Tŷ-mawr, Wybrnant, in the parish of Penmachno, not far from Llanrwst where Salesbury was brought up. His father held his farm as a tenant on the estate of the Wynn family of Gwydir, and it was at the house in Gwydir that William Morgan received his early classical education, probably from one of the chaplains attached to the family there.[23] The Wynns of Gwydir were also notable for the patronage which they extended to bards and other practitioners of the arts.[24] In 1565, at the same time as Edmwnd Prys

---

[21] Facsimile reprint in *Trattati di fonetica del Cinquecento*, ed. Nicoletta Maraschio (Florence, 1992).

[22] R. Geraint Gruffydd, 'The Life and Work of Dr John Davies of Brecon (Siôn Dafydd Rhys)', *Transactions of the Honourable Society of Cymmrodorion* (1971), pp. 175–90; idem, 'Dr John Davies, "the old man of Brecknock"', *Archaeologia Cambrensis*, **141** (1992), pp. 1–13.

[23] 'William Morgan, D.D. ... servants (both he and his ancestors) to the house of Gwydir where he was brought up in learning.' John Wynn, *History of the Gwydir Family and Memoirs*, p. 63.

[24] J. Gwynfor Jones, 'Diddordebau diwylliannol Wyniaid Gwedir', *Llên Cymru*, **11** (1970–71), pp. 95–124; idem, *The Wynn Family of Gwydir: Origins, Growth and Development, c. 1490–1674* (Aberystwyth, 1995), esp. pp. 144–89.

(who was to be a lifelong friend), Morgan went up to St John's College, Cambridge. St John's was a college with which the Wynns had a special connection: one of the family, Dr John Gwyn, had been a fellow in the 1550s (and on his death in 1574 left an endowment for three fellowships and six studentships at the college), another, Owen Gwyn, was to become Master in 1613.[25] Morgan had a distinguished career in Cambridge, graduating BA in 1568, MA in 1571, and BD in 1578; in 1583 he added the degree of DD.

St John's provided a particularly suitable environment for training a biblical scholar. The college had been established by Bishop John Fisher, in 1511, with the special purpose that it should be a *collegium trilingue*. William Morgan therefore found himself in a place which was ideally suited for fostering command of Greek and Hebrew. It is not known for certain who was Morgan's Hebrew teacher, but there was no shortage of distinguished scholars giving instruction in the language in St John's through the middle years of the sixteenth century. Three such scholars during Morgan's time there were William Fulke (later Master of Pembroke and Vice-Chancellor of the University) and the Protestant exiles from France Philippe Bignon and Antoine Chevallier. There are many witnesses to Chevallier's abilities as a teacher; Hugh Broughton, for example, says of him that one would learn more from him in a month 'than others could teach in Ten Years'![26] Another who taught at St John's during William Morgan's time there was Andrew Downes, later Regius Professor of Greek and one of the most highly regarded Greek scholars of his day. St John's was also a college which, a decade and a half earlier, had been prominent in the Protestant resistance mounted in the 'Little Germany' which was Cambridge during Mary Tudor's reign. In terms both of learning and of churchmanship, it is clear that William Morgan studied at a college which allowed him to steep himself in the principles of the kind of Protestant humanism which fitted him for the task of translation.

William Morgan was an undergraduate when the Welsh New Testament and Book of Common Prayer appeared in 1567. One can only speculate about the impression which these books, published in his native tongue, made upon him. What is certainly the case is that, when Morgan came to undertake the task of translating the whole Bible into

---

[25] W.P. Griffith, *Learning, Law and Religion: Higher Education and Welsh Society, c. 1540–1640* (Cardiff, 1996), pp. 208–9.

[26] Gruffydd Aled Williams, 'William Morgan ac Edmwnd Prys yng Nghaer-grawnt', *Bulletin of the Board of Celtic Studies*, 29 (1981), pp. 296–300; G. Lloyd-Jones, *The Discovery of Hebrew in Tudor England: A Third Language* (Manchester, 1983), pp. 204–9, and Appendix I, p. 274.

Welsh, he was remarkably well equipped for the job. There is some uncertainty concerning when exactly he began the work. In 1572 he was appointed, by Bishop Richard Davies, to the benefice of Llanbadarn Fawr near Aberystwyth; three years later he was presented to the vicarage of Welshpool, in the diocese of St Asaph. It seems, however, that he was absent from his parishes, probably still studying in Cambridge. Had Richard Davies heard of the eminent suitability of the young Cambridge scholar for the translating which remained to be done, and were the appointments to Llanbadarn and Welshpool made to enable him to prepare himself fully for the task? We do not know. What is certain is that when he was appointed to Llanrhaeadr-ym-Mochnant (also in the St Asaph diocese) in 1578, he took up residence there and devoted himself to the translation. He not only produced the first Welsh version of the Old Testament (apart from the Psalms) and the Apocrypha, but also completely revised Salesbury's New Testament and Psalter. Not without reason has R.S. Thomas written of the work which was his gift to his fellow-countrymen that

> The smooth words
> Over which his mind flowed
> Have become an heirloom.[27]

What makes William Morgan's translation special? First, there is no question about his standing as a biblical scholar. I refer again to the researches of Dr Isaac Thomas, who has painstakingly analysed Morgan's work. For the Old Testament, the main Hebrew text which he used was that of the 1572 Antwerp Polyglot Bible (which contained a revised version of Santi Pagnini's Latin translation). Morgan also used the very accurate Latin translation of Immanuel Tremellius, as well as the English translations, especially the Geneva Bible. Dr Thomas has demonstrated, however, that there are places where he is confident in his own interpretation: for example, in 2 Chronicles 1: 11, 'that thou mightest judge my people', Morgan seems to have realized that the Hebrew for 'to judge' had the secondary meaning 'to rule', and uniquely translates accordingly, *fel y llywodraethit fy mhobl* ('that thou mightest rule my people').[28]

Another great distinction of Morgan's translation is his instinctive literary feel for Welsh idiom and expression. Professor R. Geraint Gruffydd has indicated that, in his judgement, this is where the great difference between Salesbury and Morgan lay:

---

[27] R.S. Thomas, 'Llanrhaeadr ym Mochnant', *Collected Poems, 1945–1990* (London, 1993), p. 192.

[28] Thomas, *Yr Hen Destament Cymraeg*, p. 192.

188   THE BIBLE IN THE RENAISSANCE

Learned scholar of Welsh and splendid writer though he was, Salesbury lacked Morgan's literary instinct. Morgan probably knew less of Middle Welsh prose than Salesbury but seems to have known more of Welsh strict metre poetry and to have had more empathy with it and respect for it. ... He appears to have studied the poets' orthography and their grammatical usage and on the whole, although not invariably, to have followed their custom. ... Overall, Morgan succeeded in excising most of the archaic and irregular features of Salesbury's translations and in ridding the text of its innumerable variations in spelling. That is, he managed to standardize the language of the translation whilst at the same time preserving much of the richness of Salesbury's work as regards vocabulary, grammar and syntax. Whereas Salesbury's translations seemed like a verdant jungle through which the reader had to hack his way, Morgan's work was more like a formal garden whose very order gave an added pleasure to its beauty, symmetry and scent.[29]

So the style and orthography of Morgan's version of the two verses from Matthew 21, quoted above in Salesbury's 1567 translation, represent much more closely the sounds and natural rhythms of the literary Welsh of the day:

> A phan welodd y discyblion, hwy a ryfeddâsant gan ddywedyd, pa fodd y crînodd y ffigus-bren yn y fann? (21: 20)

> Ac wedi ei ddyfod efe i'r Deml, yr archoffeiriaid a henuriaid y bobl a ddaethant atto. (21: 23a)

For his work on the Old Testament (with the exception of the Psalms) and the Apocrypha Morgan did not have a version by Salesbury before him. As a brief example of his artistry, I quote the opening five verses of Genesis. It is Morgan's practice to print inserted words, for example parts of the verb *bod*, 'to be', within square brackets, as here in verses 2 and 4:

> Yn y dechreuad y creawdd Duw y nefoedd a'r ddaiar.
> Y ddaiar oedd afluniaidd, a gwâg, a thywyllwch [ydoedd] ar wyneb y dyfnder, ac yspryd Duw yn ymsymmud ar wyneb y dyfroedd.
> Yna Duw a ddywedodd, bydded goleuni, a goleuni a fû.
> Yna Duw a welodd y goleuni mai dâ [oedd], a Duw a wahanodd rhwng y goleuni a'r tywyllwch.
> A Duw a alwodd y goleuni yn ddydd, a'r tywyllwch a alwodd efe yn nôs: a'r hwyr a fû, a'r borau a fû, y dydd cyntaf.

It is, perhaps, little wonder that the biblical scholar C.H. Dodd, himself from North Wales, is reputed to have described Morgan as 'a Hebrew poet of genius'![30]

---

[29] Gruffydd, *The Translating of the Bible into the Welsh Tongue*, pp. 23–4. See also Gruffydd, 'William Morgan', in *Y Traddodiad Rhyddiaith*, ed. G. Bowen, pp. 149–74.

[30] R. Geraint Gruffydd, *William Morgan: Dyneiddiwr* (Swansea, 1989), p. 22.

William Morgan was not only a master of the Welsh language but also an accomplished writer in Latin. His best-known Latin composition is the *Epistola dedicatoria*, the dedicatory address to Queen Elizabeth at the beginning of the Bible.[31] The address opens with the following, rhetorically rich, sentence:

> Quantum Deo optimo maximo Maiestas vestra debeat (Augustissima princeps) vt opes, potentiam, & admirabilem ingenij ac naturae dotem taceam: non solum gratia, qua apud plurimos pollet rarissima, & eruditio, qua prae caeteris ornatur varia, & pax, qua prae vicinis fruitur alma, eiusque nunquam satis admiranda protectio, qua & hostes nuper fugauit atroces, & multa et magna pericula semper euasit faelicissime: verum etiam cum primis eximia illa pietas toto orbe celebrata, qua ipse V.M. imbuit, & ornauit, nec non verae religionis & propagandae, & propugnandae studium propensissimum quo semper flagrastis, clarissime attestantur.

> There are very clear proofs, most noble Sovereign, how great a debt your Majesty owes to the good and most high God. To speak nothing of your wealth, power and wonderful endowment of mind and character, there is the matchless grace by which your Majesty holds sway over very many people; and your learning which in its many-sidedness is pre-eminently equipped; and the peace which in greater degree than your neighbours you propitiously enjoy; and the way in which that peace was defended (a matter which can never be too highly admired) when you recently put your cruel enemies to flight, and also every time a way of safety has been happily found out of many and great dangers. But in addition to all these there is also that exceptional piety of yours, well known throughout the world, piety with which God Himself endowed and adorned your Majesty, and that most ready zeal which has always been burning within you to propagate and defend true religion.

Three cumbersome English sentences represent one Latin period in which the balanced use of corresponding structures and subordinate clauses interlocks within the main framework provided by the indirect question of the opening seven words and the closing *clarissime attestantur* (whose subject comes in the sentence's succession of abstract nouns, in the nominative singular). The sentence may strike us as both contrived and excessively fulsome. It is certainly the work of one who was at ease with the copiousness of Latin expression.

In the later part of the address William Morgan discusses the objections raised by those who did not wish to see the Scriptures translated into Welsh:

> Siqui consensus retinendi gratia, nostrates vt Anglicum sermonem ediscant adigendos esse potius, quam Scripturas in nostrum

---

31 *Y Beibl Cyssegr-lan* (1588), fols. *ii^r–iii^v.

sermonem vertendas esse volunt: dum vnitati student, ne veritati obsint cautiores esse velim, & dum concordiam promouent, ne religionem amoueant, magis esse solicitos opto. Quamuis enim eiusdem insulae incolas eiusdem sermonis & loquelae esse magnopere optandum sit; aeque tamen perpendendum est, istud vt perficiatur tantum temporis & negotij peti, vt interea Dei populum miserima illius verbi fame interire, velle, aut pati nimis sit saeuum atque crudele. Deinde non dubium est, quin religionis quam sermonis ad vnitatem plus valeat similitudo & consensus. Vnitatem praeterea pietati, vtilitatem religioni, & externam quandam inter homines concordiam eximiae illi paci quam Dei verbum humanis animis imprimit praeferre, non satis pium est. Postremo, quam non sapiunt, si verbi diuini in materna lingua habendi prohibitionem, aliena vt ediscatur quicquam mouere opinantur? Religio enim nisi vulgari lingua edoceatur, ignota latitabit.

If there are people who wish that, for the sake of maintaining agreement, our people should be made to learn the English language rather than that the Scriptures be translated into our own, I would wish that they be more careful lest in their eagerness for unity they stand in the way of truth; and while they promote concord, I desire that they be more anxious that they do not supplant religion. For although it is greatly to be desired that the inhabitants of the same island should have the same speech and language, yet it must equally be borne in mind that so much time and trouble are required to achieve this aim that it means willing, or at least allowing, that God's people perish in the meantime from wretched famine of his word, and that would be far too savage and cruel. Besides there is no doubt that similarity and agreement in religion do more to promote unity than do similarity and agreement in speech. Furthermore, it is not godly enough to prefer unity to devotion, convenience to religion, and a kind of external understanding between people to that extraordinary peace which God's word impresses on men's souls. Finally, how lacking in wisdom are those who think that to prohibit having the word of God in the mother-tongue is any incentive to learning a foreign language. For if religion is not taught in the language of the people it will remain hidden and unknown.

The passage presents the rational argument of a Welshman and a Protestant. It is also a fine example of a humanist's effective use of the stylistic resources of the Latin language. Take the first sentence, with its correspondences of vocabulary and syntax. It has several subordinate clauses, but is fundamentally a conditional sentence, its protasis sustained by *siqui ... volunt*, the apodosis by *velim* and *opto*. Thus the same basic idea (wish, desire) is in the three verbs. But there is an effective variation between indicative and subjunctive in *volunt* and *velim*, and of choice of word between the two forms of *velle* and, at the end of the sentence, the more confident *opto*. Then there is the pairing, in terms of sounds and constructions, between *nostrates ut Anglicum sermonem* and *Scripturas in nostrum sermonem*; between *unitati student* and *veritati obsint*; and between *concordiam promouent* and *religionem amoueant*. These things are not the work of a groping Latinist!

In the *Epistola Dedicatoria* William Morgan reveals himself as a humanist sensitive to the legacy of antiquity, not only in his polished Latinity but also in the use of imagery drawn from the classical world. He compares the condition of Wales, before the publication of the 1567 New Testament and Book of Common Prayer, to one where the waters of Lethe had erased from men's minds the vocabulary wherewith adequately to discuss the sacred mysteries (*mysteria … Letheis quasi aquis deleta*). He refers to Archbishop Whitgift as 'an excellent Maecenas of letters' (*literarum Mecaenas [sic] optimus*). Queen Elizabeth herself is a phoenix for the world, *mundi Phoenix*, that is a unique, matchless person, as Erasmus explained in one of his Adages.[32] These are minor references, of course, but they show William Morgan as one comfortable in the world of Renaissance classicism.[33]

The address to Queen Elizabeth is not William Morgan's only Latin work. Another piece by him is an epigram, in four elegiac couplets, written to greet Maurice Kyffin's English translation of *Andria* (*The Girl from Andros*), first of the Latin comedies composed by the dramatist Terence (Publius Terentius Afer). Maurice Kyffin, of Oswestry, was an unusual combination of Welsh writer, classical scholar, soldier and administrator. In 1587, in the wake of the Babington Plot, he wrote an English poem in praise of Queen Elizabeth, 'The Blessedness of Brytaine', and in 1588, in the same year as the Welsh Bible, his translation of the *Andria* was published.[34] During those years Kyffin was based in London, and it is likely that he and William Morgan enjoyed something of each other's company during the months which Morgan spent in London while the Bible went through the press. It may also be that Morgan's influence played its part in inspiring Kyffin to translate Bishop John Jewel's *Apologia Ecclesiae Anglicanae* into Welsh, resulting in a classic of early modern Welsh prose, *Deffynniad Ffydd Eglwys Loegr* (1595). In his preface to that translation Kyffin pays warm tribute to Morgan's work on the Bible:

---

32 Erasmus, *Adagia* II. vii. 10 (*Opera omnia*, ii [Leiden, 1703], col. 615c).

33 For translations of the whole of the *Epistola*, see A.O. Evans, *A Memorandum on the Legality of the Welsh Bible and the Welsh Version of the Book of Common Prayer* (Cardiff, 1925), pp. 128–37 (into English), and Davies, *Rhagymadroddion a Chyflwyniadau Lladin*, pp. 64–70 (into Welsh).

34 *ANDRIA. The first Comoedie of Terence, in English … Carefully translated out of Latin, by Maurice Kyffin … Printed at London by T.E.* [Thomas East] *for Thomas Woodcocke, at the Signe of the black Beare in Paules Churchyard. 1588.* See C. Davies, *Welsh Literature and the Classical Tradition* (Cardiff, 1995), pp. 67–70.

Doctor Wiliam Morgan a gyfieythodd y Beibl drwyddi yn hwyr o amser; gwaith angenrheidiol, gorchestol, duwiol, dyscedig; am yr hwn ni ddichyn Cymry fyth dalu a diolch iddo gymaint ag a haeddodd ef.[35]

Dr William Morgan lately translated the entire Bible: a necessary, admirable, godly and learned task – for which Wales will never be able to repay and thank him as much as he deserved.

Here is William Morgan's epigram, one of six congratulatory poems (including one by William Camden, author of *Britannia*) at the beginning of Kyffin's *Andria*:

>   *In M. Kyffini Andriam*
> Caute sectatus quondam, sapiensque *Menandrum*
>   Aeternum nomen *Publius* est meritus.
> Consimiles laudes puto te *Kyffine* mereri,
>   Afri quod Vatis stricte imitere pedem.
> Namque aliena sequi, quam sit uestigia magnum
>   Noui. Qui nescit, carpere solus auet.
> *Andria* multarum fuit illi prima sororum:
>   *Andria* sit caueas ultima scena tibi.

At one time Publius [that is, Terence] in his wisdom carefully followed Menander, and earned a name which lasts for ever. I believe that you, Kyffin, deserve similar praises, in that you closely imitate the step of the poet from Africa (Afer). For I know what a great thing it is to follow in others' footsteps. The one who does not know, it is he who is keen to find fault. For Terence, *Andria* was the first of many sisters; take care that *Andria* is not your last performance.

The epigram is a polished piece of occasional verse, thematically held together on the one hand by the relationship between Terence's work and that of Menander, his Greek precursor, and on the other hand by the relationship between Terence and his English translator. In the last couplet William Morgan recalls that *Andria* was Terence's first comedy, and plays on the word *scena* (stage, scene, performance) in a striking way to urge Maurice Kyffin not to give up writing. It has already been indicated that, seven years later, Kyffin's translation of Bishop Jewel's *Apologia* came from the press. The epigram may also afford a glimpse of the company – Gabriel Goodman, Kyffin, Camden, William Morgan himself – which gathered in the deanery at Westminster in 1587 88, and of their delight in entertaining each other with Latin verses. Over four centuries later, the personal touch in the third couplet is the most striking feature. Here speaks the translator of the 1588 Bible. He has honestly tried to convey the content of the Hebrew and Greek

---

[35] *Rhagymadroddion*, ed. Hughes, p. 91.

Scriptures, relying much on the work of other interpreters and translators, including William Salesbury. From experience he also knows of the difficulties of the task, and of the obstacles created by the faint-hearted and the hostile. *Qui nescit, carpere solus avet.* It is all expressed in Latin verse of accomplished elegance.

By the end of 1588 the Bible went out to the Welsh parishes, and was immediately greeted with great acclaim. The bards were lyrical in their praise of William Morgan's work, and his appointment to the episcopal bench was warmly welcomed.[36] During his years as a bishop he published, in 1599, an important revision of Salesbury's 1567 Book of Common Prayer. He also prepared a revised version of the New Testament, but the manuscript was lost when the printer, to whom it had been entrusted, mislaid it in the confusion which occasioned his flight from the plague in London in 1603. In the history of the literature of Wales, and of the country's religious experience, William Morgan's achievement in the 1588 Bible remains unparalleled. It was he who, in the words of the twentieth-century Welsh poet Gwenallt Jones, 'conferred upon this language the highest dignity and honour/By converting it into one of the dialects of God's Revelation'.[37]

Richard Parry (1560–1623) and John Davies (*c.* 1567–1644)

Many of the copies of William Morgan's Bible were, thirty years later, either lost or beginning to fall apart. In the wake of the appearance of the King James version of the English Bible in 1611, Richard Parry, Morgan's successor as Bishop of St Asaph, undertook to prepare a revised version of the Welsh text. The new edition appeared in 1620, printed by Bonham Norton and John Bill. Bishop Parry had been educated at Westminster School and in Oxford, and was himself a man of great learning.[38] His Latin preface, at the beginning of the 1620 Bible, is an expression of his scholarly and humanistic interests. In discussing

---

36 For a collection of poems in praise of William Morgan, see R. Geraint Gruffydd, '*Y Beibl a droes i'w bobl draw*' (Cardiff, 1988), pp. 31–83; *William Morgan: Dyneiddiwr*, pp. 30–31.

37 'Gan roddi arni yr urddas ac iddi'r anrhydedd uchaf/Wrth ei throi yn un o dafodieithoedd Datguddiad Duw.' Gwenallt Jones, 'Yr Esgob William Morgan', *Gwreiddiau* (Aberystwyth, 1959), pp. 50–51. Translation from Dyfnallt Morgan, *D. Gwenallt Jones* (Cardiff, 1972), pp. 58–9.

38 J. Gwynfor Jones, 'Yr Esgob Richard Parry 1560–1623', *Trafodion Cymdeithas Hanes Sir Ddinbych*, 23 (1974), pp. 126–46; *idem*, 'Richard Parry, Bishop of St Asaph: Some Aspects of his Career', *Bulletin of the Board of Celtic Studies*, 26 (1974–76), pp. 175–90.

the relationship between his edition and Morgan's he aptly quotes from Plutarch's *Life of Theseus* and from the works of Jerome, Ambrose and Chrysostom.[39] It is probable, however, that Richard Parry's part in producing the 1620 version was as initiator and supervisor of the undertaking, and that the main work of revision was carried out by his chaplain and brother-in-law, Dr John Davies, rector of Mallwyd. Davies was exceptionally well suited for the task. As a young man he was in Llanrhaeadr-ym-Mochnant helping William Morgan, probably as an amanuensis for the 1588 Bible. After studying in Oxford he again became Morgan's assistant, and is known to have been a member of his household in both Llandaff and St Asaph. He probably played a major part in preparing the 1599 Book of Common Prayer and the lost revision of the New Testament. It is little wonder, then, that he was the scholar to whom Richard Parry turned for help in revising the whole Bible. John Davies, in turn, writes of himself as 'an unworthy assistant to both translators of the Holy Bible into Welsh' (*utrique SS. Bibliorum interpreti Br. indignus fui administer*).[40]

The differences between the 1588 and 1620 versions are, on the whole, minor. Morgan's policy of standardizing language and orthography is pursued even further; typographical consistency is a clear aim; the use of adverbs like *yna* ('then') and *hefyd* ('also'), as particles at the beginning of a new verse, disappears.[41] Some of these points emerge from comparing the 1620 version of Genesis 1: 1–5 with the 1588 version, quoted above:

> Yn y dechreuad y creawdd Duw y nefoedd a'r ddaiar.
> A'r ddaiar oedd afluniaidd a gwâg, a thywyllwch [oedd] ar wyneb y
>   dyfnder, ac yspryd Duw yn ymsymmud ar wyneb y dyfroedd.
> A Duw a ddywedodd, bydded goleuni, a goleuni a fu.
> A Duw a welodd y goleuni mai da [oedd], a Duw a wahanodd
>   rhwng y goleuni a'r tywyllwch.
> A Duw a alwodd y goleuni yn ddydd, a'r tywyllwch a alwodd efe
>   yn nos: a'r hwyr a fu, a'r borau a fu, y dydd cyntaf.

Parry and Davies were, however, scholars who exercised their own judgement, and there are instances of more substantial departures from Morgan. For example, in the two verses previously quoted from

---

[39] For translations of the whole of Parry's preface, see Evans, *Memorandum*, pp. 146–50; Davies, *Rhagymadroddion a Chyflwyniadau Lladin*, pp. 101–4.

[40] *Antiquae linguae Britannicae, nunc communiter dictae Cambro-Britannicae, a suis Cymraecae vel Cambricae, ab alijs Wallicae, rudimenta* (London, 1621), Praefatio, sig. d2ʳ. On John Davies, see Rh. F. Roberts, 'Y Dr John Davies o Falwyd', *Llên Cymru*, 2 (1952), pp. 19–35, 97–110; R. Geraint Gruffydd, in *Y Traddodiad Rhyddiaith*, ed. Bowen, pp. 175–93 (also on Parry); Ceri Davies, *John Davies o Fallwyd* (Caernarfon, 2001).

[41] Gruffydd, in *Y Traddodiad Rhyddiaith*, ed. Bowen, pp. 183–4.

Matthew 21, they revert from Morgan's local interpretation ('on the spot') of παραχρῆμα (20) to the temporal interpretation which had also been Salesbury's:

> A phan welodd y discyblion, hwy a ryfeddasant, gan ddywedyd,
> Mor ddisymmwth y crinodd y ffigys-bren? (20)

> Ac wedi ei ddyfod ef i'r Deml, yr Arch-offeiriaid a Henuriaid y bobl a ddaethant atto. (23a)

In 23a the use of capitals in *Arch-offeiriaid* and *Henuriaid* also returns to Salesbury's practice. Meanwhile, the use of the form *ffigys-bren*, for the *ffigus-bren* of both Salesbury and Morgan, shows a greater distancing from Salesbury's obsession with displaying Latin roots.

John Davies, it should be added, is remembered not only as a biblical translator but also as the greatest scholar of the Welsh language itself in the early modern period. An Oxford-educated humanist of some renown, he also made it his life's work painstakingly to study in manuscripts the language of the Welsh poets down to his own day.[42] He was the last in a notable succession of Welsh grammarians and lexicographers of the sixteenth and early seventeenth centuries. Without question, his work on the study of the language, incorporated in his grammar, *Antiquae linguae Britannicae ... rudimenta* (1621), and in his dictionary, *Antiquae linguae Britannicae ... dictionarium duplex* (1632), was epoch-making. In the telling words of his contemporary Rowland Vaughan, John Davies was 'the one outstanding Plato of our language' (*unig Plato ardderchawg o'n hiaith ni*).[43]

At the beginning of those two books, the grammar and the dictionary, John Davies added Latin prefaces which are among the most important writings of the Renaissance in Wales. They are learned essays in which he discusses, from the standpoint of a Welsh churchman in the early seventeenth century, themes of scholarship which matter to him: the language and history of Wales, biblical exegesis and theological debate, and the interconnection of these things. It is as a humanist, a man of the Renaissance, that John Davies sets about discussing his subject matter in the two essays. He draws easily on the work of Renaissance scholars from continental Europe (for example, Juan Luis Vives and Justus Lipsius, Joseph Justus Scaliger and Paulus Merula); he knows about the

---

[42] Cf. Anthony à Wood's delineation of John Davies, that he was 'esteemed by the Academicians well vers'd in the History and Antiquities of his own Nation, and in the Greek and Hebrew Languages, a most exact Critic, an indefatigable searcher into antient Scripts, and well acquainted with curious and rare Authors', *Athenae Oxonienses* (2nd edn, London, 1721), col. 598.

[43] Preface to *Yr Ymarfer o Dduwioldeb* (1630). *Rhagymadroddion*, ed. Hughes, p. 120.

authorities on the biblical languages and their expository works (for example, Franciscus Junius, Sebastian Münster and David Parraeus), not to mention the Fathers of the Church. Throughout the essays he makes full use of classical references, skilfully quoting from both Greek and Latin literature in order to lend colour and force to his argument. It is also evident that he is steeped in the works of Erasmus, especially the *Adagia*.

The preface to the *Rudimenta* is in the form of a letter addressed to the aged Edmwnd Prys, William Morgan's old friend, and author of graceful metrical versions of the Psalms in Welsh. The following extract summarizes not only John Davies's position but also that of all the translators of the Bible into Welsh. Davies is countering the accusation, made by some detractors, that the Welsh language had no practical usefulness. He writes as one who had both worked closely with William Morgan (his words echo parts of Morgan's own preface to the 1588 Bible) and had also been jointly responsible with Richard Parry for the revision of Morgan's Bible, published just a year earlier:

> Ad vsum quod attinet, cuiusque linguae vsum duplicem esse constat; alterum quo quisque cuique animi sui sensa exprimat, quisque cuiusque mentem sensumque intelligat; & commercia, necessitudo, societas, consiliorum communicatio, inter gentes conseruentur: alterum praecipuum vt omnes gentes lingua qua nati sunt magnalia Dei audiant, mens diuina hominibus innotescat. Atque huc pertinet *linguarum, etiam vulgarium, cultura,* & Grammaticorum praeceptorum traditio. *Eo enim purius a fontibus deriuari necesse est verbum Dei, eo clarius populis tradi, quo purior & perfectior sit linguarum in quibus traditur, & in quas transfertur, cognitio.* Nec enim dextere et perspicue doceri, nec pura & incorrupta seruari potest doctrina caelestis, sine linguarum, etiam in quibus populo praedicanda est, studio. Quod superioris seculi barbaries cum erroribus coniuncta, & huius seculi, quo linguae excoli & efflorescere caeperunt, Religionis emendatio, & rerum tum diuinarum tum humanarum renascens cognitio; luce clarius demonstrat. Hebraeae & Graecae vsus est a reliquis peculiaris, vt Prophetarum & Apostolorum oracula intelligant Diuini verbi concionatores, reliquarum vt praedicantes intelligant populi. Si nullus igitur illis videatur huius linguae vsus, certe hic negari non potest, vtpote qui in hac insula ab ipsis Apostolorum temporibus, in hunc vsque diem inualuit. Et cultum profecto meretur lingua Br. vel hoc nomine, quod *Omnium prouinciarum prima Britannia, publicitus Christi nomen recepit*: vnde & *Primogenitae Ecclesiae* nomen sortita est Britannica. Nec sane vllo modo credendum est, voluisse Deum linguam hanc post tot gentis clades, imperij mutationes, tyrannorum molimina, in haec vsque vltima tempora conseruatam, nisi eadem etiam Nomen suum inuocari, suaque magnalia praedicari decreuisset.

As regards usefulness, it is agreed that each language has two uses: first, so that a man may express his thoughts to another, and may himself understand the thoughts and feelings of that other person, and so safeguard business dealings, friendship, partnership and communication of decisions between nations; and the second use – and this is the special one – so that all nations should hear in their own tongue, wherein they were born, the wonderful works of God, and so that the mind of God should become known to men. The cultivation of languages, even vernaculars, and the handing down of grammatical precepts, are relevant to this. 'For it follows of necessity that the purity with which the word of God is drawn from the original sources, and the clarity with which it is presented to the peoples, are commensurate with the purity and perfection of one's knowledge of languages, both those in which that word is first transmitted, and those into which it is translated.' For the heavenly doctrine cannot be effectively and clearly taught, nor can it be kept pure and undefiled, without the study of languages, including the languages in which it is to be preached to the people. This is made clearer than daylight, first, by the barbarousness of the age before our own, and all its errors, and second by the reform in religion and the renaissance in knowledge of matters divine and human in this age, an age which has seen the beginning of the cultivation and flourishing of languages. Hebrew and Greek, compared with other languages, are useful in a unique way, namely to enable the preachers of God's Word to understand the oracles of the prophets and the apostles; while the function of other languages is to enable the people to understand the preachers. Accordingly, even if those whom I mentioned do not themselves see any usefulness in this language, yet it cannot be denied that it has this spiritual purpose, seeing that, from the time of the apostles up until this day, the Gospel has gone from strength to strength in this island. The British [that is, Welsh] tongue deserves to be honoured, if only for this reason, that 'of all the provinces, Britain was the first openly to receive the name of Christ': that is the reason why the British church has gained the name of 'First-born Church'. And one cannot at all believe that God would have willed the preservation of this language, in the face of so many disasters for the nation, so many changes in government, and so many machinations of tyrants, had he not also ordained that his name be called upon in this language, and his wonderful works proclaimed in it.[44]

The passage is, throughout, the work of a learned humanist. John Davies applies the *ad fontes* principle and supports his thesis by quoting from the *oratio* in praise of the Hebrew language by the continental

---

[44] *Antiquae linguae Britannicae ... rudimenta*, Praefatio, sig. c3ᵛ–c4ᵛ. The whole preface is translated into Welsh in Davies, *Rhagymadroddion a Chyflwyniadau Lladin*, pp. 105–23.

Hebraist and biblical scholar Franciscus Junius.[45] A striking contrast is made between medieval 'barbarousness' (*barbaries* – both of language and belief) and the joint blessings of Reformation (*religionis emendatio*) and Renaissance (*renascens cognitio*). The special position of Greek and Hebrew is emphasized. But the Welsh language, too, has its own evangelical purpose in its corner of the world. John Davies further corroborates that view by referring to the belief, which had been given its clearest expression by Bishop Richard Davies in his prefatory 'Epistol at y Cembru' (Epistle to the Welsh people) at the beginning of the 1567 New Testament, that an early 'Protestant' church had once existed in Britain, among the forefathers of the Welsh.[46] The legend of the introduction of Christianity into Britain by Joseph of Arimathea, and (as has previously been indicated) Geoffrey of Monmouth's story about the conversion of King Lucius, were among the powerful, if shaky, pieces of evidence adduced to support this belief. Here John Davies refers (not directly, but on the basis of secondary sources like Richard Davies's 'Epistol at y Cembru') to the *Enneades* of the Italian M. Antonius Sabellicus (M. Coccio) to support the British church's claim to primogeniture. The passage's last sentence is a succinct and moving expression of a conviction which sustained not only John Davies but also William Salesbury and William Morgan and the other translators, the conviction (expressed in echoes of the second chapter of the Book of Acts) that God had 'ordained that his name be called upon in this language, and his wonderful works proclaimed in it'.

---

[45] The 'oratio' was published independently as *De linguae Hebraeae antiquitate praestantiaque oratio* (Naples, 1579), and reprinted at the beginning of Junius' *Grammatica Hebraeae linguae* (1580; 2nd edn, 1590). The quotation here is the *Grammatica* (1590 edition), sig. a4[r].

[46] *Rhagymadroddion*, ed. Hughes, pp. 17–43; English translation in Evans, *Memorandum*, pp. 83–124.

Index